KU-498-297

THE HANDBOOK OF
COMMUNICATION
SKILLS

BERNICE HURST

KOGAN
PAGE

The masculine pronoun has been used throughout this book. This stems from a desire to avoid ugly and cumbersome language, and no discrimination, prejudice or bias is intended.

COUNTY PLANNING
AND ENVIRONMENT
DEPARTMENT
TECHNICAL LIBRARY

First published in 1991
Reprinted in 1992

Apart from any fair dealing for the purposes of research or private study, or criticism or review, as permitted under the Copyright, Designs and Patents Act, 1988, this publication may only be reproduced, stored or transmitted, in any form or by any means, with the prior permission in writing of the publishers, or in the case of reprographic reproduction in accordance with the terms of licences issued by the Copyright Licensing Agency. Enquiries concerning reproduction outside those terms should be sent to the publishers at the undermentioned address:

Kogan Page Limited
120 Pentonville Road
London N1 9JN

© Bernice Hurst, 1991

British Library Cataloguing in Publication Data
A CIP record for this book is available from the British Library.
ISBN 0 7494 04566

Typeset by Saxon Printing Ltd, Derby
Printed in England by Clays Ltd, St Ives plc

HERTFORDSHIRE LIBRARY SERVICE		
No. 352 6115		
Class		
Supplier	Price	Date
BC	£25·00	10|92

CONTENTS

Acknowledgements *9*

Introduction *11*

PART I   HOW WELL DO WE COMMUNICATE?   **15**

Introduction *15*

1 The Communications Audit *17*

   Stage 1 — Examination 17
   Stage 2 — Evaluation 23
   Stage 3 — Implementation 34
   Stage 4 — Assessment 35

PART II   FACE-TO-FACE COMMUNICATION   **39**

Introduction *39*

2 Speaking and Listening *41*

   Saying is Believing 41
   Seeing is Believing 42
   Power 42
   Feedback 44
   Speaking 46
   Listening 50

3 Presentations *55*

   Preparing the Presentation 55
   Exhibitions 68
   Putting on the Ritz 69

4 Meetings *72*

   Who? 73
   When? 73
   Where? 73
   Why? 74
   How? 74

5 Employee Communications *90*

   Recognizing and Communicating Value 91
   Need to Know 92
   Family Business and the Community 92
   Doing it Right 94
   Security 95
   Complaints 97
   Perceptions 99
   Keeping People Informed 100
   The Working Environment 106
   Leadership 109
   Human Resources Development 109

6 Training *114*

   Planning for the Future 114
   The Strategy 116
   Identifying Training Needs 123

7 Negotiations *133*

   What are Negotiations? 136
   How to Negotiate 142
   AB Co v the Bank 150

8 Selling Techniques *152*

   The Customer Knows Best 152
   Sales Techniques and Communication 153

PART III   COMMUNICATION THROUGH AN INTERMEDIARY 159

Introduction   *159*

9 Telephone Techniques   *161*
   Placing a Telephone Call 162
   Receiving a Telephone Call 164
   Skills and Techniques 168
   Summary 177

10 Communicating with the Media   *178*

   Reaching the Audience 178
   Handling the Press 180
   Interviewing Techniques 185

11 Hi-tech Communications   *190*

   Communicating Through an Intermediary 190
   Creating a Specification 193
   Equipment 199

12 Marketing and Public Relations   *205*

   Marketing Techniques 214

PART IV   WRITTEN COMMUNICATIONS   221

Introduction   *221*

13 One-to-One Communications   *225*

   Letters 225

14 Corporate Communications   *231*

   Way to Go 231

15 Communications for Information   *237*

   Manuals 237
   Gathering Information 241

16 Fit to Print   *250*

   Back to Basics 251
   All the News That's Fit to Print... 253

PART V   INTERNATIONAL COMMUNICATION   **261**

  17 Communicating across Cultures *263*

    Customs and Conduct 263

PART VI   CASE STUDIES   **281**

  Z International Ltd *283*

    Passing on Information 283
    Duplicating Effort 284
    Setting the Ground Rules 285
    Talking it all Over 285
    Environment as Facilitator 286
    One Man's Views 287

  Digital Equipment Company *288*

    The Research 288
    The Plan 289
    The Changes 290

  BP Exploration *292*

    The Objective 292
    The Problem 293
    The Recommendations 293

APPENDICES

  Jargon *301*

  Glossary *305*

Bibliography *311*

Directory of Useful Organizations *314*

Index *316*

ACKNOWLEDGEMENTS

I would like to thank the many people who helped, deliberately and intentionally, in providing information and opinions for this book. Many of them prefer not to be named, but among those who will accept public recognition are:

- my partner, Ray Hurst, who researched and wrote the chapter Fit to Print;
- all those who helped him including Roddy Kennedy and Dudley Cheale of BP Exploration, Dick Coleman of National Power and Cecil Pedersen of the British Association of Industrial Editors;
- Sir Bob Reid, Chairman of the Management Charter Initiative and British Rail;
- Ms Jackie Boxall, European Public Affairs Manager, Digital Equipment Company;
- my colleagues in the South East Oxfordshire Education Business Partnership;
- Kogan Page for providing an invaluable library of reference material and permission to include extracts from many of these in the text.

I would also like to thank the many people who helped, unintentionally, in providing information and opinions for this book. None of them can be named and I hope that their identities will be apparent only to themselves.

Finally, I would like to thank:

- JW for providing the incentive;
- LH for providing the challenge; and
- PK for providing the opportunity to write this book.

INTRODUCTION

The Handbook of Communication Skills aims to build and improve a skill which we already possess.

We all know how to communicate. We know how to speak, how to listen, how to read, how to write. Therefore we communicate and are communicated with. But do we communicate well and clearly? Do we know how to put across our messages as well as possible or, indeed, how to interpret messages we receive?

Communication, as I will say over and over again, is a skill. As such, it can and should be learned, and anything that we learn can be learned in greater or lesser depth. We can all find ways to develop or improve our skills.

Communication, like every other subject, has its own jargon. Successful communication is not possible without:

- understanding;
- common ground;
- perception;
- awareness;
- self-confidence;
- clarity.

We all know about the generation gap; we know that people do not always speak or understand the language we are using — literally and figuratively. Communication should be used to overcome barriers of language, to convey ideas, to make sure we find ways of making ourselves understood and of understanding others.

Most of us want to be understood — our ideas, abilities, personalities. Most of us also want to understand others, to empathize, to identify, to communicate. Communication is the means by which we teach and learn.

In business, communication has specific applications. Employers communicate with employees; employees communicate with employers; both communicate with unions. Salespeople communicate — or not, as the case may be — with customers. We make presentations, give speeches, write letters and sales material, conduct telephone and face-to-face conversations, make decisions, sell ourselves and our companies or products.

To be successful we need to present our views and products clearly. If we do not communicate successfully, our products will sit on the shelves; we may not even be able to acquire the raw materials needed to create the products.

The subject of every chapter in this *Handbook* has had at least a dozen books written on it, covering the topic in depth from every conceivable angle. You will see, as you read this book, that the chapters overlap and points are often repeated. Presentations, for example, consist of speeches and conversations and are often supported by written material as well as visual aids.

Who we speak to, when, why and how can have totally different results according to the means of communication we choose to employ. The ways in which we communicate are inextricably related. Repetition is both necessary and unavoidable but the cross references you will find throughout this book should serve to demonstrate and clarify the extent of the overlap.

If I were to diagram the development of this book, I would have to:

- break down the overall subject of communications;

- break down the target audiences who might find the various sections of interest or relevance;

- correlate important points within each section with the relevant audience;

- reorder the sections in the most cohesive and comprehensive fashion possible;

- create links and a progression of thoughts that makes most sense to the reader.

This is not a book to be read straight through from cover to cover, but rather one to browse through, jumping from subject to subject. It offers a snapshot of the functions of communication at specific moments in time. I have adopted that oft-used technique which recommends that you:

- tell the audience what you're going to say;

- tell them;

- then tell them what you've told them.

Within each section I have also followed the advice of my colleagues to

Keep It Short and Simple

By doing this, and by touching on the various aspects of communication that we must all consider every time we attempt to explain our thoughts to others, I have signposted some of the factors which are needed to develop effective communication skills.

The ways in which I have summarized the key processes of communication are intended to identify and strengthen skills which will help achieve successful communication. Each of the parts — on face-to-face communication, communication through an intermediary, written communication — is a necessary part of the whole interaction between individuals. Unless they are all considered in their mutual dependence on one another, and all accepted in their mutual support for one another, communication cannot be wholly effective.

This *Handbook* aims to communicate and to help its readers improve their communication skills. Use it, learn from it, build on it. Consider it a tool to teach and advise. But most of all, consider it a roadmap, offering choices and showing you where various paths will lead, leaving you to decide which route to follow.

PART I

HOW WELL DO WE COMMUNICATE?

INTRODUCTION

We may accept the premise that we are all communicating with a variety of other people every day of our lives but the purpose of a communications audit is to determine whether or not we are communicating effectively. To do this, there must be a mutual understanding of the messages being conveyed. We must make sure that all the relevant people hear the same message and know the same facts. Offering them is not the same as communicating them.

As with an annual audit of a company's accounts, a communications audit consists of two stages:

- examination;
- evaluation.

To be wholly effective, it must then be followed by two further stages:

- implementation;
- assessment.

Each of these stages must be further sub-divided when trying to specify what the audit is trying to find out, why and how and, later, what it has achieved and with what degree of success.

Chapter 1

The Communications Audit

STAGE 1 — EXAMINATION

If we assume that the main purpose of communication is to convey information, the first step in planning a communications audit is to identify the audience a company's communications are aimed at. The necessity for communication between given groups or individuals is a key issue here. Overkill and supplying too much information can be just as negative as supplying too little information.

Michael Bland and Peter Jackson, in *Effective Employee Communications*, offer a very succinct list of the questions an examination should attempt to answer:

- who should you communicate with;
- who do you actually communicate with;
- what should you be communicating;
- what are you actually communicating;
- how should you communicate with your audiences;
- how do you actually communicate with your audiences.

So a step-by-step examination of target audiences would seem the best place to begin. Individuals within a company need to interact and to convey information to others outside the company.

Internal structure

Figure 1.1 identifies the internal structure of a company in a fairly simplistic form. Communication must take place between and within the levels.

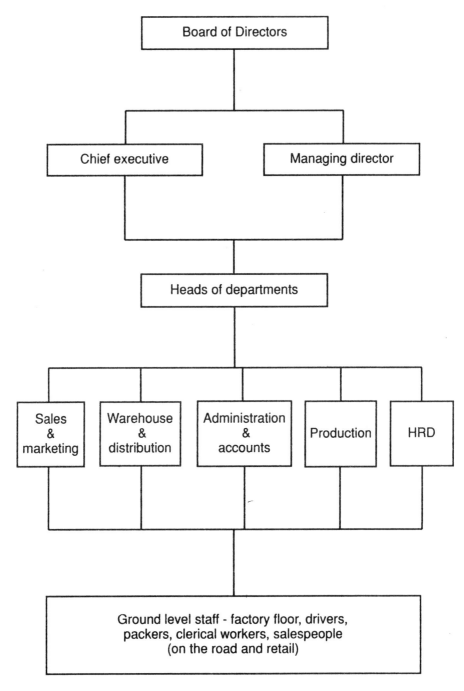

Figure 1.1 Internal structure

There are countless studies indicating that employees feel more highly motivated when they understand a company's structure and its corporate identity. One classic story concerns the factory whose output increased significantly when workers along the assembly line were shown where the part they were working on day in and day out fitted into the overall product being manufactured. Such a simple piece of information was not mutually understood; communicating it effectively resulted in a higher degree of job satisfaction for those on the assembly line when they realized the value of their contribution. In addition, there was an increased level of productivity appreciated by the management and shareholders.

On a broader scale, notice boards and newsletters keep employees informed about policy and personnel. Memoranda, meetings and minutes, company brochures and annual reports provide details of what each department is doing and how. They prevent that vacuum which can arise when information is not communicated adequately and help prevent needless duplication of effort. The specific value of these documents, and how to make best use of them, will be discussed in Part IV.

Employees need to know about the whole company but they also need to know about one another. Communication within and between departments is just as important as communication to and from supervisors and management.

Figure 1.1 was originally designed to illustrate the internal structure of a company. There are a number of levels of responsibility and authority, hence the demonstration of a hierarchy. If it were to be re-configured to demonstrate an ideal communications network, however, it would look more like Figure 1.2.

Admittedly the pattern of arrows indicating that each and every department or employee can communicate with one another is confusing. The point, however, is that the lines are open, available and ought to be used.

One essential feature of the communications audit will be to ensure that those lines are actually in place and are being used to their best advantage.

External structure

Figure 1.3 identifies, again in very simplistic terms, the groups outside a company who will be interested in corporate communications.

Government must be communicated with on a number of levels – local government for matters concerning planning and services, national government for regulations concerning financial controls as well as lobbying for or against relevant legislation.

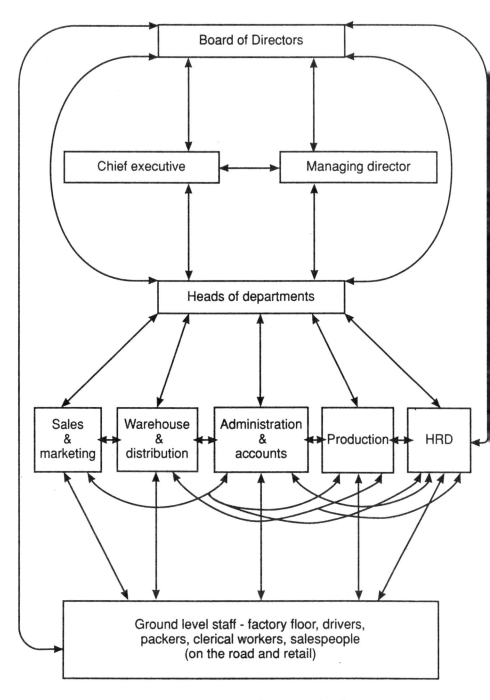

Figure 1.2 Internal communications

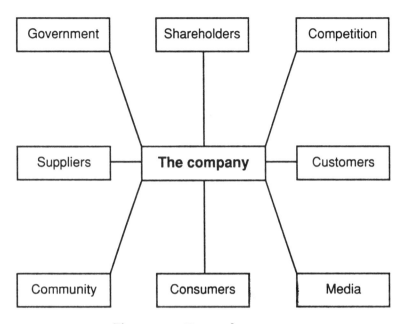

Figure 1.3 External structure

Shareholders are both interested in, and entitled to, detailed information about how the company is functioning both financially and in terms of policy. They need to be aware of potential changes to management or company structure, ownership and overall performance.

Competitors will want to know about a company's status and progress for obvious reasons. But what information is communicated, when and how, is a decision that must be made and reviewed regularly. The media, market research companies, financial service companies or any others acting as intermediaries must be treated similarly. Intermediaries take information communicated by the company, translate it and re-present it without reference back to the company. In this way they are also communicating the company's image. The image projected directly by the company therefore must be controlled so that any conclusions drawn are, as far as possible, those of which it would approve.

Suppliers are those from whom the company gets the raw materials it needs but also the equipment for production and administration. They can include manufacturers or wholesalers of plant, office supplies, packaging materials, transportation and distribution services. They can also include the suppliers of support services such as public relations, research and marketing, thereby covering the entire range of material on which the company relies for its smooth functioning.

Customers are those to whom the company sells, but, depending on what the company produces, they may not be the end users. Manufacturers often sell to corporate buyers; service companies deal with clients who in turn sell their products to a range of customers.

Consumers are the end users. They are the public who walk into a shop, restaurant, cinema or other leisure facility; they are the people who read books and magazines; they are the final recipient of the company's products although the company itself may never have direct dealings with them.

The community actually encompasses all of these categories and more. It includes those in the immediate geographic vicinity of the company, whose needs and interests are served and affected by it. This can mean neighbours, educational institutions and employees, as individuals and as groups.

The community also refers to financial institutions and banks who have a direct and indirect (via employees) vested interest in the company's affairs. Financial markets and market research companies must be seen as target audiences because they take information and pass it on to clients, drawing their own conclusions from available data.

Using information provided by the *media*, and providing them with information to use and/or pass onto others, is a vital concern to any business. The media can and should be used as a tool. If treated as an ally, it can assist communications with suppliers, consumers, customers and the community. If treated indifferently, or as hostile, it can do irreparable damage.

This is, as stated earlier, an oversimplification. Life is not like that. The same people can be part of several audiences; they can move from one to another; their interests can both overlap and conflict. Employees can also be members of external audiences, possibly as consumers or shareholders, frequently as members of the community.

Any company, when assessing and controlling the image it projects, needs to be aware of the conclusions drawn by each and every one of its target audiences. Each of those audiences is affected by, and is the target of, corporate image in all its aspects.

Differing reactions to the same information is also conceivable. If a company's financial results are good, then shareholders will be pleased. Consumers, however, will feel that prices must have been too high if profits of such a level were achieved and employees may feel that their salaries were too low.

Not only must target audiences be identified when planning an audit, but the types of information those audiences want and the ways in which they are likely to react to it and use it must also be taken into consideration.

STAGE 2 — EVALUATION

At the same time that you are examining 'who', you should be examining 'why' and 'how'. The quantity and quality of your communication with the target audiences identified must be evaluated in order for the next two stages, implementation and assessment, to take place.

Why communicate?

There is no single answer to this question, and trying to find the correct answers for your circumstances is the job of those responsible for the communications audit.

Do the various communicators in your company want to:

— solve problems?
— influence people?
— create change?
— provide a conduit for an exchange of information?
— supply information to others in a one-way direction only?
— achieve power?

How do you communicate?

Malcolm Peel, in *Improving Your Communication Skills*, tells a most appropriate story.

"'Our communication,'" roared a Chief Executive to his subordinate directors, "is dreadful. I want it improved immediately."

The Director of Office Services went away and ordered a brand new internal telephone network for £1m. "That's not what I meant at all," said the Chief Executive, and sacked his Director of Office Services.

The Director of Personnel went away and drew up a brand new organization structure, complete with both solid and dotted lines. "That's not what I meant at all," shouted the Chief Executive, and sacked his Director of Personnel.

The Director of Computing and Information Technology went away and bought a network of micros and a comprehensive suite of interactive, real-time software. "That's not what I meant at all," screamed the Chief Executive, and sacked his Director of Computing and Information Technology.

The Industrial Relations Director went away and set up a magnificent Consultative Procedure to ensure continuous contact between Management and Employee representatives by a daily cascade of briefing meetings. "That's not what I meant at all," roared the Chief Executive, and sacked his Director of Industrial Relations.

No sooner had he done this than the Chief Executive suffered a violent heart attack and found himself standing before the Great Head of Communications in the Sky. "If none of your fellow directors understood you," said the GHOC, "do you think the failure in communication that you observed could have had anything to do with you?'"

All of the directors were right in their own way, that is, within their own frame of reference. But they needed to work together and consider their communication needs in conjunction with the company's overall requirements.

Setting up the audit

Planning the communications audit must be an organized and logical process. The purpose of the audit is to form an objective picture of what is happening compared with what senior executives think (or have been told) is happening.

If companies, and specifically those in the company conducting the audit, know which questions to ask and how to get answers, then the company might find it necessary to take a different view of its communication policies. The audit not only has to identify weaknesses in the company's communications policy but also any strengths. These can then be built on, thereby achieving the commitment to change that growth and profitability demand.

Who should do it?

This is a question that has a variety of answers. The correct one is the one most suited to your business and your own requirements. There is no hard and fast rule. For all the value of delegation, and all the sense in standing back to take an objective look at things, in the final analysis it is only the company itself, in the person of its executives or partners, who can make the final decision.

Malcolm Peel, again in *Improving Your Communication Skills*, considers the best people to use. He points out that it is rare for an organization to have staff available with both the skills and time to complete such a large exercise but does suggest that it would be a useful training exercise for graduate trainees or high-fliers.

The Confederation for British Industry (CBI), in their publication *Finding Out the Facts About Employee Communications*, suggest having a team conduct the audit. Comprised of one personnel manager or consultant, one middle manager or supervisor and one shop steward or safety representative, they furthermore advise that 'no member should be so senior that he would dominate everyone nor so junior that he would be frightened to ask the right questions'. The CBI booklet also suggests training the audit team, a suggestion particularly appropriate if you are making use of in-house resources. Preparation and discussion of the objectives of the audit must precede its instigation.

Using professional consultants   Malcolm Peel goes on to point out that using professional consultants, on the other hand, can be expensive. Not many people would dispute this point.

Many consultants are confronted by doubt and surprise at their charges. The explanation offered is that the final product is the result of a long creative process. The investigation, discussion and evaluation that precede presentation are time consuming and costly. Clients pay for expertise, objectivity and mental effort. Although the final result may look flimsy and raise questions of value for money, it is the preparation and creation that the client pays for.

Whether or not this is money well spent is a matter of opinion. Michael Bland and Peter Jackson in *Effective Employee Communications* suggest that consultants can spot faults more easily as they are objective and bring in a clean, fresh outlook. They can also use their experience to advise on things you may not have known or thought of.

Bland and Jackson also stress that, for all a consultant's experience, it is still the company itself that has to communicate its message. Consultants should be used but not followed blindly; their advice, ideas and recommendations need to be analyzed in light of what you know about your own business. As Bland and Jackson say, 'no amount of consulting relieves you of an ounce of your own responsibility for good communication'.

When using professional consultants, be sure that their references and past clients are carefully checked in order to be certain they are the right people to analyze your particular set up. You may get on very well with the director or salesperson who makes the initial contact and then find out that your account is being handled by someone you have never met.

You must be certain that the consultant you choose is familiar with your company as well as with your industry or service. You must be certain that what you are buying is not just a beautifully bound report, but that it will also contain specific recommendations on implementation and assessment. In short, take as much care as possible that you will get what you want, and what you are paying for. A few well-placed telephone calls to some of the organizations listed in the directory section of this book may save you a lot of time, trouble and expense later.

How should it be done?

Once the examination and evaluation of the company's audiences has been completed, a panel or consultant put in position, the 'why' and 'how' examined in principle, the next step is considering the actuality of the company's communications. The question of effectiveness of the company's communications should be answered by the communications audit through a system of questionnaires, interviews and group discussions.

Prior to starting the audit, a plan must also be established for analysis of information received. The team must decide on actions to be taken, making allowances for contingencies. There could be a series of diagrams or model dialogues, for instance, indicating directions to take depending on responses. Suppositions and hypotheses may be formulated, preliminary reactions to specific feedback anticipated and then alternative procedures outlined for all eventualities. A structure for reports, which should always contain examples and evidence, should be planned well in advance. Statistics have their place and can often be used to illustrate points but should never be used in isolation or without explanatory notes. The team should always explain what is meant by statements in reports and why conclusions have been drawn.

In short, before beginning the work of conducting the audit, a plan for its beginning, middle and end should be constructed.

Communications factors to be audited

1. Corporate identity

Any communications audit must include an examination of the company's position in the market place. Its strategy must be examined in conjunction with the communications audit in order to decide what the company wants to achieve and the best way of achieving it.

There are a number of different issues involved in discussions of image and its importance. Certainly any company wants to be perceived in the ways it thinks best.

Wally Olins, founder of design consultancy Wolff Olins, has been quoted as saying that 'Corporate identity is involved with the way the company behaves and what it feels like' (*Observer*, 14 April, 1991). On another occasion, he explained that it is 'the visualization of strategy'.

Nicholas Ind is head of corporate identity at Oakley Young, a WPP consultancy. WPP is known as the largest communications company in the world and owns, among others, J Walter Thompson. JWT in turn is an advertising agency whose clients include many of industry's most well-known names, well known largely because of JWT's successful campaigns on their behalf. In his book *The Corporate Image*, Ind demonstrates the ways in which corporate identity can help a company 'to gain and sustain competitive advantage'. He discusses the use of corporate image as an expression of corporate strategy.

Ind goes into detail, explaining the links and differences between corporate identity, corporate image and corporate strategy. Like Olins, he believes that the identity reflects the company's sense of itself and its strategy. Ind explains that identity is formed through a combination of history, ownership, technology, personality and philosophy. Identity, he says, 'is not something cosmetic, but is the core of an organization's existence'. He also points out that corporate marks are designed as expressions of corporate strategy.

Strategy is the plan a company formulates to achieve its objectives. According to Ind, 'strategy will be influenced by the identity, while the identity will be affected by the nature of the strategy'.

More specific information regarding the analysis, construction and implementation of corporate identity, strategy and image will be found in Chapter 12 on marketing.

2. Corporate image

Image is the way in which target audiences see the corporate identity, or the interpretation that they put onto it. It is the ways (please note the deliberate use of the plural form here) in which the company is perceived by its audiences. And, says Ind, corporate communication 'is the process that translates corporate identity into corporate image...Without communication the values and strategies of the organization will not be understood...'

Corporate image is conveyed both intentionally and unintentionally. Businesses, like individuals, are constantly communicating. There is a need to be aware of this to ensure that the image received coincides with the one transmitted — the audit should provide feedback on this.

Unintentional messages can be either positive or negative. They are transmitted through products and services and are the basis for audience perceptions of the company's reputation. Perceptions are also formed on the basis of physical presence, the internal and exterior design of the company's offices, for example.

Intentional messages are transmitted through publicity, advertising, public relations and all of the means of communication the business defines as essential to its objectives.

The logo problem   One highly visible, and often controversial, aspect of corporate image is the company's logo. Controversy associated with logos is generally associated with cost and perceived value. Although the final result may look flimsy and raise questions of value for money, it is the preparation and creation that the client pays for. Expert skills and advice are always expensive, regardless of field, and any design consultant will tell you that if it is important for you to communicate your message, and the logo does this effectively, then any cost incurred is well justified.

This justification is, however, necessary. Target audiences need to understand the use of, and need for graphic representations of identity and strategy. If the only message communicated is that vast sums of money are being spent creating a logo that goes onto all of the company's products, stationery, delivery vans etc then something has gone wrong with the transmission.

The argument of value is particularly applicable to companies 'tweaking' their image. Press coverage of modifications to logos frequently concentrates on cost and whether there is any point spending company – and hence shareholders' – money in what is visually a minor modification only.

But tweaking a logo is an indication that a company is tweaking its identity. That basically it is staying the same but with a slight shift in structure and/or policy in recognition of progress, changing needs and a response to feedback. The company is therefore visibly demonstrating two ideas. First, that it is conscious of the need for progress. Second, that it is maintaining its traditional values. The evolution of an identity, and an image, is intended to communicate that there will be no dramatic overhauls but there will be an awareness of contemporary requirements and circumstances.

Drastic changes to logos can indicate drastic changes to company policy. They can also be used to signal mergers or changes to ownership. Visible alterations make audiences stop and take another look at a company. If this happens, and audiences re-examine their perceptions, then the message has got through. Whether it is then accepted or not depends on the nature of the change, but at least people have been made aware that the change has occurred.

Minale, Tattersfield & Partners are international design consultants specializing in corporate and financial literature, corporate identities, packaging and a range of related design services. They have produced corporate identities for such organizations as the Home Office, Central Television, Harrods, Jewsons Builders Merchants, the Port of Dover and the House of Fraser to name but a few. In the promotional package detailing some of these, they emphasize the importance of implementing corporate identity. Communicating the objectives and different applications of the image, they say, must be considered in conjunction with the overall design process. Nicholas Ind's comment, which supports Minale, Tattersfield's view and is a classic example of understatement, is that 'failure to communicate the rationale behind a change in the visual identity can have damaging consequences'.

If target audiences do not understand the images, or the reasons why they need to exist or be modified, then both the company and its design team have failed in their purpose. Understanding logos and the message they have to convey to all those with whom a company communicates is an essential feature of the corporate communications policy and therefore of the communications audit.

3. Written communications

All written material circulated within the company, and to groups outside the company, must be gathered up, examined and evaluated.

Every form of written communication must be identified and collected:

- signs;
- labels;
- logos;
- slogans;
- sales material;
- company brochures;
- annual reports;
- letter headings in all their variations;
- house journals, newsletters and magazines;
- orientation and style manuals.

These must all be considered in the context of the message they have to convey to all of the people and groups with whom the company communicates. The consistency (or inconsistency) of the corporate identity, image and message will become apparent once written materials are assembled.

Language must also be examined – the use of English, comprehensibility and the relationship of use to the target audiences. Perhaps not everyone in the target audiences is a native English speaker. Have you established this and laid ground rules for coping? Do you have a house style or corporate manual to which employees can refer? If so, does it need updating? If not, should you create one?

In addition, any written material you can locate about your company should be assembled. It is just as important to know what others are saying about you and how they are representing you. Press coverage, directories, market research reports on your industry, historical material and statistical data that could include information on your company should all be considered. The ways in which intermediaries have interpreted any information coming from you, and the ways in which they have passed it on to others, cannot be omitted from the audit.

4. Communications equipment

Every form of communications equipment must be inventoried.

Not so very long ago, anyone starting a new business rented an office and filled it with desks, typewriters, pens and paper, filing cabinets, photocopiers and telephones. That, and of course the people in the office, was all the equipment that was needed to make a start.

Now typewriters are either supplemented or replaced by word processors, with a terminal on each desk. Work stations come complete with all the equipment needed to communicate with anyone and everyone, internal and external, regardless of distance.

The filing cabinet where information used to be stored has also been replaced by those terminals which are generally networked, making all data available to anyone with the right password. At *The Times*, for example, anyone who knows the magic word can refer to the morgue of past papers, searching by subject or date, read articles currently being written by colleagues, and check worldwide news as it comes in, all without moving from their own desk. People in different parts of a single building, in different parts of a city or country, even in different countries, can communicate instantly.

Pens and paper are still useful for note taking but how many people have you seen carrying their own portable computer? There is a wide range of pocket organizers and computers now available. How often have you been in a meeting and heard strange bleeps coming from those around you as their pocket alarms, organizers and pagers remind them of other commitments?

Telephones may still be linked to a central switchboard but mobile phones can be seen everywhere. Have you ever sat on a train listening to stereophonic ringing as the passengers surrounding you each maintain communications with colleagues elsewhere? Have you ever driven along watching one-handed drivers trying to concentrate on both the road and their conversations? Portable and cellular telephones, ship-to-shore telephones, phones on planes and trains, chats with astronauts, satellite and transatlantic cables for telecommunications...

Technology has added telex and facsimile machines, modems, electronic mailbox and teletext to the range of support facilities on which we can now rely. An inventory of a company's communications hardware is an essential element of its communications audit.

All of the equipment will be covered in greater depth later in Chapter 11 on Hi-tech Communications but its very existence and the frequency of its use within the company must be treated as part of the communications audit. It is essential to assess staff attitudes to technology.

● Do staff show resistance or react with excitement to the potentials of technology?

● Are staff terrified of technology or challenged by it?

● Do machines make staff fear redundancy? Or do they just fear the machines themselves?

● Is it the equipment or the idea of it that people react to?

● Are there expensive pieces of equipment covered in dust in corners of offices? Is there enough training and explanation offered to encourage its use?

It is important to look at who uses what:

- Do employees have the necessary skills?
- Do they understand all of the functions each machine can perform?

The audit should examine the specification for equipment, whether or not it was comprehensive, whether or not there is a need for change. Do you need more equipment or less?

While most of these questions apply generally to training and communicating the use of equipment to employees, they also refer specifically to communications equipment. The extent to which information technology on storage and retrieval can be computerized must be examined within the confines of the audit. The systems developer and his assessment of the company's requirements should be reviewed. The ways in which that assessment was implemented and an evaluation of it once in progress must be added to the tasks for which those conducting the audit are responsible.

5. Reliable communications

Tomtoms and smoke signals may be out of date but it is still essential to establish reliable and accurate lines of communication. No one will ever eliminate the grapevine entirely but ensuring that a network is not based exclusively on word of mouth and hearsay is one way of establishing effective communication.

Michael Bland and Peter Jackson believe that 'the grapevine does not even merit a place among communication methods'. But while it is not an intentional form of communication it is nonetheless a fact of life. Employees are among a company's foremost communicators, speaking to one another and to those outside the company. They are also one of a company's prime audiences, recipients of messages and perceptions. They receive those messages, form perceptions and then act as intermediaries. Any company which ignores such informal methods as the grapevine, does so at its own risk. There must be an awareness of informal networks within the company and their accuracy should be judged and ensured as far as possible. They can be used then and, if necessary, defused when rumour and negative information is being communicated. Ways of using and understanding the grapevine will be discussed in Chapter 5 but it is important to mention it here, in the context of the communications audit, as another form of communication which must be considered as part of the overall pattern within the company.

6. Employee opinions

Before devising or choosing questionnaires or scheduling interviews with employees the audit team must determine its objectives.

- Who are the questionnaires aimed at?

- What information do you hope to get from them?
- Who should be interviewed?
- What are the advantages and disadvantages of group discussions?
- Who should be involved in group discussions?
- How does the information hoped for from questionnaires differ from that hoped for from discussions?

The CBI's booklet, *Finding Out the Facts About Employee Communications* contains a checklist to be used when interviewing employees during a communications audit. It suggests that interviewers:

- communicate the purpose of the interview and its terms of reference;
- ask questions logically, without darting about;
- listen;
- ask supplementary questions to elucidate points;
- not believe everything they are told, especially opinions, but ask for evidence to support claims;
- take notes;
- tell interviewees what will happen next;
- do not interview anyone without permission from the appropriate department head or supervisor.

The booklet also gives examples of questions that can be asked during a communications audit. It is stressed that these are examples within a framework of questions. Audit team members must use discretion in deciding to ask all, or some of them, or to supplement them in any way.

Face-to-face briefing

- Who is your boss?
- When was the last time your boss got everyone together as a team?
- When will he get everyone together again?
- When he does meet everyone, what sort of subjects does he talk about?
- Do you get the chance of asking questions?
- How well is the team doing anyhow?
- How do you find out about changes in company policy eg a decision to sell a new product or scrap an old one?
- Do you think the firm is profitable? How much profit do you think it made this year?
- How do you find out news about pay and conditions of employment?
- Has anyone raised the question of [name the current company problem] with the team?

Consultative machinery

- When was the last works council meeting?
- When is the next one?
- What was discussed last time?
- How did you find out about it?
- How often do you actually see your steward or representative?
- To whom do you talk if you have an idea about the job you do?
- Does your team ever discuss ideas for improving efficiency with the supervisor or section leader?
- How often do you read the minutes of works council meetings?
- Have you ever put forward an agenda item?
- What is on the agenda for the next meeting?

Accountability of management

- When was the last time you held a progress meeting?
- How often do you hold meetings of this kind?
- Do you have a drill for walking the job? (What is it?)
- What drill do you operate for seeing that your team find out about progress, policy, profits, points for action and plans?
- How do you monitor whether foremen actually pass on messages once you have briefed them? (When do you brief them anyhow?)
- What subjects do you introduce for discussion at consultative meetings?
- Do you have your own personal work targets?
- Have you consulted the team about how they can be achieved?
- What management training have you received?
- What subjects did it cover?

Provision of financial information

- How well did the group do last year?
- How well did your part of the group perform?
- Can you remember the net profit figure in the report?
- Can you remember the net added value per employee?
- What are the financial targets for this year?
- How do you find out about financial information?
- Do senior managers explain what is contained in the employee report?

- Why do you think the company publishes an employee report?
- When you read it did you think it contained any further kind of 'message'?
- When did the last report come out?
- When you read it, what did you understand by -?

The CBI has an Employee Relations Group which covers all aspects of employee communication and can offer additional information and advice on communications audits. Their address will be found in the directory at the end of this book.

Sample questionnaires and guidance in structuring interviews are also available from organizations specializing in human resources development. Further information on these can also be found in the directory at the end of the book.

7. External opinions

Market research, and obtaining feedback from target audiences outside the company, can also be used in the communications audit. Market research is most valuable when you are thinking about new product development, as a means of getting consumer reaction to products and services. But it is just as important to examine perceptions of the company itself and to find out how effectively you are communicating the image discussed earlier. It is important to look at beliefs and reactions among individual customers/consumers, intermediaries and all of those external audiences described at the beginning of this chapter.

A system of questionnaires and discussions with members of the target audiences mentioned earlier in this chapter will provide data regarding those perceptions. Selection procedures and the quantity and quality of interviews are of particular importance, however, if the audit is going to reach any conclusion. The team will have to make its own judgements on how many people to speak to, what questions to ask, how much allowance needs to be made for bias and accuracy of the information on which audiences base their perceptions.

STAGE 3 — IMPLEMENTATION

After all the interviews have been conducted, the questionnaires tallied, the written communications perused and the overall corporate strategy identified, it is up to those conducting the audit to draw conclusions and make recommendations for the implementation of change. Strengths and weaknesses should be identified but they cannot stand alone. It is the method of change and improvement that makes the audit valuable.

To paraphrase Nicholas Ind again, one of the aims of the communications audit is to create a sense of order and consistency in the communications process. Recommendations for change should point in a single direction; they should devise a plan for overseeing all of the company's communications, 'reflecting the company's identity in creating a corporate image which helps achieve the corporate strategy'.

The CBI recommends that a team or joint working party be set up to discuss the report and take action. They advise that the working party should include representatives of management and employees with the chief executive officer or personnel manager (human resources development manager) as chairperson.

It may be that appointing two teams is necessary, however. One team would assess and recommend steps for implementing results of the internal communications audit. Their familiarity with the organization's structure and staff will enable them to follow through most effectively. Those selected for the team may not be best qualified to approach external communications, and a second group of people should work independently on that aspect. The two teams would, finally, confer and produce a single report.

Either way, priorities and a logical presentation of the changes are essential. Not every recommendation can be implemented at once; some may be contingent on others. Therefore both the audiences and the objectives must be ordered and implementation structured to follow that order.

STAGE 4 — ASSESSMENT

Once those improvements have been structured and put into effect, they must be assessed. Not immediately, of course, although some changes may become apparent quite soon. And it obviously isn't necessary to repeat the whole audit process again straightaway. What is necessary is to give the changes time to work and then to check them, sharpen them up and make any adjustments that seem advisable. One result of the audit, for example, may be to identify training needs, whether they be language skills, writing skills, computer skills or any other skills. This in itself will lead to further research and take some considerable time to achieve satisfactorily.

As communication is an ongoing process, so too should be the communications audit. And while the first step, the original, structured, objective audit may not have to be repeated in its entirety, one thing it should teach us all is that we should be constantly aware of its aims and conclusions in order that we implement them to the best of our ability. Complacency has no place in any aspect of business. Perceptions may change, audiences may change, the means and quality of communication may change. Examination, evaluation, implementation and assessment should be built into company policy as a perpetual task equal in importance to any and every other.

Summary

The communications audit team has three main functions to fulfill. They must:

- examine all of the company's communications;
- identify the strengths and weaknesses of the company's communications and recommend change where necessary;
- ensure that the communications policy is consistent and coherent.

Aspects of corporate communications to be examined include:

- corporate identity, image, strategy, logo;
- internal communications – notice boards, newsletters, house journals, memo system ie copies to -;
- hierarchy, communication within and between departments, employee reports, accountability of managers for communication;
- external communications – advertising and public relations material, marketing material, media relations, sales material, brochures, annual report;
- information technology – internal and external phone system, computer system, software, record keeping;
- accessibility of information, use of information, information storage and retrieval, skills in using hi-tech, hardware available for communications;
- evaluation of training needs, how often revised, how these are acted on;
- relationship with training providers including educational institutions;
- consultation arrangements.

The audit team must also ask:

- How does the company's communications work?
- Does it actually work?
- Why does (or doesn't) it work?

They must look at the communications 'network' in its widest sense, examining the system of communicating up and down the ladder and taking into account unofficial networks. Questions must be designed to determine:

- Who is communicating?
- Who is being communicated with?

and in relation to answers given to both of those questions:

- Why are they communicating/being communicated with?

- How are they communicating/being communicated with?

Members of target audiences often overlap, with buyers selling on the company's products or services, employees living in the community and transmitters receiving messages. These multiple roles, and frequently conflicting perceptions, have all got to be taken into consideration. The team must look at any and every form of written and verbal communications going into and out of the organization. Quality and relevance must be key factors in their assessment. Information to be obtained from the audit should be broken down according to what the company feels in relation to its audiences:

- what the audiences want to know;
- what the audiences need to know;
- what it would be good for the audiences to know.

PART II

FACE-TO-FACE COMMUNICATION

Introduction

As I began outlining the topics to be covered in this book and structuring the research which would be necessary, I drew up a list of people on whom I could call. When I stopped to think about it, the people I knew and the range of tasks/industries/responsibilities they covered staggered me. I had never before looked at my friends and colleagues as a whole. I suddenly realized the breadth of my own communications network.

You never know what will happen when you meet someone. Several years ago, my partner and I published a directory of freelance illustrators and designers. To promote this directory, we took a stand at an exhibition of creative services. One of the visitors to that stand was an advertising salesman who was interested in becoming a publisher. We got to know one another and worked on several projects together over the next two or three years, working under the umbrella of another, larger company.

During the time we worked together, my partner and I had occasional dealings with the financial director of the larger company. These dealings were generally acrimonious as we only spoke to him when we were chasing payments that were due to us. After a while, the salesman-turned- publisher sold one of the projects on which we had worked to a different publisher. We were not privy to the negotiations and my partner and I fell out with the salesman-turned-publisher. We severed relations with him and moved over to work with the new publisher in order to maintain continuity on the project which had changed hands.

One day, as we were leaving a meeting with the new publisher, we passed a friend of his on the way in to have lunch with him. We were introduced. It was none other than the financial director of the company we no longer dealt with. To everyone's surprise, we discovered that none of us had horns, that we were all very nice, sensible, reasonable people and that we had several common perceptions of our mutual ex-colleague. There was a general recognition that we could, if necessary, deal directly with one another in the future now that the intermediary who had caused the conflicts between us had been removed from the equation. We shook hands and went our separate ways feeling a sense of satisfaction that an obstacle had been removed and new lines of communication opened.

There are indisputable advantages to first-hand communication. It can be face to face or over the telephone, just so long as it is two-way, live and direct. Only through these means can we quickly and satisfactorily:

- exchange views;

- alter one another's views and requirements through discussion and negotiation;
- close the knowledge gap through explanation and justification;
- show willingness and interest in communicating, working together and building relationships;
- build relationships which will facilitate future encounters even if they aren't all – or can't all – be face-to-face or first-hand;
- eliminate extenuating circumstances and distractions or make allowance for them in order to open direct lines of communication.

This isn't to say that communication is only effective on this basis. Going back to my first point about networks, none of us ever knows what a conversation or meeting with someone will lead to. Communication is about relationships and relationships are what build networks. It is through this interrelationship directly between people and through intermediaries, including technology, that messages are transmitted, word spread and, effectively or not, communication achieved.

Chapter 2

Speaking and Listening

Does saying something often enough and loudly enough make it true?
What message does it communicate? That the lady doth protest too much
perhaps? Better to communicate by example and demonstration, following that old adage one picture is worth one thousand words. There are two
sides to that coin as well, though. On the one side, there is the question of
whether or not pictures can be trusted. Hi-tech equipment makes 'fixing'
pictures child's play. At the other end of the spectrum, other hi-tech
equipment turns us each into eye witnesses, transmitting images around
the world as they happen. Thus current events are harder to tamper with
than printed images.

SAYING IS BELIEVING

As an example of using repetition in an attempt to communicate your own
choice of message to target audiences, let us look at a well known high
street bank. Their current television advertising slogan is that their job is
to make the customer's life easier. Yet like the small business mentioned in
Chapter 7 on Negotiations, the chairman of this particular bank has also
had complaints from small businesses about real life treatment from staff
at branch level. Perhaps the message being communicated to those of us
sitting at home watching television has not yet filtered through to the
bank's employees?

Another bank was fond, for some time, of referring to itself as 'the
listening bank'. But this was the same bank which made record losses and
whose chairman resigned soon afterwards. Perhaps their message was
communicated so successfully to staff that they listened too often.

SEEING IS BELIEVING?

Like it or not, first opinions are formed on appearance. Before beginning a speech or presentation it is wise to create a checklist of the good and bad points in appearance — physical and otherwise. Ask yourself:

- What should or would I change about myself, how and why?

Equally important, in trying to understand how others see us, we should look at the way we look at others. Ask yourself:

- How do I perceive others — on what do I base my judgements?
- Are my criteria fair, do they need to be changed, how and why?

POWER

Power is a perceived attribute; if the person wielding power believes he is powerful and/or the person receiving the attentions of another person believes that person to be powerful then those perceptions make it so. Your perception enhances and perpetuates his own perception and you will be continually intimidated. Ineffective communication, whether deliberate or otherwise, can also perpetuate the myth of power.

Power is entirely determined by perception and whoever thinks they have the power. Those who believe they have power have to communicate this belief to others and convince them to share that belief. Large organizations, for example, use their size and buying power to negotiate discounted terms or better deliveries. They frequently demand longer periods of credit with the implied threat that they will withdraw their patronage if they do not get what they want. Smaller organizations find that cooperation provides the individual members with greater power and respect. After all, this is the basis on which unions were formed and the principle has applied to life and industry from time immemorial.

Perception

We all want and need to know how others see us. Equally we need to determine how aware we are of the impression we are making and the accuracy of our perceptions. We all need to assess the impression we are making and ensure that our assessments are based on realistic criteria.

Each of us needs to know something about others to establish a frame of reference and to make the most of others' experience. On the other hand, however, we have to avoid judging people by labels.

Attitude

A government minister was recently lambasted for calling readers of a popular newspaper 'morons'. At approximately the same time, one of Mr Major's cabinet said even 'jerks' needed to be represented.

Frank Keating's story in *The Guardian* in June 1991 described Sunil Gavaskar, the Indian batsman, and his rejection of honorary membership of the MCC because he had too frequently been 'belittled by the rudeness and hostility of the Lord's gatesmen and stewards'. His stand was supported by numerous fans who then began telling tales about these often defensive and offensive guardians.

The stewards were sent on a training course as a result which could be likened to the charm school attended by employees of British Rail and other organizations where staff not only have to do their jobs but deal with the public as well. They are representing their companies, giving out impressions that may be lasting and attributed to the company itself rather than the individual employee who may simply be having a rotten day.

When thinking, speaking or writing, attitudes towards our audience become apparent. Ask yourself whether you think in terms of:

- us or them;
- you or we or one;
- you or I;
- he/she or just one;

Sexism, agism and prejudices of all sorts can be exhibited in the simplest sentence. Another question to ask yourself is: Do I think positively or negatively about people and situations?

Look at the point where you enter any new situation and think about how you see your role and others' role. Do you have an optimistic or pessimistic nature? Does your initial attitude turn into a self-fulfilling prophecy?

Look as well at your attitude to problems:

- Do you always make them seem big so that when you have solved them you are seen in an especially good light?
- Do you see problems as a challenge, there to be solved rather than bypassed or succumbed to?

Understanding your own attitudes and determining whether or not they need change is the first step in changing others' perceptions of you and achieving more effective communication.

The attitude of both the person communicating (delivering the message) and the person/people receiving the message affect communication. Audiences can also be affected by the attitude of an intermediary transmitting a message, for example a reporter, an interviewer or salesman representing another person's behaviour or opinions.

Excess baggage

When completing the publisher's author questionnaire for this book, I was asked how I would like my name to appear on the title page. I considered the options and nearly replied B R Hurst rather than Bernice

The Handbook of Communication Skills

Hurst. My reasoning concerned the still frequently encountered attitude towards women in business. Although there are more women in executive positions now than ever before, it is not unusual for a first reaction to be the assumption that a woman is a secretary or assistant to a more important male executive.

If a woman makes a telephone call, it is assumed she is calling on behalf of someone else higher up the ladder. If a woman answers the telephone, it is assumed that she is a gatekeeper. How many men, after all, answer corporate telephones? If a letter is signed by B R Hurst, the response is inevitably addressed to Mr Hurst. Not many people check first to find out whether B R Hurst is male or female.

Not to be unfair, though, it should be pointed out that women react in the same way to one another. It is not just men who doubt women.

The main change in the last twenty years has been the rate of acceptance once people realize that the woman they are addressing holds a position of responsibillity. There may be initial surprise or suspicion, but this is now overcome at a much faster rate than ever before. Apart from countries where women are generally expected not to leave their homes, our mental capabililties are widely accepted. Although some individuals may still resent working for a woman — and these individuals come from both sexes — this is more the exception than the rule.

But communicating with someone new, making that initial contact, reacting to a female colleague or counterpart is an area that still needs work.

This involuntary initial surprise can also crop up when encountering a colleague of a different race or religion. Just how relevant is sex, race, religion to the way in which we communicate? Must we restrict ourselves to written communications in order to avoid bringing instinctive prejudices to a business relationship? Are we all equipped with so much attitudinal luggage accumulated from childhood that we have to find a way of depositing it at the boardroom door before we start negotiating?

FEEDBACK

The problem with poor communication is that the communicator doesn't know he isn't getting across. He can and should know, though, through a combination of feedback and an awareness of others' perceptions, response and body language.

The real problem with communication is that people don't want to communicate. We have to protect our own patch and therefore we don't want people to know very much or let them have selective information only. Our egos get in the way of communication.

No matter how sophisticated and streamlined the methods and equipment we use, communication often breaks down at its most basic level — people. Operators who transmit and receive messages, whether with hi-tech equipment or more traditional methods, are largely responsible for communication failures. People often fail to prepare sufficiently for communication. We do not develop our skills and sometimes do not even recognize that skills are necessary.

Although we all communicate to some degree every day of our lives, communicating effectively is far more complicated than it may seem. Our own perceptions and others' perceptions, the degree of observation and awareness employed, are determining factors which make what may seem to be a straightforward conversation or document something far more meaningful. At the beginning of each potential encounter with another person, we should ask ourselves:

- Why are we communicating?
- What are we communicating?
- What do we think we are communicating?
- What is the best way of communicating this particular message?

Feedback plays a significant part in speaking and listening. People hear what you are saying but do they hear what you think you are saying? When you are the listener, do you let the speaker know how you feel about what he is saying?

Response, or feedback, is the means we use to exchange views on understanding and communicating with one another. It helps us each to know whether the messages we are transmitting are actually being received. Marion Haynes, in *Effective Meeting Skills*, offers the following criteria for useful feedback:

- Be descriptive rather than evaluative, leaving the listener free to accept or reject your reaction; making a value judgement about someone's performance automatically puts them on the defensive.
- Be specific rather than general leaving the listener the ability to realize for himself that this is perhaps a fault that occurs more often than he would like; do not generalize and say you always or never do the specific thing being discussed.
- Direct feedback about behaviour that the receiver can do something about, do not harp on shortcomings over which he has no control.
- Offer feedback at the earliest opportunity.
- Ensure it is communicated clearly and phrased so that it is not interpreted as criticism for its own sake or as a personal reaction rather than a response to what is being said.

Many of us have a fear of feedback. We don't want to know what others think because we may not like what we hear. Asking for feedback is like asking for a compliment. It is better not to ask because if you have to ask you may be told what you want to hear rather than receiving spontaneous comments which are more likely to be genuine and sincere.

Losing your audience

We communicate in different ways with different people under different circumstances. How do we decide the best approach for any given situation? The answer is to find out as much as possible about your audience in advance; to create terms of reference, not, as discussed earlier, to form preconceived notions, but to prepare. A little bit of background knowledge cannot go amiss so long as you refrain from making a value judgement and formulating a plan from which you are unable to deviate. Flexibility is crucial.

The pitfalls of unsuccessful communication can bore, threaten or offend an audience. It can result in a failure to achieve the object you hoped to achieve.

Give and take

Communication must be a two-way process, with people hearing and listening, perceiving and understanding one another's words and intentions. The frequent recurrence of certain terms commonly used in business support this principle:

- cash flow;
- flow chart;
- fluid;
- moving along.

Communication must flow, meetings and discussions must progress and move on.

SPEAKING

The personnel director of a medium-sized business recently told me that a newly promoted manager had come to her asking to be sent on a public speaking course as his new responsibilities included making presentations to potential clients and to the marketing department which would be promoting their products. Stephanie discussed the request with others in her department and concluded that there was far more need for training in diction and elocution than actual public speaking. It was not just confidence in front of an audience that the manager needed but a refinement of pronunciation so that others could listen more easily and understand what was being said. The technicalities of speaking slowly and clearly were just as important as the training in style and, perhaps, acting that a course in presentation would provide. They decided that the public speaking course might well be helpful but not until after some basic steps were taken in speaking. The manager had to learn to walk before he began to run.

Making contact

Mikhail Gorbachev is said, like many other powerful speakers, to make eye contact and hold it, forcing a response of some sort from the person to whom he is speaking.

Eye contact during conversation or when speaking to an audience shows that both sides are paying attention to one another. If the audience avoids the eye of the speaker, it can indicate lack of interest. If the speaker avoids the eye of the audience, it can imply lack of honesty. Enforced eye contact can pressurize the person you are addressing into responding in some way. It prevents him from ignoring you and forces a reaction of one sort or another.

Proximity can also be intimidating. Standing near to someone implies intimacy, sincerity and honesty. Not that the other person necessarily wishes to accept this. There is the classic situation of two people talking, one backing away because the other is too close, while the one who seeks proximity continues following to maintain closeness until someone ends up with their back against the wall, literally and figuratively. I have spoken elsewhere, in Chapter 5 on Employee Communications, about space and the defensiveness of people not wanting their territory invaded. Space and proximity are used to convey status and power. They can communicate all sorts of things without a single word being spoken.

Conversations

Conversations, like every other sort of communication, have different purposes and hence can be conducted in different ways. Nor are they always as simple and straightforward as they may seem. We use different language, non-verbal cues and intonation in different situations and to different people. It is often possible to listen to someone having a telephone conversation and know, without paying particular attention to the words themselves, who they are speaking to. The question to answer is, are you conveying the message you want to convey or are you giving the listener the impression that you have a hidden agenda? Are they giving you the impression that they have a hidden agenda?

Whether you are the speaker or the listener, the transmitter or receiver of a message, there are certain conventional rules to follow:

- Don't interrupt or contradict;
- Give signals to indicate that you are listening and interested;
- If necessary, give cues to indicate disagreement or boredom.

There are few of us who, when we stop to think about it, are unaware of the signals that we give others and that others give to us. Common sense and an awareness of what is going on under any given set of circumstances can be combined to increase our understanding of ourselves and others.

Speeches

The best speech I ever wrote was the one I was unable to give. After four years at university, where my extra-curricular activities centred around the formation and administration of what was called the human development centre, the time came to make my farewell speech. I spent days writing it, re-writing it and fine tuning it to make sure all the points I wanted to get across were covered along with all the emotions and feelings, respect, love and sense of accomplishment that had built up during that time. It was so good that when the time came to give it, I choked and couldn't get a word out.

During those four years I had participated in umpteen different sizes and types of groups from committees to conferences, small encounter groups to huge orientation sessions, formal and informal, as participant, chairman, trainer and leader. My audience was friendly — made up of students and teachers, friends and colleagues all. Some I had known closely for four years. Others were new acquaintances who I knew saw me as an authority figure, freshmen who had perhaps heard of the HDC and what it offered, knew of me but didn't actually know me. I wasn't trying to impress anyone but rather to break down barriers, reach out, share my experiences and feelings and help newcomers get to know me, what I'd done and why. It was a closeknit group with new members there because they were being welcomed and wanting to be welcomed.

In a sense, my failure was a success in terms of communication. Everyone knew what I wanted to say and why I was unable to say it. My obvious inability to convey the words did not in any way prevent me conveying the sincerity of my message and in the end, the session turned into a party and the speech was unnecessary. But it isn't always like that. The moral of the tale is, by all means believe in what you want to say but make sure you can say it. Use emotion to rouse feelings and convey your own feelings only if you can cope.

When speaking or making a presentation of any sort, we must know ourselves as well as we know our audience. Although the types of presentation are covered more fully in the next chapter, along with the various tools and aids you can use to help you along, before making any kind of speech you need to ask yourself if you feel more comfortable:

- speaking informally from notes; or
- with the cushion of a fully written, prepared speech.

Jacqueline Dunckel and Elizabeth Parnham describe the difference between speeches and presentations in their book, *The Business Guide to Effective Speaking*, by saying that speakers are expected to:

- entertain;
- inform;
- persuade;
- surprise.

Whereas presenters are expected to:

- explain;

- elicit information and opinions;
- persuade;
- inform sufficiently to achieve sound decisions.

Rehearsing

Before the day, try to run through your speech several times in front of:

- a friendly trial audience;
- a tape recorder;
- a video camera;
- a mirror.

Look at yourself and listen to yourself. Time yourself. Know what you sound like, compare it with what you want to sound like, make the adjustments and do it again until you are satisfied.

Dunckel and Parnham offer a number of specific suggestions regarding what to judge yourself by and how to improve. They recommend speaking the same words:

- while standing or sitting in different positions, possibly even walking or moving about, so that you can see how the sound changes;
- with and without gestures;
- with different intonations and emphasis.

Posture, breathing, diction and pronunciation all affect the way in which the audience — be it one person or a room full of people — will hear, understand and interpret what you have said.

Preparing for the worst

One other step in rehearsing your speech or presentation, even if it is a conversation with just one other person, either face-to-face or over the telephone, is to plan for contingencies. After all, what if the other person does not respond in the way you expect them to or follow the script that you had mentally devised for him?

The answer is manifold:

- Be prepared.
- Be flexible.
- Be calm.
- Be reasonable.

Run through as many scenarios as you can in advance, and try to have all the possible answers to all the possible questions. Expect someone to come up with the one you haven't thought of. When it happens, explain that you need to look into the matter further. Do not answer off the cuff, do not commit yourself to something you may not be able to fulfill, do not back yourself into a corner just to appear more knowledgeable than you are. Do not get defensive or offensive, do not reject the question or claim outright. Promise to come back with an answer or a suggestion and keep that promise. But do not promise more than you can deliver and do not try to fool anyone in order to save face.

Presentation

It is not unusual for a speaker to use the gimmick of beginning to read from a fully written speech then discarding it and speaking 'off the cuff' — or seeming to — in an effort to be spontaneous. Cue cards can be used to remind you of the highlights of your speech but should be large enough for you to read the words without studying the cards closely. They can also serve as a prop to shuffle and keep your hands occupied so that you look as if you're checking important points. You must determine which is a better approach for each individual occasion — using important reference notes or a relaxed, totally prepared speech. The various types of presentation, and the decision on what is best for different occasions, is discussed more fully in the next chapter.

LISTENING

Listening is a process of absorbing words and selecting meanings. Evaluation should come later so that you do not miss the next part of what is being said while you consider your views on the last part.

Listening is a skill and can therefore be developed and improved upon. As with other skills, self awareness and discipline are necessary in order to be a good listener and convince the speaker that you are listening, hence cooperating in the effectiveness of your (and his) communication and making it a genuinely two-way procedure.

There are certain cues that listeners can give speakers to let them know that they are paying attention. Ask the occasional intelligent question. Repeat something the speaker has said when asking a question in order to elucidate a point for yourself and others. Remember, though, that asking a question on something the speaker has already covered can indicate just the opposite — that you have not in fact been paying attention. Do not ask just for sake of asking; do not waste your time and everyone else's.

Diane Bone, in *A Practical Guide to Effective Listening*, says that most people listen at about 50 per cent efficiency during the first part of an oral communication. In other words, if tested immediately on what they just heard they would accurately remember 50 per cent. However, the efficiency rate drops quickly after the initial statements. Most people average a 25 per cent efficiency rate overall.

To improve listening skills, Bone offers a concentration checklist to her readers. She suggests rating the points on a scale from 0 to 3, as follows:

0 no problem
1 a minor problem
2 something of a problem
3 major problem

Once the statements are rated, total the score. If you have scored

0 – 5	you have excellent concentration skills.
6 – 10	your concentration skills could do with some improvement.
11 or more	you need to put into practice a specific action plan to improve your skills.

The key statements to rate when checking your concentration are:

- I'm in a hurry;
- I become distracted by what is going on around me;
- I'm self-conscious;
- I'm bored;
- I'm thinking about what I'm going to say next;
- I'm in surroundings that are out of my comfort zone;
- I already know what the speaker is going to say;
- I'm used to having things repeated;
- I'm on mental overload most of the time;
- I'm not responsible for the information given;
- I'm tired;
- I'm confused by the topic or the speaker;
- I'm daydreaming.

Do you hear what I hear?

Expectations colour responses and the degree to which we listen to people. If you know someone goes to great lengths explaining the technicalities of a simple procedure, you may stop listening. If you know someone prefaces a business conversation with a period of small talk, you may stop listening. If you know someone repeats what they are saying a second or a third time, you may stop listening.

There are passive, non-responsive listeners and active listeners. Active listeners interact in a two-way conversation or exchange and, therefore, more effective communication takes place. Listeners do communicate with speakers.

To be a successful listener, to understand what is being said and why, it is best to listen not only to the words but also to the intentions behind the words, to look at the speaker's body language and listen to non-verbal cues.

Figure 2.1 illustrates the interaction between speaker and listener. The transmitter can be a person, that is an intermediary or representative in the form of a union representative, arbitrator, salesman, personnel manager or any other kind of representative or someone from the media, or a machine (telephone, fax, computer or even manual or other form of publication). The source is the person from whom the intermediary or transmitter gets the information for the message which is then conveyed to the audience. Even by taking away the middleman or transmitter, allowing direct communication between source and audience, it is the dual existence of message and feedback that determine whether or not the communication is successful and effective.

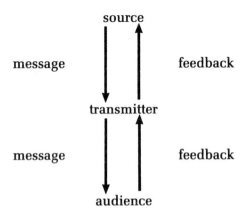

Figure 2.1   Speaker/listener interaction

Working at it

Diane Bone maintains that to be a good listener, we must involve our whole body. Someone she terms 'a whole body listener' listens actively by:

- conveying a positive, encouraging attitude;
- sitting in an attentive posture (facing the speaker);
- remaining alert but comfortable;
- nodding in acknowledgement of the speaker's words;
- making good eye contact;
- ignoring or eliminating distractions;
- tuning in to the speaker's feelings;
- looking like a listener.

She goes on to say that listener behaviour which can distract a speaker includes:

- fidgeting;
- blinking;
- biting your lip;
- frowning deeply;
- playing with your hair, tie or jewellery;
- looking at your watch.

Bone recommends pacing as a means of showing that you are listening but warns that it can also be extremely irritating and distracting. She advises that, within reason, mirroring the gestures, breathing, voice rate, vocabulary, favourite phrases and facial expressions of the speakers can indicate your interest in what they are saying and eliminate any possible conflicts between speaker and listener.

Obstacles

Michael Armstrong, in *How to be an Even Better Manager*, identifies some of the factors which prevent us from listening effectively. These include:

- an inability to concentrate;
- preoccupation with self or external issues;
- concern with what we are going to say next;
- lack of understanding of what is being said and why it is important;
- inability to follow the speaker's arguments or points;
- lack of interest.

To this I would add external distractions due to unsuitability of venue.

Taking it in and taking it down

Note taking can be an aide memoire or a distraction if it stops you listening and leaves you one step behind the speaker. Unless you develop both your writing and listening skills accordingly, note taking should be in some form of shorthand that you can read back later — do not even try to take down word for word what is being said.

It is possible to mislead through note taking as well. It may seem that you are listening and taking down what is being said when in fact you are just doodling and trying to give an impression of listening when you are actually doing no such thing.

Similarly, fidgeting can indicate that you are not listening or can indicate that you are listening and anxious to respond or interrupt and ask a question.

Eye contact can also be faked. You can watch the speaker without actually listening but conversely you can be gazing into space or even have your eyes closed in an effort to concentrate more carefully, eliminating possible distractions.

Asking questions shows you are listening as does repeating what the speaker says but this could be for show only.

Making a point

Speech is the power to convey (or not), according to requirements, our thoughts. The same applies to non-verbal communication. We can cause a deliberate distraction or disruption by riffling through papers, looking at the time, speaking to a neighbour... The message that behaviour conveys does not always coincide with the message we are trying to convey. Whatever form speaking and listening take, if we want to communicate, we must work at developing a sufficient understanding of our own and others' behaviour as both speakers and listeners in order to be effective.

Chapter 3

Presentations

This section will concentrate on standing up in front of an audience to tell them something. The size of the audience may vary, but the principles regarding preparation and presentation will remain the same.

In Part IV on written communications, you will find chapters on the construction of written presentations — reports, documents, business plans, letters etc. Speeches were included in the last chapter but will be covered to a certain extent again in this chapter.

One type of presentation not covered in this chapter is the presentation made to an invisible audience. That is, video presentations. Increasingly used as a sales tool and as an implement for training, the advent of hand-held cameras means that videos can be made more frequently, inexpensively and informally. The fact that, when participating in a video, you cannot see any reaction, or receive any feedback, needs to be taken into account. It must not be forgotten that you are, none the less, addressing people and relying on your own ability to communicate well and clearly in order to get your message across.

One major advantage of video recording is that it can be played back instantly, faults identified and, if it is not entirely satisfactory, a new version immediately recorded. This is particularly important to anyone who may be nervous or not quite sure of how he comes across to an audience. It is an ideal medium for rehearsing, for learning about yourself, and for seeing yourself as others see you. Videos are less intimidating than full-blown television or film studios and therefore more successfully used with non-professional participants.

PREPARING THE PRESENTATION

According to Michael Bland and Peter Jackson in *Effective Employee*

Communications, the reason for any form of communication is the desire to communicate and having something of importance to communicate. In order to do this, you must find ways of communicating. Presentations are one way of doing this.

Anyone who has ever made a presentation of any sort will tell you that the key to success lies in preparation and planning. Identifying your objectives is the first step to take in preparation. These provide a constant reminder of what you want to achieve and thereby help you work out how to achieve it.The use of organization and logic to work through problems, outlining the sequence and priority of tasks and points before fleshing out the presentation provide a means of formulating a structure in the simplest and most efficient possible way.

There are all sorts of tools available to make presentations both successful, informative and interesting. The use of:

- language;
- visual aids;
- design (for support material and visual aids);
- information technology;
- statistics;
- graphics, illustrations, diagrams, slides, videos;
- a formal or informal approach.

All this depends on who you are addressing, where and why.

Understanding the audience

Challenging speeches need to be constructed without being over-aggressive or off-putting. Difficult messages often need to be conveyed. Supportive speeches should neither go overboard or appear patronizing or condescending.

The ability to satisfy all those criteria largely depends on what the speaker knows about the audience. The speaker must judge where to start and have an understanding of the audience's knowledgeability. There is no point starting from square one if the audience knows what you are talking about, but a surefire way to lose an audience is to start in the middle and blind them with science.

Peter Gummer, whose nightmare recollection of speaking when ill-prepared is related later in this chapter, maintains that the ability to judge the audience is a skill which only comes from experience and awareness.

Jacqueline Dunckel and Elizabeth Parnham in *The Business Guide to Effective Speaking* offer guidelines on audience analysis. Their views on what constitutes vital information include:

- size of audience;
- age range;
- common interests if any;

- educational range;
- economic background;
- male/female ratio;
- political views if relevant;
- ethnic/racial mix if relevant;
- what benefit do they expect/can they expect from speaker;
- whether or not the presentation is linked to any specific event or occasion.

We can add to these the need to know if the audience is comprised of:

- professionals or knowledgeable laymen;
- specialists;
- employers and/or employees;
- clients and/or customers, existing or prospective;
- colleagues (superiors, equals, subordinates);
- competitors or rivals,

and whether they are there:

- to be entertained;
- because attendance is compulsory;
- because they are interested in the subject;
- because they need information

in order to:

- make a decision;
- evaluate their options;
- pass information onto others;
- satisfy some other personal need.

To this I would add that the speaker needs to be aware of any hidden agendas, including whether or not the audience is friendly or hostile and how well informed the audience is about the speaker and his views on the subject to be discussed. You can assess likely reactions to your presentation by asking yourself questions such as:

- Does the subject have special significance for the audience?
- Do they want to achieve something by being there?
- Will they gain or lose by the proposals?
- Are there preconceived views to overcome regarding either the subject or the presenter?
- Is the presenter's help needed in making a decision?
- How much decision making power and authority does the audience have?

- Is there a coincidence or a conflict of views between presenter and audience?

And to these I would add:

- Why me?
- Why have I been asked to speak on this subject?
- Why does this audience want to hear about this subject?
- Why have this speaker and this subject been combined to address this audience?

Once those questions are answered, you will begin to see the way to tailor your presentation to meet both your own needs and those of the audience.

Perceptions and shared understanding

Your perception of others and others' perception of you are equally important. We all need to be aware that others in a group or at the receiving end of written communications are doing the same thing we are. Although it is not advisable to succumb to paranoia, it does no harm to realize that others may be reading between the lines and looking at the presentation as well as the message.

Communication cannot succeed without understanding. We need to know what our own motives and intentions are. We may want to be (and be) perceived in different ways by different people. The accuracy of our perceptions of others, the ways in which we formulate our opinions and the ways in which we use our perceptions of others to shape the way in which we communicate with them has a direct bearing on how others see us. Perception goes hand in hand with communication.

Communication styles vary according to the role we are playing and the role in which we see our audiences. We speak differently to friends and colleagues, up and down the business ladder. We display different attitudes, tone, vocabulary, manner, body language and even degrees of openness in different groups. We can be totally different people within peer groups, departments and teams, to people at higher and lower levels, to people within or outside our company depending on whether they are customers or clients, buying or selling.

Preparing your speech

When writing a speech or document, it isn't actually necessary to start at the beginning and work through to the end. Starting with the main point, then listing or outlining subsidiary points which are then put in order and prioritized, will help the beginning and end fall naturally into place.

Trevor Bentley offers advice in his book *Effective Communication for the Accountant* on judging the timing, speed and structure for a speech:

- The written speech should contain no more than 60 words for each minute of speaking time (note that everyone's speed is different however, and it is best to time yourself reading a speech aloud before calculating the precise number of words per minute which suits your style).

- Divide the presentation into three parts allowing 10 per cent of the time allowed for the introduction, 70 per cent for the main body of the speech and 20 per cent for the summary.
- Spend no more than five minutes on each main point in the body of the presentation.

Although these should be taken as guidelines rather than hard and fast rules, they do make sense and provide a basis from which to work.

In addition to visual aids, which will be discussed later, there are a number of methods popularly used to get the message across.

- Surprise or shock.
- Humour.
- Statistics and hard facts.
- Emotion.
- Illustration and example.

There are also a number of tips that may prove useful when making the speech:

- Highlight notes or manuscript, making them as easy to read as possible so that you don't lose your place.
- Order notes in the sequence you want to follow.
- Allow plenty of space so that a mere glance at the page will help you find what you are looking for.
- Keep paragraphs short — closely typed or handwritten sheets are not conducive to jogging the memory quickly.
- Use key words or cues as prompts.

If you are speaking from notes, partly in an impromptu manner, keep an eye on the time. Don't wander too much or spend so much time on some points that you haven't got enough time to cover all the points you feel it necessary to make.

Rehearsals

One of the golden rules in preparing for a presentation is to rehearse. An unresponsive audience can make a speaker very nervous and it is best to be prepared for that as well as hecklers and awkward questions. Not only the presentation itself must be prepared but scenarios rehearsed for possible responses to the presentation and responses to those responses.

I mentioned rehearsals in Chapter 2 on Speaking and Listening and feel it does not do any harm to repeat the key points here. Stand in front of a mirror or use a tape recorder; ask a friend to listen to you and comment; if you have someone with a video camera to record you so you can see yourself, all the better. The more familiar you are with the way you appear to the audience, the more able you will be to understand their reactions. And the more control you will have over the way in which you come across.

One word of warning however — too much rehearsal can make you stale. So, like everything else, do not overdo it. Know what you have in mind but avoid rehearsing so much that the final presentation lacks spontaneity and enthusiasm.

Setting the scene

On the day of the presentation, be sure to leave enough time to arrive early regardless of delays en route. On arrival, check that circumstances have not changed — the meeting hasn't been postponed or cancelled, the other speakers delayed, the chairman taken ill, a hurricane or monsoon washed out the approach road, a meteor landed on the roof...

Prior to the presentation, conference, meeting or training session the organizer should confirm:

- room reservations (both for the presentation and anyone who needs accommodation);
- size and shape of the room are suitable for the presentation you have planned;
- travel arrangements;
- catering arrangements;
- presence and functionality of equipment;
- seating arrangements — that there are enough seats and that they are arranged so that the audience can see and hear the speaker and any visual aids that may be used;
- that there are sufficient lights, heat and ventilation;
- that external distractions have been minimalized;
- enrolment and expected attendance;
- that the audience knows the time, date and place of the presentation;
- provision of any support material which may have to be distributed.

Knowing your place

Before planning your presentation, try to find out the agenda for the session and your place on it. Find out:

- who else will be speaking and on what subject;
- who will be in the audience and their likely attitude;
- what the audience knows about you and your views as well as about the subject.

In short, follow the steps outlined earlier in the chapter for researching the audience.

If you are one of several people making a presentation, try to find out your position in the queue. At a board meeting I attended recently, two of the directors nodded off immediately after lunch to the discomfort of their companions and the consultant attempting to advise them, at their request, on a new design concept. On another occasion, several managers of a different company glazed over by the time the third pitch of the day began. A colleague was humiliated during a presentation when the prospective clients began to laugh hysterically. Not, it transpired, because of what he had said but because it was 3.30 in the afternoon and their meeting had begun at 8.30 that morning with an almost identical presentation from one of his rivals.

Supporting material

Should supporting material be distributed before or after the presentation? If it is circulated prior to the meeting, the audience will be familiar with your views and proposals, better informed and able to comment and discuss. If it is distributed immediately before the meeting, however, they are likely to be reading rather than listening. It is better, therefore, to make your presentation first, with all the pros and cons, value judgements and recommendations before letting them get into nitty gritty discussions.

Confronting the audience

Peter Gummer, chairman of Shandwick, currently the world's largest public relations group, wrote his story for a regular column in the *Independent on Sunday* called My Biggest Mistake. Invited to give a 90-minute speech to 50 middle to top ranking businessmen at a management conference in Brussels, he learned a hard lesson in the need for adequate preparation.

'Secretly I thought: wasn't presentation the key skill in public relations? Couldn't I "snow" my way through any minor difficulties, such as lack of knowledge?' When the organizer asked for Mr Gummer's lecture notes, he responded with jargon about 'participative conference techniques' and said he would 'send notes to delegates after synthesizing their views'.

The audience realized immediately that he was unprepared and they knew more about his subject than he ever would. He realized after just 15 minutes that he had lost them and then attempted to get them back by asking for participation, shared experiences and questions. Nothing worked and he was forced to give up halfway through his allotted time, retreating to nurse his wounds.

'Mistakes like that arise from personal failings — in my case, arrogance,' wrote Gummer. 'I believed I could, by force of personality and persuasion, bluff my way through a lack of knowledge. My audience saw straight through me and made me suffer for my sins.' On the flight home, he listed the reasons why he had performed so badly. He had, he felt:

- cared more about what he wanted to say than what the audience wanted to hear;
- not had enough material;
- not prepared enough;
- not been flexible.

Someone who had prepared more appropriately and successfully would have:

- asked himself who the audience is and what they want from his session;
- had at least three times as much material as he anticipated needing on the assumption that something will inevitably go wrong or someone will ask the wrong question;
- learned to read a live audience and react to them — something only experience will teach;
- allowed, for every five minutes allotted for the presentation, 60 minutes of concentrated preparation and three full rehearsals;
- had confidence in what he had to say in order to adapt as the mood of the audience changed.

Take a deep breath

Not very many people will admit to not feeling nervous before a presentation. Exercises ranging from deep breathing to yoga can relax you and are to be found without difficulty in books devoted exclusively to the subject of presentation and tranquility.

Confidence, timing and awareness of both the audience and your own strengths and weaknesses are all essential and, once mastered, will result in interesting and successful presentations.

The secret of timing is linked to relaxing. Do not speak too quickly or too slowly, do not speak too loudly or too softly, do not try to shout over audience response. If they laugh at your joke, wait until they settle down. If there is a heckler, answer his comments or tell him to shut up or to join you on the stage. Do not try to compete with him. If people are rattling their sweet wrappers or chatting among themselves, if they are discussing some point you have raised, razzing you or cheering you on, ride it out. Do not try to carry on regardless. Go with the audience, respond to them and keep calm.

Presentations can inadvertently get interrupted by well meaning colleagues. You may be invited to sit when you prefer to stand; you may be asked a question that anticipates something you planned to cover further along in the presentation. Do not let this shake you. Explain that you prefer to follow the outline you have drawn up, ask for the audience's patience and have them bear with you. Do things your way. If you let them put you off your stride you may not get back on track again.

Speakers and audiences must empathize with one another. They must not only listen to words but take note of body language and non-verbal gestures. Eye contact is the most obvious of these.

Tone of voice and posture can also indicate attitude. Mrs Thatcher, in her early days as Prime Minister, underwent much publicized speech lessons to make her voice sound less high pitched, deeper, sexier and more feminine. She began to lean forward, towards her audience, when she spoke. The proximity discussed in Chapter 2 was exercised to convey her sincerity and conviction in what she was saying. By conveying her own conviction, she attempted to convert her audience to her way of thinking. Sometimes she succeeded. On other occasions, her audience viewed her behaviour as so contrived and insincere that she was less successful.

Both voice control and tone are important. It is not only what you say that counts but how you say it. Diane Keaton in the film *Baby Boom* was offered a price for buying out her business. 'That's it?' she asked. By posing a question rather than making a statement of exclamation with emphasis to indicate finish, she told her potential customers that she wanted more. The old musical *Singing in the Rain* concerned the advent of talkies when actors' voices killed their careers.

As an exercise, think about which type of voice makes people listen or not listen to what is being said. Read a passage into a tape recorder and then read it again with different intonations. Try emphasizing different words or using different pronunciations, speeds and strengths. Play it back and list the differences you can hear. After all, hearing is just as important as seeing.

The devil you know

I've said it before and I'll say it again. Find out who you are presenting to, their degree of understanding of your subject and how important it is to them. Find out why they are there, whether out of duty or interest, and whether they are friendly or hostile.

Not all presentations are made to groups of strangers; they can be made to colleagues or to potential clients. Presentations can be made to boards of directors, shareholders, groups of decision makers within your company, or clients. The latter can be potential customers or someone for whom you are already working but to whom you have to present plans, for instance in the case of an architect showing drawings, models and costings to be approved.

You may also be presenting to intermediaries, for example members of the press or marketing and sales teams who have to go out and sell new products based on your presentation to them. You may have to sell to the team who will do the selling. Some years ago I made a video for a publisher promoting their new list of titles. The video included interviews with authors, cookery demonstrations and shots in the garden. The publisher told the marketing and sales people the whole background to the book and to its target audience in order to give them maximum ammunition. Another publisher I know sent a junior manager on a presentation training course solely to teach her how to present their new list to the sales team.

Presentations to colleagues can also be on the subject of change. Certain questions are likely to be asked by the audience and should be pre-empted by the speaker:

- Is there a problem?
- What is it and how has it arisen?
- How can it be solved?
- Is there a need for change?
- What will happen as a result?
- Where do we go from here?

Reaching out

Many people regard presentations as performances. The speaker must reach out to the audience and form a relationship if the message being transmitted is to be accepted.

Who or what the speaker looks at when speaking to a group — a point on the wall, a specific individual, his notes, visual aids or nothing in particular tells the audience just how confident or nervous he is.

Reactions to non-verbal communication, hidden agendas or body language can be:

- sympathetic;
- susceptible;
- suspicious;
- cooperative;
- questioning;
- responsive.

Participants at conferences, meetings and presentations frequently joke about how obvious it is who has done which course. They often know what the other knows, and what the other doesn't know, and play games which can have varying degrees of malicious intent to them. Members of a panel, for example, when they are not speaking, can still communicate with the audience and affect the way the speaker and the audience are communicating.

Showing that you are interested in your subject and interested in the way the audience responds, will go a long way to convincing them.

Audiences can also be involved in the presentation in order to obtain their cooperation. They can simply be asked for responses or they can be divided into groups with tasks to perform. Reporting back and discussing proposals or opinions can inspire a feeling of loyalty and ownership which is discussed in more detail in Chapter 5 on Employee Communications.

Making your point

When you are making an oral presentation, the audience needs to know where you are taking them. The presentation should start with an outline of what you are going to say. You then need to make your points, or say what you are going to say. Finally, summarize what you have said and tell the audience that you have said it.

Written presentations take much the same form. The introduction announces your intentions, the body of the document expands on this loose outline and, finally, the summary restates the main points of what you have said.

There are many ways of getting an audience to listen to what you have to say. The first is to surprise them and grab their attention. Tantalize them. Promise them something. Arouse their curiosity.

The second is to threaten them. Worry them, frighten them, force them to listen.

A third is to challenge them, involve them, motivate them. Depending on which of those three objectives you want to achieve, different methods need to be selected and employed.

Repetition as reinforcement

A good speaker must know when to draw the line after his point is made rather than belabouring it *ad nauseum*. Try taking a simple proposal and see how many different ways there are of saying the same thing.

Repetition is an approach that many books on communication have in common. Cross referencing is a useful tool, particularly when subjects overlap. There is, therefore, a need for some repetition but how much? I cannot tell you how often different authors have recommended the same structure:

- tell them what you're going to say;
- tell them;
- tell them you've told them.

Establishing a rapport

Charm, compliments, frankness and subtlety all have both advantages and disadvantages. It is up to the speaker to decide how to use each style, and how to use them while simultaneously avoiding an air of being either patronizing or contemptuous. I have met smooth talkers who are so obviously playing a role that they are laughable. And I have found myself distrusting people who are sincerely charming. Some of us have got so used to subterfuge and something less than total openness that honesty is unfamiliar. Trust must be built, and perceived, if it is to be effective.

Negative messages can be conveyed both verbally and non-verbally. You can communicate confusion, concern and fear deliberately or not.

Anecdotes can be used as illustrations to make a point, increase or maintain interest, establish a relationship or rapport. They don't necessarily have to be humourous, but when presented as evidence and supporting material can back up a point that may benefit from clarification by example.

Telling people doesn't necessarily convince them. Showing them may.

Both speaker and audience need to consider their own expectations with regard to:

- what they expect to hear, say and see;
- the response they expect to get;
- how to react if anything differs from expectations;
- how to communicate with each other;
- how to react to/see/feel others' reactions.

They both need to be aware, look at clues then assess quickly the need for any change in order to make the necessary adjustments. The whole process must then repeat itself and awareness start the cycle all over again.

Getting out alive

The conclusion is sometimes the hardest part of a speech or presentation. Learning how to call it quits and stop rabbiting on is another of the skills that a good speaker must learn. There are, of course, alternative ways of drawing a presentation to a close. You can:

- ask a question, sit down and leave the audience to mull over the answer;
- summarize and repeat the main points of the presentation;
- present an action plan, say this is it, thank you for listening and sit down;
- ask for questions and comments.

Visual aids

One way of ensuring that your audience follows what you are saying during a complicated presentation is through the use of visual aids.

Visual aids must support your presentation, not be used to make your point for you. As Jacqueline Dunckel and Elizabeth Parnham say in *The Business Guide to Effective Speaking*, aids should be used to help the audience understand or believe the points you are making. It is the combined impact of the vocal and visual that should be used to get the message across. According to Dunckel and Parnham, 'The great danger is that presenters place the major emphasis on visual aids and relegate themselves to the minor role of narrator or technician. You are central to the presentation. It needs you, your interpretation, your explanation, your conviction, and your justification.'

Jane Allan believes that while most of us generally only retain some 20 per cent of what we hear during a presentation, visual aids can increase this to as much as 80 per cent. Peter Sheal, in *How to Develop and Present Staff Training Courses*, quotes a study by the University of Minnesota which shows that the use of visual aids can increase a presenter's persuasiveness by 43 per cent.

Visual aids are indisputably helpful to the speaker. They can and should be used to reinforce your message to the audience and give them a chance to take it in, remembering what you have said even when you have moved on to another point. Like any other tool, however, they should be used to supplement other methods, not to replace them. As Sheal and others agree, they should enhance a performance not compete with it.

Michael Stevens, in *How to Improve Your Presentation Skills*, points out that 'the proper use of aids is to achieve something in your presentation that you can't do as effectively with words alone'.

When deciding whether or not to use visual aids, and what kind of aid to use, you must consider:

- whether they are a means of visualizing something which cannot physically be brought in to the presentation;
- what purpose the visualization serves;
- whether the point can be adequately verbalized;
- does the visual aid achieve unity;
- is the aid of benefit to the presenter, audience or both;
- is it readable by everyone in the room.

Michael Stevens summarizes the pros and cons of using aids. When used correctly, he says, they can:

- provide a change from listening and grab the audience's attention;
- allow the audience to absorb information in a way, and at a rate, that suits them individually;
- clarify complex information;
- trigger response from the audience;
- save time in explaining details;
- ensure that the message is received and retained at a higher level than it might be through verbalization alone.

When used incorrectly, Stevens says, visual aids can:

- distract the audience from your message;
- distract the presenter from his purpose by having to refer to the aid and, possibly, operate it or create it in the case of a drawing;
- mislead or confuse the audience if they are not clear, well designed or well presented;
- unnecessarily add to the complexity of the presentation.

Steve Mandel, in *Effective Presentation Skills*, adds his advice against using visual aids to:

- impress the audience with excessively detailed tables or graphs;
- avoid interaction with the audience;
- make more than one point;
- present simple ideas that can be stated verbally.

Mandel repeats, in this context, the message stressed throughout this book and every other book on communications I have read — Keep It Short and Simple. KISS is a principle that applies throughout discussions of effective communications and should not be forgotten whatever the type of presentation and audience.

Props

This is not the place to go into great detail on the wide range of aids which can be selected. Flipcharts, graphs, slides, videos all have to be prepared and specified according to requirements. They can be tailor-made by consultants or in-house, or bought off the shelf from an ever increasing range of products. It is only after you have decided why an aid would be helpful, what type is most suitable for your presentation and how you want to use it that you should begin to narrow down the field and make your choice.

Props and visual aids should not be used as a means of avoiding the audience. Eye contact is still crucial and although you may have to turn slightly to face the aid for part of the time, you should never speak while facing away from the audience.

The point of using visual aids is that the audience should be able to see them for themselves. They do not have to be read to the audience but rather discussed.

In addition to unexpected props which can be used to illustrate the presentation, podiums and lecterns, notes, pointers and even pens can be used as props. They give you something to do with your hands and can make you feel less awkward and self-conscious. One last time, the most successful presenter is the confident and relaxed presenter. If it takes props to help you achieve this, then do not cast them aside.

EXHIBITIONS

Exhibitions are a very special form of presentation. They must be eye-catching and attractive, aiming to make visitors stop at your stand and look to see what you have on offer. You are literally in the open market, competing with umpteen others who are after the same audience as you. There are two reasons for attending an exhibition:

- Generation of new contacts and new business.

- Flag waving, publicity and prestige.

Both the representatives you send to the exhibition and the support materials communicate the quality of your organization and product or service.

If you are visiting an exhibition, your aims are probably the same as the exhibitors'. You are there to gather information, see what others are doing, collect as much material as possible to take back to home base and consider at your leisure. So you are just as interested in who and what you see as in what you can take away.

At an exhibition in London recently, the Training Enterprise Council mounted an expensive and highly visual laser show. There were multiple screens and display units full of brochures. It was all very impressive and satisfied most of the criteria for successful exhibiting. It failed on one important count however. During the afternoon I walked past the stand at least three times and not once did I see a single representative of the TEC standing there speaking to visitors. There were no people to talk to, thus reducing the impact of the display to the superficial only, and a great opportunity to make a presentation to a new audience was lost.

PUTTING ON THE RITZ

First impressions, no matter how open minded we try to be, are invariably based on appearance. What we should aim at is getting beyond first impressions to second impressions. Even if these are, in the end, the same they ought to be based on additional evidence and investigation, understanding and consideration. The words we hear and the sights we see form first impressions.

Convention with regard to fashion changes almost weekly in some countries. In others, dress has been the same since time began. The way we dress is tied up with the way we want to be seen, the culture we come from, our own sense of style and the rules we have to follow.

We often choose how to dress in a particular situation because of the impression we want to make. There are people who deliberately dress down to show a lack of interest or importance, for example. The old story of the rich man who dressed like a tramp so that people would like him for himself alone comes to mind as does that of the poor young girl who borrows a friend's jewels and furs so that no one knows she comes from the wrong side of the tracks.

Uniforms immediately tell people something about us. But even uniforms have to be kept clean, neat and tidy. Unshined shoes, shabby collars and cuffs, missing buttons all convey their own message.

Whether we choose to dress in the height of fashion or in a more traditional style, the care we take of our appearance is what communicates something about us to others. Comfort, suitability, grooming and custom all have a bearing. In many Western countries, dress rules are fairly relaxed. Women are no longer required to wear hats, gloves and stockings. Men may wear jumpers and jackets instead of suits, colour is permissible in shirts and ties. A large wardrobe is not necessary so long as clothes are well cared for.

Environment and circumstances are also allowed to dictate to a certain extent. Bermuda shorts have become acceptable for men and women; women are not permitted to wear trousers in many countries. The degree of formality and the severity of rules such as the following are no longer accepted as hard and fast:

- Don't keep a sweater in your office to wear on cold days; it won't go with everything and will develop bumps and droops.
- Dress and suit lines should not show below a coat unless it is three-quarter length.
- Ankle strap shoes are not for business; choose business shoes with a medium heel height.
- Short-sleeve shirts may be great for leisure wear but work in long-sleeved shirts; the touch of white or pale colour at the cuff is good.
- Avoid flamboyant colours and patterns when choosing ties...ties with narrow stripes with a fine red line are considered sincere and honest by the experts.

Some rules are perennial, however:

- Make sure your clothes fit, suit you and are comfortable.
- Make sure they are not in need of repair or cleaning.
- Choose a hairstyle that suits you.
- Choose makeup and jewellery (both men and women) that suit you.
- Consider the environment and don't wear clothes that are too light or too heavy for the room and the town where you will be speaking or working.

Appearance consists of more than clothes and accessories, however. Posture when speaking or listening in different situations tells its own tale. Do you sit up/stand straight or do you slump and need something to lean on?

Whether you stand or sit conveys a message regarding the formality of your presentation. Where you position your hands, whether you are stiff or relaxed, stand still or pace, gesticulate or not all gives the audience clues to your own attitude and helps them form a perception of your personality as much as your message.

Appearance is another of those facts of life that we must accept and do our best to control. No matter how much we may deny it, we all make judgements based on appearance. The secret is to tailor appearance so that it says what we want it to and accurately conveys our message. We each have to develop our own style, one with which we are comfortable but which is suitable for each occasion and audience. Style can be adaptable and the facility to be flexible is a skill which applies as much to appearance as it does to every other aspect of communication.

Consideration of dress is just as applicable in the chapters of this book on employee communications, marketing and public relations, international communications and meetings. I have covered it here in Presentations because, in effect, every time we communicate with someone we are making a presentation. We are presenting ourselves, our organizations and our messages. And the first thing that people judge us, our organizations and our messages on is our appearance and whether it communicates trust, reliability and sense. We have to convince people to listen to us and we frequently decide whether to listen to others or not, based largely on those first impressions created by appearance.

Presenting the establishment

Virtually the same comments apply to working environment as to dress. We are all judged, to a certain extent, on appearances. What appeals to one person and is interpreted in one way, can be just the opposite to someone else. My own office is small, situated in a village in the country. It is attached to a house and looks out over a beautiful garden. The atmosphere is informal.

Potential clients often come to visit before deciding whether or not to work with us. We have lost some jobs because of the size and location of the office and because the decor is homely rather than slick. Our furniture is not expensive and the pictures on the wall are photographs and posters, all with their own tales to tell. They are not original oil paintings.

Yet we have also won jobs because of the impression we give of knowing what we are doing. Our efficiency and reliability, the fact that everyone in the office knows all about each client and gives them a great deal of attention, wins us more clients than we lose.

Some people believe that a high price tag or glitzy window dressing means high quality. A slick, glossy presentation may not be more than surface deep. Other people look beyond the surface, take up references, judge by quality and reliability. They are more interested in delivery on time and within budget.

Those clients that we lose, if their decision is based on first impressions only, are not necessarily those that we would be able to work with on a long-term basis.

As with dress, the appearance, location and image presented by premises could be discussed in other parts of the book. Environment must be conducive to employee communications, it is part of the marketing and public relations tale that we tell to visitors. Status can be communicated the minute a visitor walks in the door. Most of us, if we are as aware and perceptive as I keep preaching we should be, will notice the way in which an organization considers internal communications and look at the way employees perform when making a judgement. It is not just the appearance of an office to outsiders that is important but the way in which insiders function within that environment.

Chapter 4

Meetings

A solicitor on a television sitcom I watched recently was setting off for an appointment. 'Have a good meeting,' said his secretary. 'There's no such thing,' he replied grimly, 'but thanks for the thought.'

Although I have said from the outset that the theme of this book is effective communication, and stressed that there are a number of different ways in which to achieve this end, meetings only sometimes qualify as one of them. There are meetings and meetings. There are long meetings and short meetings, meetings between two people and hundreds of people, meetings that proceed apace and meetings that drag. There are meetings that are worth every minute spent at them and meetings that are a complete and total waste of time.

Using a meeting as a means of effective communication is not difficult. It requires thought, planning, organization and firmness. A current issue, one requiring discussion and decision, is generally the reason for instigating a meeting. If we were to equate an agenda to a news item and take the analogy one step further, anyone thinking of arranging a meeting should first consider the questions generally asked of himself by someone about to sit down and write a news report:

- Who?
- When?
- Where?
- Why?
- How?

Or, to be more explicit:

- Who should attend the meeting?
- When should it be held?

- Where should it be held?
- Why should it be arranged and why would anyone invited want to attend?
- How should it be arranged?

WHO?

The answer to this depends on the issue and the reason for having the meeting.

- Do you want public opinion on some corporate development?
- Do you want press coverage?
- Do you want to brief your sales team on a new product?
- Do you want to exchange ideas with colleagues?

Examine the subject to be discussed, the reasons for discussing it and the ends you hope to achieve. Then decide who you need to discuss it with.

WHEN?

Breakfast meeting, evening meeting, morning or afternoon? The answer to this one depends partly on demographics and proximity.

- Do people have to travel far to get to the meeting?
- Are they occupied with different jobs during the day, making it difficult for them to get away?
- Would they (and you) prefer to meet early in the morning when everyone is fresh and ready to start the day?

It is generally accepted that decisions are reached more quickly at morning meetings; the period just after lunch tends to be when we are all at our lowest ebb.

Look at the list you have drawn up of people who should attend the meeting and then decide the best time for scheduling it.

WHERE?

Your place or mine? Office, meeting room or conference centre? The size of the venue depends on the number of people attending and the facilities needed.

- Do you need audio visual equipment?
- How is your presentation going to be structured?
- Is an audience going to be addressed or is the meeting to be a discussion group?

And again you need to consider who is coming to the meeting.

- How far do they have to travel?
- Should the meeting place be centrally located, near public transportation?
- What kind of refreshments will be offered?
- How long will the meeting last?
- Should there be rooms available for those who have come from a distance and may need to spend the night?

WHY?

This is the big one.

- Is a meeting really necessary?
- Is it going to accomplish something that cannot be accomplished with telephone calls and letters?
- Is there a good reason for getting people together to discuss the issue?
- Is it worth their while to attend?

Think about the time it will take to arrange and attend the meeting, to prepare any necessary documentation, to circulate minutes afterwards. Consider whether or not a meeting is the best way of communicating to this group at this time, in this place, on this subject and then ask

- Is there a satisfactory alternative?

HOW?

If, when you have answered all of these questions, you believe that a meeting would be helpful then you must devise a plan for setting it up. It might be as simple as making a few telephone calls with your diary open in front of you. It could be that you simply have to invite someone to see you and fix a mutually convenient time and place. Or it could be that you need to reserve a venue, create an invitation list, set a date and inform others of your decision.

Regardless of the size and place, every meeting should have an agenda no matter how informal it may be. There must be a degree of planning to ensure that the actual event serves its purpose and does not meander along out of control. You need to decide whether supporting documentation needs to be circulated in advance, the style of the meeting and presentation, who will chair it and how long it will last.

Meetings that are not planned in advance can turn into open-ended marathons which are not helpful to anyone. No one who attends a meeting has an infinite amount of time available. Everyone who has ever attended a meeting of any sort will tell you that the business to hand should be conducted in the most expedient way possible. This does not necessarily mean that the agenda must be covered at the speed of light, eliminating questions and discussion time, leaving people feeling that they have not had sufficient time to consider the issues. But it does mean that filibustering is out, prolonged political statements are out and that the task in hand is what should be focused on.

Choosing a format

Although all meetings need a reason to justify their very existence, there are many different types each suitable for a different purpose.

Conferences

Used for intensive discussion and decision making, when a large number of people need to be gathered together to see or hear a presentation. Conferences, to use their literal definition, provide an opportunity for people to confer, to get together and exchange views, to hear what others with whom they may not be in frequent or regular contact have to say on a subject. They are generally attended by people of similar interest and position and often provide an opportunity for presentations by experts on the subject who may not otherwise be available at first hand. When several experts are in attendance, unique opportunities for debate can present themselves.

Conferences may consist of various other types of meetings such as the others mentioned here. There may be a keynote speech followed by plenary workshops which report back to the general meeting for instance.

A well organized conference can stimulate ideas and actions in a way that no other type of meeting, by itself, is able to do.

Workshops

Tasks and workshops are often used as means of developing a group or team and encouraging them to work together. Each group should contain between six and twelve people for maximum interaction to occur.

Committees, or groups of people who attend regular but infrequent meetings and do not get the opportunity to know one another and exchange views, often benefit from having the occasional workshop session. With a specific task to accomplish, they begin to work together, building a cohesive team. Even if they don't always agree, they at least begin to identify one another's strengths, weaknesses, skills and beliefs. When they go back to their committee structure they take with them a relationship.

Task oriented workshops also serve to break the ice rapidly so that in short conferences the best use is made of a limited amount of time. A group of people, whether strangers or not, begins to learn about themselves and one another with the result that decisions are made with more assurance and sharing than a more formal structure might allow.

Brainstorming

Brainstorming sessions consist of small groups interested in a particular subject gathering with a large board or sheet of paper in clear view so that they can toss out ideas as they think of them. Each idea is noted for later discussion but no immediate discussion takes place. The point of the exercise is to get as many ideas as possible on the agenda for full consideration.

When brainstorming, an idea contributed by one person often stimulates another idea and another until the interaction produces, almost of its own accord, a result. This unstructured method can be extremely productive and creative, with lateral thinking playing a vital part in the development of ideas. At the end of the session the ideas listed can be prioritized and those that are of least interest or practicability eliminated.

Committees

When a group or an organization is too large to consider all the options and make a sensible decision, representatives are appointed to do the necessary research, compose recommendations and present them for final approval. In itself, the intention is to keep fewer people tied up and, by using a few experts, get the best possible recommendation and advice on which to base the decision. Sometimes committees solve problems, sometimes they don't. Roger Bennett in *Personal Effectiveness*, summarizes the pros and cons of committees. In their favour are:

- ease of coordination and management control;
- utilization of talents, experience and creative abilities;
- shared responsibility;
- extensive in-depth discussion;
- compromises can be reached rather than arbitrary or extreme decisions;
- representatives from a range of interest groups, often with conflicting requirements, can be heard;
- distribution of the concentration of power.

Bennett says that the disadvantages of committees include

- high operating costs when members are at meetings or doing committee work instead of doing their jobs;
- the possibilities of trivial arguments and personal conflicts developing, including the struggle for leadership;
- indecision leading to compromise rather than positive courses of action;
- abrogation of individual responsibility;
- slow decision making.

All of Bennett's points hold true in different circumstances and it is up to the individual or organization to decide when and how committees should be used to good purpose. Compromise, for example, is a form of consensus, frequently encountered in a democratic situation. Unanimity is a rare thing in a group. When a majority of those in a group agree to a specific action or decision, a consensus or compromise can be said to have been reached. This may be less than satisfactory to the minority but it is nonetheless acceptable and a far more practical way of approaching decision making.

Advisory panels

Three organizations with advisory panels can be used to illustrate some of the functions they can fulfill.

- RSS is a pharmaceutical research company, testing new products for its clients; it has an ethics committee composed of objective consumers with no stake in the company whatsoever who meet twice a year to discuss projects that the company is considering and advise on whether they are acceptable or not in moral rather than commercial terms.
- Directory Books Ltd is a business publisher, specializing in directories, which sets up advisory panels, each consisting of different people, to consider the need for information in different fields; representatives of the specific industry and its trade associations and publications are invited to discuss their needs and help identify gaps which the publisher then finds a way to fill.
- PG Partners organizes events which involve exhibitors and entertainment for the general public; they have to obtain sponsorship in order to fund the event and support in order to stage it. Their steering committee is comprised of people who understand the logistics of the physical criteria, representatives from sponsors who have a financial stake in seeing that the event is successful and a number of program planners whose job it is to see that there are enough exciting activities planned to guarantee attendance. These people do not actually see that the event takes place but help to plan an event that fulfills all their separate requirements.

Each of these panels provides assessment and feedback. In order to do so, the aim of the company or organization has to be communicated. So they not only have to function as self-contained, efficient groups, they must also relate to the parent company or organization. Each of their members, because they have no permanent association with the parent company or organization, undertakes to accept a responsibility which is additional to the other tasks in their lives. They are busy people and as such want to do their jobs with the fewest possible meetings. When they do get together, they insist that their sessions are conducted in the most efficient, well organized way possible.

Public meetings

This is a particular type of meeting arranged by a business perhaps to announce and get feedback on plans which might affect the community.

A local hotel, for example, wanted to build a leisure centre and an additional wing to house staff. There would be an increase in the noise level both during construction and when the new buildings became operative. There would be a need for increased parking and more people would be moving in and out.

The new centre and the hotel's expansion, however, would attract new people to the area for tourism and would offer more jobs to local people.

Management felt that the community needed to be aware of their plans and wanted the opportunity to weigh up the pros and cons with people who might be affected. They wanted the community's opinions and also wanted to build a good relationship.

The gathering

Time and space allowed before a meeting starts allows participants to mingle, break the ice, chat and generally get to know each other especially in a group which doesn't meet very often. If there is no space and people have to take their seats as soon as they come in, they may introduce themselves and speak to their neighbours but can only have access to those in their immediate vicinity. If there is sufficient space to mingle before the meeting starts, or during a break, they are then able to speak to several others consecutively and/or simultaneously rather than being limited to those either side of them.

Unless the group is very large and a presentation is taking place, the meeting should start with new members being introduced to the group. There are advantages to distributing nameplates in a group which doesn't meet often, including a line about the person's job title or the organization from which he comes.

Hard or soft

The degree of formality built into a meeting depends on a combination of format, purpose, location and attendance. Large groups tend to be more formal in order to keep them in order, small groups can sometimes be leaderless and self-contained. Presentations can take the form of speeches, papers, videos in any of their various alternatives. Chapter 3 explains some of the alternatives, and the skills needed to make sure they work, in greater detail.

Let's take a break

Breaks are especially important in meetings that are likely to carry on for some time. The chance to stretch our legs, take a few deep breaths and perhaps have some refreshments, as well as the opportunity to have conversations with others, brings people back to the subject at hand with fresh enthusiasm and interest. And occasionally, having had a chance to think things over, with new ideas or more willingness to accept what others may be saying.

Those who may not have spoken to others, or to all of the others, prior to the meeting, may appreciate the opportunity for informal conversations during breaks. Once they have heard various views during the course of the meeting, they may then need the chance to speak directly to various people outside the context of the meeting. Some of the liaisons and conversations which take place prior to the meeting, or during breaks, may actually determine the course and/or outcome of the entire session.

Timing

It is not always possible to schedule important meetings for morning sessions when people are fresh and clearheaded. Afternoon meetings, especially when they take place immediately after lunch, may be attended by people not prepared to give their undivided attention to the subject or able to give it due consideration. But in any lengthy meeting, decisions may eventually be made just so that the meeting will be drawn to a close – clearly very dangerous. Lengthy meetings must take breaks in order to prevent participants from nodding off.

Watching the clock

Part of the chairman's role in organizing the meeting is setting the agenda and ensuring that it is followed. Making best use of the time allowed, and not letting sessions turn into marathons, is also the chairman's responsibility. One person I know who frequently visits companies to make presentations followed by discussion groups takes her kitchen timer everywhere with her. It is a great icebreaker because everyone laughs when she sets it, but in actual fact it has the benefit of focusing minds because participants are aware of their time limits. Her meetings are almost invariably constructive and the task assigned, or the decision required, successfully achieved by the time the bell rings.

Setting the style

Chapters 2 and 3 on speaking and listening, and presentations both contain specific information on addressing an audience or being a member of an audience. There are more general things to think about than the actual speech or presentation when arranging a meeting however. And some of the points made in those chapters are worthy of repetition here.

Do you see what I see?

Each of us needs to know whether the effect we intend is achieved. We need to know what others are seeing and hearing when we are speaking in almost every situation. It may seem to me that I am indicating friendliness and informality by not speaking from notes, or by sitting within a group rather than standing in front of it, but it may seem to others in the group that I am simply unprepared. My jokes may not seem funny. My tendency to ask the group for suggestions may be perceived as either an inability to make decisions or a lack of understanding on my part. If I say too much I may seem bossy, if I say too little I may seem unsociable. Different people will interpret the same behaviour from me in different ways.

All of this must be accepted. The question then becomes, how do I deal with it? At some point I must take the responsibility and decide which style of behaviour is appropriate for a particular occasion and then go as far as I can to ensure that my intentions are communicated to the rest of the group. If they know why I feel we need a brainstorming session or a formal presentation by a panel of experts, then they are far more likely to cooperate and be receptive to the structure I have established.

I do not advocate anarchy in meetings. There are obviously times when I may make an incorrect assessment of a group or a task but it is my job, as chairman, to keep such errors to the minimum, and, when they occur, to notice them and change course as quickly as possible.

Knowing what is going on in a meeting can be judged by:

- paying attention to who says what, when and why;
- attempting, in advance, to predict questions and likely responses.

Acting on impulse

It is important to give an impression of spontaneity even if your behaviour and responses are not actually spontaneous. Preparation for a meeting should include trying to guess what will happen and having a few alternative scenarios ready to put into action. You need to be aware of the reaction you are getting and be able to change your action or style appropriately.

One of the least spontaneous people I know not only makes an agenda before a meeting, and decides who will speak on each point and for how long, he then holds a rehearsal and makes sure that each of the people he has selected informs him of what they are about to say.

When he is taking a team into a presentation, he likes to know exactly who will say what on his team in order to predict who will say what among the hosts. He has followed this pattern for many years and finds it very successful. But speaking to one of the clients he made such a presentation to after the meeting had ended, I was delighted to know just how aware the hosts were of his style and methods. As one of them said, 'we know what he is doing and let him do it because it is such a pleasure to watch him work'.

Are you sitting comfortably?

Meeting rooms are often airless and those using them know that they get their best decisions in the first half hour because after that people start to glaze over. Modern exhibition centres are designed without windows and seminars can occasionally suffer from such a claustrophic atmosphere.

One organization I visited has a purpose designed meeting room with a large table that can be extended and altered in shape by re-forming its component parts. The chairs are comfortable and swivel based so it is a simple matter to turn and face others without having to lean and stretch.

Meetings held in offices are fine when they are for discussion purposes only, but when participants have papers to refer to or presentation material to be displayed, a conference room with a table is essential.

The external environment is just as important as internal. In exhibition centres, natural light is deliberately excluded. The architects have taken into account the effect that outside distractions can have and ensured that visitors concentrate exclusively on the business at hand. Similarly, meetings held in offices can be affected by interruptions from ringing telephones, traffic outside the door or the general life of the business which continues no matter what you are discussing. Allowance must be made for all of these factors when deciding where to hold the meeting.

Take your seat please

A television news report showed the Soviet government meeting in a room with a large oval table around which all the ministers, including Mr Gorbachev, were seated. As with the room shown in *Yes, Prime Minister*, the sitcom about the British cabinet, there was no 'head' of the table. Mr Gorbachev and Jim Hacker both sat in the middle of one side, as part of their cabinet, rather than at the top of a long table.

There was one striking difference however. In the Soviet cabinet room, to one end of the table but set back into a corner, was a small podium at which anyone who was speaking stood to address his colleagues. He did not speak from his seat. He stood, set off to one side, while the others remained at the table, most of them with their backs to him. They did not turn to face him. The poor man stood there, facing their backs, while he gave his speech.

Predetermining features

When you think about who is attending the meeting and what is expected to be accomplished, also think about:

- the type of seats and the degree of comfort they offer;
- whether a table is needed so participants can make notes or spread out their reference material;
- closeness to others in a room especially if it is a large gathering;
- whether there is sufficient space in a large meeting to break into small groups;
- whether people in a large group, broken into small groups, will be able to hear themselves think or speak;
- what participants can see from where they sit — other participants, speakers only, windows or walls;

- what is in the room ie pictures, plants;
- whether there is a clear view of other participants and of the speaker or chairman;
- whether there is a clear view of visual aids eg flipcharts, videos or screens;
- acoustics so that everyone can hear what is being said as it may be difficult to hear speakers without a microphone or to hear questions and comments from the floor.

Seats can be arranged in rows, circles or horseshoes. Each design will affect the ease of communication from presenter to group and between members of the group.

Jane Allan expresses her view in *How to Develop Your Personal Management Skills*, that sitting face to face over a table increases the opportunities for conflict. She also maintains that sitting side by side makes disagreements harder.

Yet, as shown above, many fairly important people believe that this is not a reason for removing themselves from a group and standing or sitting in front of it. It all depends on the purpose of the meeting and whether the chairman, secretary and speaker or panel have to be seen by all. Or whether there is a reason to indicate their status as separate from the other participants.

Entire books have been written on this subject. The best advice I can offer is to look at the room where you are meeting, why you are meeting and who you are meeting with, then decide on the best arrangement.

Decision making

The reason for having a meeting is to make a decision. Information may be given in the form of a presentation and questions or discussions follow, but it is to get a sense of consensus that the meeting has been arranged in the first place. Achieving this in the most time and cost-effective manner possible is a goal that everyone attending must share.

Staff at Z International, one of the companies whose case study appears in detail at the end of the book, thrive on meetings. They say that this is because of their belief in team work. Every matter is considered, discussed, presented to others, often several times with shifting atten-dance at each meeting to ensure that every possible opinion has been solicited. The result is that decisions are a very long time in coming. And proposals are often shot down quite far into the production process when someone looks at work in hand and says 'no, that really won't do'. So the cycle repeats itself.

Marion Haynes, in *Effective Meeting Skills*, maintains that decision making meetings need to follow a specific structure. The rational decision process includes the following steps:

- study/discuss/analyze the situation;
- define the problem;
- set an objective;
- state imperatives and desirables;
- generate alternatives;
- establish evaluation criteria;
- evaluate alternatives;
- choose among alternatives.

One other aspect of decision making is the necessity for participants in the meeting to be aware of one another's needs and perceptions. If these are not effectively communicated, if there is an insufficient degree of understanding of one another's requirements, then an acceptable conclusion is unlikely to be reached.

Chapter 7 on Negotiations covers the importance of this exchange of information. Awareness, understanding, empathy and perception are discussed repeatedly throughout this book. The role they play in becoming an effective communicator cannot be repeated frequently enough, or isolated in a single chapter. It is only when we accept that communications are a two-way process that any form of communication, including decision making, will become genuinely successful and effective.

Decision making is not always an identifiable activity. Frequently the discussion can evolve into a consensus which can be recognized and verbalized by the leader without the need to 'put things to the vote'. The part a leader plays in formulating a decision is discussed later.

Role playing

In *How to be an Even Better Manager*, Michael Armstrong explains how those playing the roles of chairman and participant can contribute to the efficient conduct of the meeting. The chairman should:

- define the objectives and set an agenda and timetable;
- ensure that each step in the agenda is covered, conclusions reached and recorded while simultaneously preventing discussion on any single item from taking so much time that the remainder needs to be cut short;
- introduce each item on the agenda briefly and have a list of points for discussion ready;
- structure contributions so that no one with something to say is ignored while simultaneously preventing anyone from dominating the discussion;
- bring the meeting to order if it drifts;
- keep control of participants and not let sidebars occur;
- allow, and even encourage, disagreement but prevent arguments getting heated;

- contribute to the discussion and keep it moving by asking probing questions without allowing his own views to dominate;
- summarize decisions, ensure that they accurately reflect what has been said, then have them recorded and minutes circulated by the secretary;
- indicate what action is to be taken and by whom;
- arrange any further meetings which may be necessary and identify the purpose of them.

Jane Allan adds to this that the chairman should:

- ensure that participants understand issues and why they are being discussed;
- clarify complex issues and prevent misunderstandings;
- not avoid difficult issues but make some attempt to resolve them or establish a means for resolving them before the next meeting;
- postpone discussion to another occasion if there is incomplete information available to reach a reasonable conclusion.

Armstrong says that participants, in order to make their contributions significant and worthwhile, should:

- prepare thoroughly, having any facts and supporting data ready and immediately available;
- make points clearly, succinctly and positively;
- avoid talking too much or being repetititve;
- avoid speaking if they have nothing to say;
- avoid speaking if you don't know what you are talking about or have not heard enough to formulate a considered opinion;
- ask questions rather than make statements if they are not sure of their ground, or still thinking through their views;
- fight for their views but know when to quit;
- remember that decisions made in committee can be reversed in general meetings.

Marion Haynes adds two other key points to this list. Participants should:

- provide feedback for the leader;
- fulfill any agreed actions.

There are certain tasks concerning observation that both chairman and participant will find useful for understanding the reasons why a meeting is going the way it is. Look at:

- who talks to who;
- who avoids eye contact or doodles;
- reactions to what you are saying but also see how various people react to what others are saying;

- who waits for whose response before speaking or expressing an opinion;
- who looks at who when speaking to see what response they are getting;
- reactions to the leader or chairman who might, incidentally, not be one and the same person;
- who is the actual leader of the group and who wants to be leader of the group.

Hidden agendas are often brought to meetings, as are preconceptions, prejudices and other excess baggage. It is incumbent on all participants, and especially leaders, to look for these and respond to them.

Empathizing

Briefly, putting yourself in the other guy's place.

- Salesmen role play at being customers.
- Managers 'buy' and 'sell'.

We all need to see both sides of each coin in order to play our own roles properly. Words and actions always come in pairs. We:

- speak and listen;
- read and write;
- can't have one without the other.

Communication must be a two-way transaction.

Leadership styles

Jane Allan, in *How to Develop Your Personal Management Skills*, explains what she considers the basic steps to being a good leader. Although she is writing in general terms about leadership styles, the qualities she identifies are relevant to the way in which meetings can and should be conducted. If you are organizing a meeting you will need to:

- establish who is in charge;
- know what you want to accomplish;
- know what you want the meeting to accomplish;
- let people know what you expect;
- find out what others expect the meeting to accomplish;
- find out what others expect of you;
- take being a role model seriously;
- expect others to be self-motivated but don't count on it;
- understand that the quality of your leadership is determined by the methods you choose to motivate others.

Allan goes on to describe the various styles of leadership and the effect that each can have on the success or failure of a meeting:

- The dictator dominates and harangues in order to get group agreement;
- The scoutmaster is more concerned with involving all participants than in reaching agreement;
- The abdicator uses all arguments from the participants as an excuse to support nothing so that there is never any decision made;
- The persuader talks so much that no one else can get a word in;
- The collector gathers in others' suggestions and puts them forward as his own on another occasion;
- The destroyer has accepted his role reluctantly and does what is expected with the least possible amount of cooperation and input.

The effective chairman, Allan concludes, is recognizable by his ability to:

- enjoy what he is doing;
- guide the group through its discussions without having a direct influence on its decision;
- use control and discipline to ensure that the task or agenda are completed efficiently.

Marion Haynes adds to this that an effective leader 'must be able to analyze each situation, decide what is needed to move forward, and take the necessary action to achieve the objective'. He must also be able to stimulate discussion, elicit information and opinions, and generate an exchange of views which lead to a fair basis for making a decision or reaching a conclusion satisfactory to all. The leader must tie things together, perhaps sketching best and worst way scenarios, and facilitating decision making without actually imposing or directing too overtly.

Interaction

Meetings are all about interaction. The subjects discussed so far in this chapter all focus on this one theme. The design of the room, the composition of the attendance list, the design of the agenda are all intended to ensure that there is interaction between participants. It doesn't really matter if you are speaking to people from out front, sitting on a higher seat or stage, having a group discussion with seats arranged in circles, rows or horseshoes. We must determine the best position in any circumstances to achieve our aims. Whether standing or sitting when speaking, with coat off, tie loosened and shirtsleeves rolled up, the point is to get down to business, let people have their say and satisfy the objectives set.

Documentation

One of the first tasks of any chairman is to appoint a secretary. Everyone present at a meeting, and often many who were not present, need to have written minutes showing:

- who was in attendance;
- who should have been in attendance but had to send apologies;
- what was on the agenda for discussion;
- what was actually discussed and the main points of that discussion;
- what conclusions were reached;
- what tasks were assigned and to whom;
- the time, date and place of the next meeting;
- the provisional agenda for the next meeting.

Note taking

As usual, there are pros and cons to this activity. Taking notes can help you to remember things and make you seem attentive. They can also make you seem, to others, withdrawn. Groups may regard leaders or chairmen taking notes as observers rather than participants. We may be concentrating so hard on what we are writing that we miss what is being said.

Just remember, you may take notes for good reason or to give others the impression that you think they have said something important which must be immediately written down. They may also be doing the same thing to you. Nothing in a meeting is necessarily straightforward. Be on your toes at all times. Even the simplest activity can be interpreted in a number of ways.

Confrontational communications

Conflict within a meeting is not necessarily a bad thing. It stimulates discussion and ensures that all points of view are aired. We all know the devil's advocate technique where someone deliberately takes a view opposite to the consensus just to make sure that it is considered. According to Marion Haynes in *Effective Meeting Skills*, a moderate level of conflict can have certain constructive consequences:

- increase motivation and energy to carry out a task;
- increase innovative thinking through a greater diversity of viewpoints;
- increase understanding of a position on an issue by forcing the advocate of that position to articulate and support it with facts;
- increase understanding of opposition positions on an issue by being forced to listen and then working to integrate diverse positions to achieve consensus.

Less constructive conflict may occur when speakers are heckled or people disagree with a viewpoint on principle, regardless of reason, circumstance, subject or importance.

Group dynamics

Chambers' *Twentieth Century Dictionary* defines dynamics as 'relating to force...a moving force...relating to activity or things in movement...any driving force instrumental in growth or change (esp social)'.

Collins' *Dictionary* defines dynamic as 'characterized by force of personality, ambition and energy.'

Group dynamics are the actions and forces that determine how the group works. When we say that something or someone is dynamic we generally mean that they are an instrumental force. When we say that the position is dynamic we generally mean that it is exciting and changeable.

Overall, though, there is a sense of change, movement, energy in the connotation of dynamics and when we study group dynamics, we are studying the ways in which groups operate. No handbook on communications can ignore the existence of groups or group dynamics any more than it can ignore the fact that no two situations or individuals are the same and that whenever two or more people get together, there is going to be a dynamic interaction resulting in a varying degree of effective communication.

For and agin

As usual, I am unable to draw a single conclusion as to whether we should meet or not meet. I am in favour of face-to-face communications, I am agin time wasting. Malcolm Peel, in *How to Make Meetings Work*, lists the valid reasons for meetings:

- Decision making;
- Communications;
- Negotiations;
- Creativity;
- Team building;
- Consultation;
- Democratic process and visible justice;
- Meeting newcomers;
- Legal or procedural requirements.

and the invalid reasons:

- Rose-tinted reasons, hoping that problems will disappear if only we can get together;
- The cycle and past precedent that may have locked us into a system that needs to be changed;
- The duck, or passing the buck or not accepting individual responsibility but requiring backup;
- The steamroller whereby the chairman or one small group of people pressurizes others into reaching a decision that they might not otherwise have reached;
- The exhibitionist which is used as a platform from which certain individuals can promote their own ideas and egos.

To go right back to where I started, I must think about my Latin teacher at school who used to pace the room while we translated difficult passages, chanting 'context will tell'.

Chapter 5

Employee Communications

One of my first observations after moving to the UK from the US was the different pace of life. People wrote letters rather than making telephone calls. Is this, I wondered later, so that they could prove what was said, avoid denials or misunderstandings, watch their backs? Decisions could take weeks and months rather than hours and days, in spite of everything I have said in Chapter 11 on Hi-tech Communications. Committees and boards were referred to, not because of a natural love for democracy but rather because of what seemed an instinctive fear of decision making.

There seemed to be a definite reluctance to accept responsiblity and an eagerness to defer to other people's judgement. Perhaps this makes the British more amenable than the Americans? I was not, and am still not twenty years later, entirely convinced that this less than dynamic approach is preferable.

To this day there does not seem to be a great deal of incentive to fulfill job requirements other than fear of unemployment and the masses outside waiting to step into the discarded employee's shoes. Sales staff do not necessarily know a great deal about the products they are selling. When attempting to select an appliance recently from a range of ten on display, I could not find out the difference between them, other than price. I had to know which questions to ask to elicit information on specific features and frequently even then could not get any sensible reply.

The point I am somewhat circuitously making is that employees need to have a stake in the company for which they work. This need not be financial. It is far more psychological and emotional. We all need motivation in order to do well at anything, particularly our jobs. The communication between levels of staff in any given business is what propels that motivation. If the communication is ineffective, the loyalty and willingness to cooperate from employees decreases and overall company performance suffers.

RECOGNIZING AND COMMUNICATING VALUE

Texaco Ltd, recently recruiting a Managing Editor — Employee Communications, headlined its advertisement 'Your audience is our most important one'. While pointing out to potential applicants the company's belief in quality communications, it stressed the importance of its own employees as part of that process. The job description emphasized the requirement to 'provide employees with high-quality, up-to-date information to foster team spirit'. Areas to be covered included news on 'current activities, achievements in the industry, future plans, who's doing what and where'. Two in-house newspapers, corporate brochures and magazines as well as video programmes, were cited as media currently used to provide successful employee communications.

Adding value

Business Line, the newsletter published by Thames Valley College, interviewed managers at ICI Paints about their views on ensuring high morale amongst employees. Philip Crookes, the Personnel Officer responsible for technical staff, said that policy includes ensuring that 'staff should see the business environment as a challenge and know what their role is in facing that challenge'.

Training is one of the ways that value is added to employees, both in terms of skills and confidence. Roger Pritchett, European research manager, pointed out that if young employees have been trained on the job and worked at the same time for professional qualifications 'they have shown perseverance to hold a job and part-time study and this is a highly desirable quality'.

John Danzeisen, finance director, believes that it is important to encourage any kind of training that employees are interested in as 'it is the people who win and keep customers for us'. The training does not have to be job specific but it is important 'as long as an individual wishes to enhance their skill-base, or improve their skills or knowledge, even if it isn't particularly related to the job they are now in, that an enlightened company would see their way clear to supporting that employee'.

What all three of these men are saying is that training is a means of demonstrating to employees that you want them to improve themselves and their abilities, that you value them and want to support them both in job terms and in personal development terms. Support is a form of communications which we all appreciate. It must be viewed laterally, going beyond a token pat on the back, and used as a means of recognizing and increasing value.

NEED TO KNOW

There are, in each and every situation, different definitions of who needs to know what. Obviously many plans and details of plans must be restricted to small groups of people for the sake of protection. More general, conceptual, information does need to be known — and understood — by as many people within a company as possible. There are two main reasons why employees need to know what a company does, how and why:

- to understand the part they play in order to appreciate their own value and to understand that their value is appreciated
- to act as successful intermediaries when they are, either deliberately or inadvertently, representing the company to others.

An overall strategy

Many companies do make the effort, however. Boots the Chemists Ltd, for instance, were one of the 1990 National Training Awards winners. Following a head office decision to establish independent merchandizing units within their stores, display areas began diversifying and deviating from the image preferred by the company. Inconsistency caused confusion among customers and targets were not met.

In order to re-establish the company's previously high standards of presentation, a training programme was developed. Everyone from shop assistants through store managers and area managers participated. It was stressed that they should all understand Boots' marketing strategy as well as merchandizing techniques. According to 'Winners 90', the annual report published to detail case studies, Boots' programme was successful on a number of different levels:

- profitability of space improved;
- expenditure on display aids was reduced;
- customers' perceptions of Boots in relation to other major retailers were improved;
- a comparison with leading US companies revealed that Boots was providing more and better training than its counterparts;
- the sum of these results was an improvement in the company's financial results.

Involving employees at all levels in fulfillment of head office policy obviously paid off on all of these levels.

FAMILY BUSINESSES AND THE COMMUNITY

In The Communications Audit (Chapter 1) I pointed out that the community was one of the target audiences to which a business must direct its communications. Apart from anything else, many of a business' employees are drawn from the community in which the business is located.

Family firms have even stronger links with their local community. There may be a complex network of relationships between the family who are owners and the families who are employees. It is especially important in towns and villages where livelihoods are dependent on one or two employers for communications with those employees to be open, effective and smooth.

Sir John Harvey-Jones, writing in The *Observer* in May 1991 pointed out that more than three-quarters of British businesses are family owned and that they are the employers of over half of the country's workforce. The special communications required to make allowances for the different aspirations and ambitions of individuals working together by reason of birth as much as choice creates yet another element in the corporate mix.

Similarly, many of the employees are there because there is only one feasible employer in the community. They are there because it is the custom for their family to work for the local laird, or because it is too difficult, in too many ways, to look for work further afield. Not many of them are there because the job on offer was one that they truly chose to do. With that sort of luggage to deal with, a sound relationship between management and employees has special handicaps to overcome and it is even more important to establish clear lines of communication to keep the wheels turning smoothly.

Loyalty is frequently automatic and instinctive but it just as frequently has to be earned. If, as Harvey-Jones points out, non-family members are brought up to management level until grandsons or cousins are old enough or able enough to take their rightful place, those non-family members are almost adopted into the family. In Mario Puzo's novel *The Godfather*, the right-hand man was an adopted son who had lived with the family since his childhood. The real sons of the family never entirely trusted him. Many other novelists have told the Cinderella story about the adopted or stepchild that was never entirely accepted despite being more clever or more beautiful than the others.

There are of course exceptions. One firm I know which is now third generation has six people on its board, five of whom are related to one another and to the company's founder. The sixth has been with the company for thirty-five years and was promoted to board level so that his assistant, who had been with the firm for a mere twenty-five years, could move into his shoes.

John Harvey-Jones is one who recognizes and endorses the value of family businesses and sees that their role in the community, including the international community, is one worth supporting and expanding. He attributes much of Germany's success, for example, to the support major companies receive from their suppliers who are often small- and medium-sized privately owned businesses. He refers to JCB which emphasizes both design and the community, as a successful family company still working from its original Midlands base. Harvey-Jones believes that we need 'family businesses with a long-term view for the future of the business, as well as commitment to their roots and the social fabric of the community within which they live'.

DOING IT RIGHT

When Walter Goldsmith and David Clutterbuck conducted interviews for their book, *The Winning Streak*, companies were rated according to eight criteria established by Tom Peters and Robert Waterman in the US when compiling *In Search of Excellence*. In addition to these preconceived criteria, points 9 — 35 below surfaced during the course of the interviews.

1. Bias for action.
2. Closeness to customer.
3. Autonomy and entrepreneurship.
4. Productivity through people.
5. Hands-on, value-driven.
6. Sticking to the knitting.
7. Simple form, lean staff.
8. Simultaneous loose-tight properties.
9. Natural curiosity.
10. International perspective.
11. Long-term perspective.
12. Market orientation.
13. Attention to employee communications.
14. Sense of ownership.
15. Ability to get back to fundamentals.
16. Innovation.
17. Team concept.
18. Clear leadership and direction.
19. Clear and demanding objective setting.
20. Clear corporate mission.
21. Effective supplier relationships.
22. Right tools for the job.
23. Generalist rather than specialist managers.
24. Attention to general corporate image.
25. Information orientation.
26. Productivity orientation.
27. Heavy emphasis on training.
28. Above average pay.
29. Incentives.
30. Promotion from within.
31. Stimulating enjoyment of work.

32. Integrity.
33. Get attention to detail.
34. Unswerving commitment to growth.
35. Others:
  a) people and job values;
  b) clarity in organization;
  c) diversification after expert management has been secured.

Each of Goldsmith and Clutterbuck's points is related, with differing degrees of directness, to the subject of communications and particularly to employee communications. As you read this chapter, many of them will ring loud bells. You will hopefully recognize them as steps that you already take. Those that you are not aware of will hopefully make more sense as you read the rest of the book. By the time you get to the last page, you will have a much clearer idea of ways to measure your own company's performance as well as ways in which to improve it.

SECURITY

Ronald Hurst in *Industrial Management Methods* says that: 'Personal security motivates every employee and any vacuum in the overall knowledge of the company's activities or management intent — and hence of the employee's own place in the scheme of things — is all too quickly filled by conjecture or by rumour as to how this security may be affected.' Now this book was written in 1970 and the truth of that statement has not diminished since it was made.

There is a particular need for sound employee communications in bad times (such as the recession) and times of change.

Communicating problems

Brian Jenks of Touche Ross, writing in The *Observer* in May 1991, says that managers should pay particular attention to communications in times of recession. 'If people do not hear from him (the manager) they may think he is experiencing problems.'

If the manager is experiencing problems, it is more likely that help and support will be forthcoming if people know what is going on than if they are kept guessing. Chinese whispers and unsupported conclusions can have far worse results than any announcement of bad news might have. At least then people will know the worst.

Although many of us are loathe to let others know when we are in trouble, when that trouble has been caused by external sources beyond our control, there is an urge to obey the precept that a trouble shared is a trouble halved. Or, to use another cliché, we all know that misery loves company. Difficulties caused by bureaucracy, taxes, government, banks, all those organizations that we love to hate, can occasionally be combated through networking. Knowing what others have gone through and what they have done about it can, every now and again, provide someone with a clue to the best way of proceeding. These unofficial communications often provide the impetus for structuring more formal communications and problem solving.

Furthermore, publicity can be helpful for us and, if difficulties have been exacerbated by unethical or questionable practices, the exposure can often provoke an investigation and an alleviation of the difficulties.

Informing colleagues and target audiences of difficulties can also clarify situations and prevent misunderstandings. We have all occasionally jumped to conclusions which have been inaccurate or incorrect. The results can be disastrous and create a cycle from which the business which is the victim cannot extricate itself. If customers think a business is in trouble, they tend to go elsewhere, thereby speeding the demise of a business which might have survived had it not lost additional customers through lack of confidence.

Communicating change

Walter Goldsmith and David Clutterbuck stated in *The Winning Streak* that 'A living culture adjusts and assimilates new ideas; it learns from its experiences and develops new responses to new situations...So open communications is simply a positive response by adaptive company cultures to a change in the external environment.'

Employees in National Power had to be informed about the process of privatization, about the comparative advantages and why their help and cooperation was needed, and about the constant changes imposed by the government which created an ongoing need for informing and re-informing repeatedly. The final stage was the distribution of a video to each of the 15,000 employees.

When a company's structure is changing, those who will be staying on need to be reassured while others will have to be prepared for the worst. Employees should not be unnecessarily worried or they will jump to conclusions. If employees know what is going on, there is likely to be an increase in their interest, loyalty and willingness to help and stay involved.

Brian Jenks of Touche Ross, in his article for The *Observer* referred to above, also emphasized that plans and intentions regarding the expansion or contraction of a business must be communicated to all of those interested in the business' financial status — past, present and future. 'A business plan is a *sine qua non*', and one of those corporate documents referred to in Chapter 14.

Jane Allan, in *How to Develop Your Personal Management Skills*, says that 'If it is accepted that change is essential in the developing organization, then it is equally essential to find a way of making it at least acceptable to the majority of the workforce and preferably to make it desirable to all.' Her recommendations for fulfilling this obligation are:

- over-inform people so they cannot claim later that there were things they did not know;
- brief people in groups so that there is minimal chance for misunderstanding or claims afterwards that some were told different things to others;
- always take questions and if you can't answer them on the spot, make sure you acknowledge them, promise an answer after you have had time to check and then do not forget to keep that promise;
- believe in what you tell them;
- use every opportunity to train people.

Nicholas Ind, in *The Corporate Image*, stresses that the support of senior management is crucial to encouraging the acceptance of change. When discussing the introduction of a corporate identity programme, he says: 'Without the endorsement of the chief executive officer, the programme will lack the necessary status within the organization.' This statement actually holds true for every aspect of corporate change which must be demonstrably supported by management if it is to be accepted and supported by staff across all levels.

Ind goes on to cite several examples of companies taking this positive step. As with National Power, large organizations with multiple sites often in different countries must recognize the importance of simultaneous announcements by management to all employees as a vital, essential and worthwhile exercise.

Accepting the inevitable

There are of course times when redundancies are justified and cannot be avoided. There are times when hatchet men coming in to clean up are necessary in order to streamline procedures and trim away dead wood. When Sir John Harvey-Jones first joined ICI, so the story goes, a group of Japanese visitors asked him how many people worked for the company. 'About half,' shot back Sir John in reply.

From the employees' point of view, it is difficult to tell the difference between the justified and the unjustified. One of the aims of the hatchet man, and/or management, is to clarify this position so that those remaining are mollified. While they may feel a sense of relief that they are still employed, it is incumbent on management to ensure that there is no ill will on behalf of colleagues who have gone.

COMPLAINTS

One means of ensuring that complaints are acknowledged is by communicating up the ladder. Writing to a chairperson or managing director or to the press when you are fighting with a business forces direct action from someone with responsibility and decision-making powers. Frequently chairmen have little awareness of the day-to-day activities of middle managers and have totally different perceptions of their audience's perceptions than are actually the case. They believe what they are told by those with a vested interest. Taking power away from underlings and confronting higher level executives forces an awareness that cannot be ignored.

The facts of life

The chairman of a large corporation is hardly likely to deal with complaints directly but he is equally unlikely to ignore them. He will pass them to someone who will deal with them, and ensure that pressure is brought to bear to resolve the complaints. Few businesses can afford dissatisfied customers particularly if those customers indicate that they are not going to be fobbed off or sit quietly accepting inadequate performance. Waking up a chairman to the facts of life can only be a positive step.

The hot seat

But what if you are the recipient of complaints? Justification is not the answer that complainants want. Explanations are well and good as far as they go, but the problem must be solved, not explained away. The reasons for any complaint must be investigated and a decision made regarding policy and compensation. Sometimes the complainant is right; sometimes not. Sometimes the complaint is justified; sometimes not. Sometimes complaints are the direct result of misunderstandings and poor communication. It is up to whoever fields the complaint to find out the truth and make sure that negotiations take place so that everyone involved is satisfied with the outcome.

Empathy is a useful skill to have when dealing with complaints or, indeed, when making a complaint. Each side of every argument has some belief in its merits and an understanding of the other side will help you formulate your own actions and reactions. Think about where sympathy will lie:

- With a large multinational perhaps victimizing employees in regard to working conditions, terms of employment or redundancy
  or with the employees?
- With companies dumping waste into local rivers
  or with the community?
- With banks calling in loans
  or with customers?
- With management and owners of large, profitable organizations taking increases and performance related bonuses many times in excess of those given to staff
  or with shareholders, investors, employees, customers and creditors?

Communication determines the degree of sympathy and support felt for each side in a complaints dispute. Communication, that is, between the complainant and the business but also between both the complainant and the business and every other target audience even slightly interested in the business' activities.

Conflicts

Taking the issue of complaints one step further, it must be emphasized that this is not a suitable activity for communication through an intermediary. Whichever end of the action you are on, whether the conflict is between employees within the company or between someone inside the company and someone from outside, first-hand knowledge of the issues is imperative. There are often hidden agendas, and some degree of personality or competition, involved that have to be considered in light of the actual complaint.

As Nicholas Ind says in *The Corporate Image*, 'It is often extremely difficult to understand the degree of inter-manager conflict that is acceptable to an organization by listening to someone in the organization tell you about it.'

The differing perceptions of a situation, and the reasons for and importance of the conflict, must be taken into account. To complete Ind's statement, 'The experience of being told by senior management that their organization is a picture of harmony, where everyone works to a common goal, is very familiar. In reality there is often not only conflict, but potentially damaging attitudes.'

PERCEPTIONS

Employee communications are a vital part of a company's success, or lack of it. So one of the first groups which needs to be considered when conducting a communications audit is the employees. They communicate the company message after it has been communicated to them. An assessment of their perceptions is thus high on the list of objectives for the audit. The ways and means of discovering what employees really think and feel is discussed further in The Communications Audit.

It is fairly apparent what the perceptions of employees are regarding senior managers who take proportionately higher percentage increases than lower level employees on top of their so called performance related bonuses and executive perks.

Chapter 16, Fit to Print, goes into detail about the various means of keeping employees informed. The responses to the information they receive and the degree to which they agree, accept, support what they are told is what management needs to know, however. Returning to my theme of two-way communications, it is just as important for management to understand staff as it is for staff to know what management is getting up to. They may not have the same perceptions of the success of strategy, or of their relationships, or of the very existence of conflict.

Open communication across levels as well as between departments and via networks are all the factors which contribute to the formulation of perceptions and it is perceptions which make people act — we act on our beliefs. If those beliefs or perceptions do not coincide then the overall smooth operations of the business are affected and can be put in jeopardy.

KEEPING PEOPLE INFORMED

Successful companies have techniques aimed at passing information down and listening to what people below have to say which run parallel to formal reporting and monitoring systems, although there is often a crossover between the two.

Communication between levels can be encouraged through mass meetings (annual general meetings) combined with semi-structured informal gatherings. The latter can be cyclical so that everyone in the company, or the branch of the company, comes together at least once every two years, in a small group gathering for example over lunch or drinks. In this way no one appears to be interviewing anyone else, or checking up on anyone else, but the opportunity is presented during the encounters for discussion of any issue that may be of concern.

Sir Kenneth Corfield, chairman of Standard Telephones & Cables (STC), quoted in *The Winning Streak*, explained that STC had a policy which ensured that employees' questions and comments received a response. Any question asked at a meeting but not answered could be presented in writing and an assurance given that all such questions would be answered in writing in the report published after the meeting.

STC also had employee representatives attend management meetings, managers attend union meetings and organized a series of informal open evenings for directors to meet with employees.

The case study of Scottish and Newcastle in *The Winning Streak* described the chairman's forum held twice a year with forty people, across levels, getting together to discuss company position. They were able to do this informally, without fighting for their own corner but looking objectively at overall company strategy and performance.

MFI had similar meetings at area level and then sent minutes up the ladder until important issues reached board level.

Mutual dependence

The significance of cross level communication is not always sufficiently appreciated. Roger Temple, of Flowtech, recently told colleagues at a meeting of the Education Business Partnership that many students coming for work experience, as well as people applying for jobs, had no understanding of the range of jobs done by employees in his company. Many came simply to find out what the company was doing and did not realize the value of the tasks completed at each level. If any single task was left undone, the company would cease to function effectively. Every task has its place in the scheme of things and there is a mutual dependence which everyone involved with the business must accept and understand.

There is also a tremendous amount of time and money wasted when efforts are duplicated through one department not knowing what the other is up to. A case in point is the use of direct mail to advertise services and products. Lists often contain slight variations in single names resulting in multiple copies sent to the same person. Nor are they always cleaned as often as they ought to be, resulting in junk mail being sent to people who have long ago moved on to different jobs or employers.

Lack of communication between departments results in wastage and increased perceptions of the company as inept and not sufficiently interested in its market to know who they are approaching and why. A case in point is needed here.

The expansion of AB Co's bank into other, associated, areas should be noted. This case is discussed further in Chapter 7 on negotiations but what is relevant here is that the preoccupation with selling was acted out without communication between departments, for example:

- When the partners re-mortgaged their home, the bank lost its security; there was insufficient communication between the manager of the bank and the mortgage department;
- During the negotiations to recover funds the bank had loaned the company, the partners received no less than three mailshots from the bank offering them personal loans;
- During the same period, their cheque cards expired and new ones were automatically issued;
- The manager insisted they take out an insurance policy which made the bank a beneficiary in the event of the partners' deaths — a questionable additional expense under the circumstances and of no particular advantage to the bank as it was not payable on anything other than death;
- An agent of one of the bank's subsidiaries telephoned the partners at home, at seven o'clock in the evening, to see if they would like to increase their pension provision.

Knowing your place

Employees need to know about the whole company but they also need to know about one another. Each of us should know our job thoroughly as well as the relationship of that job to other people's. Communication within and between departments is just as important as communication to and from supervisors and management. The entire progression of a company's product or service from new product development and research through production, sales and marketing, along with the individual roles necessary to fulfill this process, should be part of each employee's initial orientation.

Equally important is an understanding of corporate structure:

- How large is the company?
- What other companies are part of the group?
- What do they do?
- What are the company's various social and political philosophies?
- How are they doing financially?

Tactics and strategy

Only when each employee sees himself within the context of the business will he begin to feel a part of the company. It is at that point that loyalty, interest and motivation come into operation.

While management may determine company strategy, employees are one of those groups which implement it. Formulation of tactics must take into consideration the role that employees will play.

I have already said repeatedly, and cannot say often enough, that it is employees who do the day-to-day work of the company and who represent it to customers and clients.

If their understanding is incomplete or inaccurate, or if their perceptions do not coincide with the intentions of management, then communication has already broken down and must be re-established before the misconceptions are passed on even further.

Networks and grapevines

Is there a difference between the two? Networks are established by wise managers who understand the value of each and every conversation and contact they ever make. They work on the principle of 'you never know' and cultivate everyone they ever meet on the off chance that it will be useful at some later date.

Grapevines bear the stigma of being associated with gossip and unsubstantiated information. This is sometimes true but by no means always the case. They are a fact of life and although they grow naturally without the same requirement for artificial cultivation and stimulus which applies to networks, they can be just as useful.

Grapevines are occasionally used for the deliberate placing of misinformation and disinformation. This is certainly not a recommended procedure but it is something that needs to be considered when you listen to anything you may hear. It is all the more reason for establishing the validity and reliability of your source.

Open communications

None of us is so unfortunate as poor Pinocchio whose nose grew with every fib he told. Yet many of us have become ensnarled in the webs we weave when we fail to keep track of what we may have told different people or groups. The simple solution would be to follow a policy of open communication in order to minimize confusion and contradiction.

'Leaks' such as those we all see in sitcoms such as *Yes, Minister* and political dramas such as *House of Cards* are the property of the grapevine. The former Prime Minister's former press secretary in his autobiography confirmed, if anyone had any doubt left, the degree to which leaks can be used to manipulate beliefs. There are some facts which some people feel need to be officially kept secret but other people feel must be revealed. Industrial espionage may not frequently get publicity but it does exist.

Yet there are occasions when the need for confidentiality is genuine. Confidentiality and perceptions of secrecy act like a red flag to some people who cannot accept even national security as a valid excuse for keeping their counsel. Others take it upon themselves to withhold information from others 'for their own good'. The entire principle of 'need to know' implies that some people know more than others and are better able to judge the wisdom of revealing what they know.

Confidentiality agreements, industrial espionage and leaks are all obstacles to open communications yet until we live in a perfect world where we all feel secure in our relationships with others, there will be degrees of openness only.

Responsibility

Jan Carlsson, chief executive of Scandinavian airlines SAS, was quoted in *The Winning Streak* as saying that 'Those who have no information can take no responsibility. Those who have information have no choice but to take responsibility.'

How many managers refrain from delegating responsibility because it is simpler and easier to do things themselves? Ask yourself the question:

What does this say for their communication skills?

Then give the answer:

If their skills were better, the tasks might get done faster or more efficiently, leaving the manager to go on to other things.

The question of responsibility is largely one of attitude. Do we take responsbility or do we accept responsibility? The answer must be individual and guides the style with which each of us leads.

Leaders who are led

There are people who want to be leaders and want to have responsibility yet find themselves frustrated by circumstances and corporate structure.

The older generation of bank managers, for example, are now complaining volubly about head office policies, passing the buck, complaining that they are not allowed as much flexibility or discretion in dealings with customers as they have enjoyed previously. Good managers are becoming increasingly upset at the mud that is sticking to them because of corporate policies.

Individual managers will have to work extra hard to overcome what is almost the stigma of their profession and rebuild trust, confidence and relationships. They have had quotas and performance linked bonuses forced upon them and been turned into salesmen. Computers are dictating margins, charges, rates and limits of security. Machines and head office staff with no direct first-hand knowledge of customers or circumstances hold the threat of promotion prospects being put at risk if bad decisions are made. Concerns for personal security have taken priority over doing the job properly.

Incentives and motivation

Most of us are more likely to take the initiative and to accept — or take — responsibility if we have a reason to do so.

Some incentives are straightforward. Gifts, perks, bonuses, freebies are indicative of the value that the giver places on our friendship and support. They can be seen as a thank you for loyalty or services rendered, or as a means of buying loyalty at a later date. Nick Goodway reviewed stockbroker Seymour Pierce Butterfield's guide to *Concessionary Discounts 1991* in an article for The *Observer* in January 1991. Depending on the number of shares held in a company, shareholders can enjoy discounts on clothes, shoes, sporting goods, meals, wine, travel and holidays, dry cleaning, shoe repairs and key cutting, cars, building materials, books and tickets for championship sporting events. To encourage stockholders to attend annual general meetings, buffets and bags of goodies are often provided. The only implications here are that shareholders should support management as and when the time comes to vote on anything.

The carrot or the stick?

The implications of identifying underperformance and having individual remedies applied has undertones which could conceivably be interpreted as sinister or threatening to staff. Instilling fear of competition as an incentive is a negative approach which can have ramifications that exceed the value of any short-term improvement in performance.

The offer of incentives or commissions is a positive approach to encouraging loyalty and high performance among staff, offering a carrot for achievement and success. The other side of the coin, however, stresses stress and nervousness to say the least. Yes indeed, we can all benefit from constructive criticism.

Incentives often provide motivation. If you know that, in addition to your pay cheque, there will be a bonus in the form of cash or a weekend in the Bahamas or simply the recognition that you have made a vital contribution to the success of the business, then there is all the more reason to think as well as complete the routine aspects of your job. It is the thought process, the initiative, the imagination, that are stimulated by incentives.

Encouraging participation

In Japan, quality circles are a popular means of taking advantage of and involving employees at all levels. The circles, which are similar in structure to a system of committees, consist of a specific group who take responsibility for identifying issues that need discussion and action. They act as intermediaries between departments and between levels of staff. They meet regularly to discuss the issues identified, create recommendations and suggest ways of implementing them.

In other companies, suggestion boxes are used. Each of these methods provides a means of getting ideas that are both good in themselves as cost savers or innovations and also act sometimes as stimuli for other ideas which can be built on them. There are incentives for winners and those whose ideas are accepted. They are a way of keeping employees involved and knowing their ideas and opinions count.

There is a devious aspect to incentives. They are the honey for the fly who will perform better than if he is threatened with losing his job. Competitions, gifts or prizes are often offered for high achievement either in sales or on the assembly line.

Ownership of the idea

Giving credit where it is due, attributing the initial idea to its rightful owner and thereby encouraging employees to feel a sense of ownership in the business are a form of motivation which can prove highly effective.

Michael Bland and Peter Jackson in *Effective Employee Communications* give an excellent example of the differing results which can be achieved through approaching the same situation from opposite directions. They describe a weekend management conference where, in the first scenario, the agenda consists of a series of presentations through which participants must sit patiently. The alternative scenario, which briefly presents those same managers with a description of management's problems and then divides them into working parties whose objective is to provide solutions to the problem, has miraculous results. When the working parties report back to the main meeting they will invariably:

- make several suggestions that management hadn't considered;
- identify controversial areas that management must be prepared to meet;
- be more committed to supporting any decisions made as they feel they were instrumental in determining procedures.

Stress

I recently read a report of a greengrocer's assistant having a nervous

105

breakdown caused by stress. His employer had asked him to sort the fruit into small, medium and large sizes....

One effect of technology is that the ability to communicate whether at the office, on the road or in the bath brings with it the compulsion to do so. Free time is considered immoral; all time should be used for work.

When staff at Digital Equipment Co evacuated to their car park while police checked their building for an intruder, certain executives paced around the car park carrying on their business with mobile phones.

The theme of Toshiba's advertisement for its laptop computers is that you can work anywhere. People can keep in touch, communicate with one another, anytime, anywhere as Chapter 11 on hi-tech communications explains. The downside of this is that the pressure to keep on working is constant.

Is it worth the bother?

Why should any of us care about quality or efficiency? Is not individual and personal quality of life far more important? Does the term job satisfaction have any real meaning? Just what exactly is the point of working apart from the necessity of bringing home a regular income? Why do we suffer from stress regardless of the type of job we do and the hours we work? What exactly has stress got to do with a lack of *effective* communication?

Please note that the operative word in the previous paragraph was *effective*. I have said repeatedly that we all communicate constantly in a number of ways, intentional or otherwise. But if we communicate our problems or insecurities effectively, perhaps stress could be alleviated or even eliminated.

If that greengrocer's assistant had been told that sorting the fruit was helpful but that his job did not actually depend on it, perhaps he would not have worried so much about the possibility of making a mistake. If he had told his employer of his fears, perhaps they could have been set to rest before he had his nervous breakdown. Neither one of them communicated effectively. Hence the assistant fell ill and the shopkeeper lost what might have been an otherwise perfectly acceptable employee.

THE WORKING ENVIRONMENT

Where you sit and how you communicate with others in the room, on the same floor, in the building or on other sites of the company are an aspect of employee communications which has a significant influence on the effectiveness of those communications. Some of the most important factors to consider are whether the environment is:

- comfortable, cheerful and attractive;
- conducive to work;
- suitable for meetings;

- presentable to visitors.

Each of these factors has to be taken into consideration when analyzing the potential success or failure of communications. Let's look at two examples.

Both PT & Sons and Z International (the company whose case study appears on page 283) are well-established companies which needed new offices for a variety of reasons. The board of directors in each bought a new building, never tenanted, and starting with an empty shell, had to specify the interior design. This included everything from the positioning of walls and partitions to providing office and meeting space, to the position of desks, chairs, power points and telephones.

Seating plans

Every business setting up an office has to decide on the best seating arrangement as well as whether to have open plan offices or not.

Another company I deal with did opt for an open plan office. They said that this was because they had no secrets from each other and wanted to convey this message to everyone dealing with them. In fact, they were such a secretive group that they spent most of their time whispering in corners to such an extent that one member of their staff of three felt compelled to leave.

Both PT and Z had to decide whether low walls and an open plan design meant that people would have to speak quietly or not at all so as not to disturb others. Perhaps someone had read *Bonfire of the Vanities*, with its graphic description of a room full of people, all using their telephones at once, talking to colleagues all around the world, shouting to be heard over others. They also had to debate the issue of confidentiality.

PT & Sons have rearranged their offices and the positions of desks within offices twice in the first year. Z has also rearranged with major disruption at least twice in two years. This is not unusual as needs change, more people join, projects involve different combinations of people who need to be in proximity to one another.

The advice taken at the outset and the practicalities of any possible future reorganization, however, have to be considered as a whole rather than in isolation.

Conference facilities

Z International has a meeting room where the atmosphere makes it difficult to sustain the thought process. The optimum time for meetings is first thing in the morning; after lunch, or after the first half hour, everyone in the rooms begins to lose concentration. The room is fully enclosed with glass walls to the corridors on either side, but no natural light. Furthermore, the glass onto the corridors makes those in the room somewhat paranoid about people seeing anything confidential. Meetings are therefore characterized by perpetual head swivelling to make sure no one is looking over anyone's shoulder from outside.

On one famous occasion, someone stood in front of a glass wall with her arms spread out to prevent anyone passing by from seeing artwork that was being considered.

The room contains a large meeting table that runs its length, and chairs along either side. There is nothing else in the room and people must enter in single file because the width of the table and chairs fills the room so that once people are seated, no one can get past them.

PT's meeting room, on the other hand, is large and airy, with windows that open, giving natural light, and a good air conditioning system. There is a telephone in the room as well as a television and video and a screen for slides. In other words, it is fully equipped.

The entrance to the room is on a glass wall facing out onto the corridor. That wall has Venetian blinds so that if the room needs to be darkened for a presentation, or anything confidential is being shown, the blinds can be drawn.

Status

Status within the company can be conveyed by whether or not your working area includes:

- walls;
- windows;
- carpets;
- plants;
- an unshared telephone extension.

Equally, if you do have an office of your own, status can be conveyed by:

- which pictures hang on the walls;
- the thickness of the carpet;
- size and type of desk;
- whether or not there is a separate seating area;
- whether or not there is a meeting area.

Those low down in the totem pole have to share a telephone extension, have no walls or partitions to put up flow charts, graphs and other work related material let alone any way to personalize their space.

Perceptions of status can be conveyed by hosts indicating to visitors where to sit — or not sit as the case may be. The host can not only convey what he perceives as his own superiority but lets the visitor know how his status is perceived.

Space and proximity also convey status. The larger the office, presumably the more important the occupant. If there is a reception area leading into another office within which is an inner sanctum for the executive himself then you can be pretty sure he is high up in the establishment.

When I visited Sir Bob Reid at British Rail headquarters, I had to sign into the building on the ground floor and then was sent up to the chairman's floor. There I was escorted to a waiting room and then through a reception area and his assistant's office into Sir Bob's own domain. The room did not have a desk but rather an extremely large — not less than six foot — table with his papers and equipment at one end. At the other end, some twenty feet beyond, were two settees facing one another with a large coffee table in between.

In other companies I have visited, the higher you are in the structure, the more of your own furniture and decorations are allowed to be utilized. The co-chairmen had their rooms furnished in antiques with original oil paintings on the walls.

Proximity can be used to communicate informality or, in some instances, intimacy. Occasionally this can be perceived as aggressive, hostile or flirtatious. The person closing the distance can be interpreted as saying: I am more important than you are (or I believe I am more important than you are).

LEADERSHIP

A discussion of leadership, its different styles, the steps to becoming a good leader and interpretations of what makes a good leader in varying situations has filled volumes. It is discussed in some detail in this book in Chapter 6 (Training) but there is no way that this one volume can possibly begin to cover such a vast subject comprehensively.

With reference to employee communications, I will have to be satisfied with saying that there are different levels of leadership and many leaders within every organization. Just as there are different groupings, responsibilities and relationships, so too can people's roles as leader of a group or member of a group overlap. You may be leader of one group but a participant in another. Learning the skills of being a participant are just as important as are the skills of responding to different types of leader.

This is a huge subject and one that anyone interested would do well to study in detail. Many of us, for instance, are seen as leaders by others even if we do not see ourselves in that role. Perception and awareness are prerequisites to fulfillment of every role that each and every one of us plays. Every chapter of this book goes back to that theme and it is one that must also be stressed with regard to leadership and employee communications.

HUMAN RESOURCES DEVELOPMENT

What is the difference between the personnel manager and human resources development manager? The short answer is, not a lot. But as with corporate identities which are periodically 'tweaked' to indicate that the company has moved on from a previous position/image or that it is moving with the times without losing sight of its main goals, therefore making a slight visible adjustment to indicate this without changing direction entirely, the role of the personnel manager has now gone beyond recruitment and interviewing. Although these essential tasks are still an integral part of the Personnel Manager's job description, a number of other tasks have either been added or given more weight than in the past. These include:

- skills and attitude assessment;
- counselling and/or referral to professional counsellors;
- maintaining links with employees once they have begun working with the company;
- establishing and developing links with audiences outside the company which have direct bearing on such issues as work experience, shadowing, teacher placements, business education links and training;
- assessing training requirements then identifying and implementing the best ways of satisfying them.

In fact, the entire emphasis has shifted to give more emphasis to individuals than jobs. Long- and short-term requirements are considered of equal importance.

While the title human resources development manager may be an acknowledgement of a current buzzword, it is also an indication of awareness. It is exactly what the words imply, and not just someone responsible for hiring and firing. The personnel manager may have been the first and last person an employee saw during their life with a company, but the HRD manager is a reference point. He is available on request, often available when not requested, a lynchpin in the communications process within the organization as much as a link with external audiences.

Interviews

Interviews are a nerve-racking experience and it does no harm to realize that this applies to both interviewer and interviewee. Each have a great deal at stake as they try to find out as much as possible about the other in order to determine whether they will suit each other's requirements on a potentially long-term basis. Although a certain amount of trust can be placed in instinctive reactions and first responses, each side is making a commitment that deserves a considered judgement. The interviewee will want to know:

- What will the job entail?
- What does the company do?
- Who else works here?
- What training will I have?
- Will I have room to grow?
- Who will I work with?
- Where will I work?

- What hours will I work?
- How much will I be paid?
- What does he think of me?

The interviewer will want to know

- What work has he done before?
- Where has he worked before?
- What training has he had?
- Who has he worked with?
- What did previous employers/teachers/colleagues think of him?
- Can he work on his own initiative?
- How far is he likely to want to go/be able to go?
- How much will he want to be paid?
- What does he think of us?

The interview then takes the form of questions and answers, with both the interviewer and interviewee trying to answer their own questions and each other's. Each will be anxious to find out what is likely to follow if the applicant is successful.

Two golden rules can be applied to interviewer and interviewee which may make the proceedings happier all around:

- Relax.
- Don't interrupt.

Nerves can never be entirely eliminated but a few deep breathing or relaxation exercises before beginning will not do any harm.

During the session, which is the best and perhaps only opportunity to ask questions and state your position, neither side should be so anxious to say his piece or move on to his next question that he doesn't listen carefully to what is being said. There is no point in asking a question and not listening to the answer. Apart from general rudeness, interrupting no matter how eager you are to respond not only makes a negative impression but results in a lost opportunity to hear what the other person was actually trying to tell you.

Making an impression

It is not just words which are important during an interview. Interviewer and interviewee tell one another a great deal non-verbally. Each is looking at the other's appearance, the interviewee is looking at the room and the general working environment, they are trying to read each other's manner and assess whether they are sincere, able, intelligent, lively, obedient.... Each is trying to make a positive impression and is on their best behaviour. While the other is aware of this, and trying to find the man or woman behind the image being conveyed.

Recruitment

The last few years have seen the development of recruitment fairs, or milk rounds, as a means of recruitment. Groups of employers send representatives to colleges or universities and man tables full of corporate literature promoting the company and what it has on offer. They are trawling to see what is in the job market and likely to come their way in the near future. Recruitment fairs can be used as a way of:

- finding people to interview in depth later;
- screening a large number of people in minimum time;
- selling the company and its jobs;
- finding out what sort of jobs potential applicants are looking for;
- finding out what skills and abilities are available;
- finding out how the company is perceived;
- improving the company's image;
- communicating directly with an audience that may only be reached through an intermediary in the normal course of events.

The selection of specific individuals for interview comes later. Recruitment fairs are part of the weeding out process, the general marketing and public relations process. They are a useful additional tool regardless of whether the people who attended apply for a job or are invited to an interview later.

Applying for the job

Curriculum vitae form the basis of the first impression a company has of potential employees. They need to be factual and informative, sufficiently positive and detailed to get over the first hurdle of applying for a job and getting an interview. They cannot convey personality in any way and should not be boastful but, conversely, should not be too modest either.

During the interview, the cv can be discussed in greater depth. This is the time when the interviewee can explain his background and experience and what he has learned from them. He can demonstrate the applications and progression of both skills and abilities that were derived from the experience — intangible conclusions that cannot necessarily be conveyed on a form or in the cv.

The cv can be used as a discussion document. For the interviewer, it can give clues and guidelines to the candidate's strengths and weaknesses, showing which questions can and should be asked.

Many employers ask candidates to fill in questionnaires regarding their feelings at various times in their lives and careers. Others ask them to answer simple questions and problems from which they can test numeracy and literacy as well as get an indication of thought processes and response to problems.

A young friend who recently applied for a number of jobs was asked to take such tests by one or two employers. He largely felt that some of the questions regarding feelings were unnecessary although he understood their relevance, particularly those which dealt with his feelings when made redundant.

The possible reaction of candidates to being 'tested' must be taken into account by the interviewer, however, as some are less willing or able to cooperate than others. Written tests can have their advantages but, again, should be seen as just one of a range of tools and not be the only criteria upon which a decision or offer of a job is based.

Planning ahead

No matter what our general and individual current economic situation may be, most of us prefer to think of the future as being better. Progress demands that tomorrow be at least as good but preferably better than the present. If this is to be the case, then we must plan now. Business involvement with training and education is not simply philanthropic or altruistic but represents an awareness that industry is the best, and perhaps the only, or final, arbiter of needs. No one else is going to do it for us. Government may say that it recognizes the country's needs but it is up to the individual and industry to ensure their future.

There now seems to be a widespread acknowledgement that management and skills do not come naturally but must be nurtured and encouraged. Chapter 6 on Training refers to the steps involved in becoming a manager, that it is a combination of experience plus training. Every chapter in this book continually reverts to the theme of effective communications and the ways in which our whole economic structure is dependent on their success. Skilling the workforce and ensuring that employees are willing and able to meet the challenges of the future are the means to achieving that end.

Chapter 6

Training

This is the chapter that, to me, is the heart and soul of this book and the heart and soul of communications.

Training should be treated in its broadest possible sense, as education and learning. It is not just for blue collar workers unable to make the grade as academics. It is not just for those who have been made redundant and need to find a new trade. It is not just for those looking for a job related skill.

Training is about learning and learning is something we do every day of our lives. It is something we *should* do every day of our lives so that we make the most of our potential, develop our abilities as well as skills, understand ourselves and others. Training is about communication and communication is about training.

PLANNING FOR THE FUTURE

There is a great deal of jargon being bandied about these days regarding training. Particularly popular is the expression 'skilling the workforce'. Skills upgrading should not be reduced to lip service only. Training should certainly be seen to have some immediate effect but its real value has got to be acknowledged as a long-term investment.

Just as production takes time, training takes time. It is generally recognized that 'education' lasts from age five to age sixteen. That is the official period we are allotted. But in real terms, education lasts a lifetime, albeit unofficially and within different contexts. If it did not, then business would not exist, let alone progress. Training and experience are two of the most important of these contexts.

Businesses have, and must perpetually have, a positive commitment to training. We must view training as an investment rather than as an overhead. We must look at both the long- and short-term prospects for our businesses, at long- and short-term strategy and, therefore at long- and short-term skills and training requirements. We not only need to fill our immediate requirements but must also ensure that people, skills, abilities, knowledge and experience, will be available in the future.

Training for change

We train for change in two different senses. First, because individual skills, including leadership and management capabilities, are developed and changed through training. Second, because motivation and perceptions often need to change in line with corporate requirements. We all need to be adaptable and that is a skill which can be developed through training. If circumstances change then we must change with them and this often involves learning or training.

Tomorrow's people

In their December 1990 issue, *IT Training*, the magazine for training and developing management, interviewed a number of leaders in industry, and IT training and development managers on their views of the future.

P J Rushworth, group personnel director, Westland Group plc was quoted as saying that

> Training in industry is all about change; preparing people for change; providing the skills which allow people to change jobs; helping people deal with changing working methods and so on...corporate training must respond to the needs of corporate business...the training function must establish a policy statement...which makes a direct contribution to improving the company's business performance.

Others interviewed were from the Institute of Directors, Institute of Training and Development, Training Agency, Grand Metropolitan Information Services Ltd, Computing Services Association, Rank Xerox, CU Assurance, B & Q plc and Westland Group plc. Among the issues they raised as key to the successful future of industry were:

- Training needs to be carried out by professionals (G B Webster, executive director, Institute of Training and Development).
- Training, vocational education and enterprise development need to be in the hands of employers (Roger Dawe, director general, Training Agency).
- Never mind whether people are qualified or fully trained, do they have the potential to fill the role...how to use people productively...equip them with the right skills (Robin Wilkins, director of technology, Grand Metropolitan Information Services Ltd).

As Sir John Harvey-Jones repeatedly tells anyone who will listen to him, low skills combined with high expectations have created a lethal

115

combination in British industry. Quantity, quality, relevance and accessibility of management training are the key issues. Training must be about knowledge and understanding as well as specific skills.

THE STRATEGY

Sir Brian Wolfson, patron of the National Training Awards, wrote the introduction to *Winners 1990*, the synopses and report on 1990's award winners. In it, he stated his belief that we need a strategic approach to training, 'linking development of people to the wider business goals of the organization'.

Investment in people is the current theme. There is an increasing recognition that training is essential as an ongoing process to show employees that you want to help them to improve themselves and their abilities. Sir John Harvey-Jones, speaking at the launch of Thames Valley Enterprise, a TEC covering a relatively affluent area of the country, emphasized the need for skills improvement, but also cited a poverty of aspiration as one of the major reasons for training.

TVE covers an area where the number of young people is declining while the number of unemployed is on the increase. There is even more need, therefore, for training and skills development in order to fill the gaps. A bridge needs to be built between employers and potential employees.

There is, in fact, a general acknowledgement of the skills shortage going into the 1990s. The Thames Valley College conducted a survey of training managers in the region and came out with the general conviction that companies 'viewed qualifications, and hence qualification-linked courses, as becoming increasingly important'.

Despite the recession, this belief in the need for training was confirmed by a CBI study which showed that 47 per cent of members were maintaining their training programmes and a further 29 per cent had increased the level of training.

The business of training

More and more people are becoming convinced that business has an obligation and an opportunity to become involved in education and (skill) training. Attitudes have changed dramatically because unless everyone is involved then change will not be achieved.

Oxfordshire is one county which takes the links between education and training as a joint responsibility. The Education Business Partnership spent the Spring of 1991 conducting an audit into the relationship between industry and education so that they can form an action plan to benefit individuals in their roles as students, teachers, managers and employees. Their goal is to ensure that neither school nor work is seen in isolation.

Roger Dawe, director general of the Training Agency, in a statement he has almost certainly made repeatedly in recent months, said 'TECs and

LECs (Scottish Local Enterprise Companies) are revolutionary. They put training, vocational education and enterprise development in the hands of local employers so they can develop the workforce they need.' The aims of the TECs and LECs are to:

- encourage training by business;
- help young people and the unemployed acquire the skills the economy needs;
- foster enterprise;
- work with the education sector to ensure that vocational education is relevant to employers' needs;
- improve the training system.

Different initiatives undertaken over the last two or three years are frequently employer-led because it is the employers who know their own needs best. There is a special need, as a result, for strong communication links between education and training providers.

Whose responsibility is it anyway?

Ours. Not yours or theirs. Not his or hers. If we are the people then we have the responsibility. Umbrella organizations such as TECS, LECs, Education Business Partnerships, Understanding Business in Industry, Management Charter Initiative, Confederation for British Industry, training providers and educationalists are all available to offer advice, support, consultancy and occasionally funding. Training and Enterprise Councils, for example, will enable support for training to be tailored for local needs and the need of industry and commerce. But in the end, it is up to each of us to do our bit and make sure that action is taken.

Winners 1990, by providing synopses on the accomplishments of those who won the National Training Awards, sets out to 'provide a source of information and encouragement' for:

- senior executives, who may identify new approaches to developing staff within their organization;
- training specialists, who need to link the training investment to business objectives, design training to meet those objectives, and evaluate the benefits from the training;
- anyone who may find useful examples of how business can profit from developing their people.

Facing the competition

Particular influences on the workforce include the impact of international communications and technology. These are both covered in more detail elsewhere but the point I would like to make here is that competition can take a number of different forms.

There is an innate resistance to change in all of us that must be overcome. We may fear that we will be replaced by machines, that there will not be enough jobs to go around, that if we do not keep up with the Jones' we will be in the dole queue next week.

In fact, this can be an incentive to train and improve our assets. There is nothing like a bit of competition to motivate.

On an international level, many British companies see Japan and Germany as a threat to their survival. This applies not only to production levels but to attitudes. The views of the Japanese and Germans with regard to company loyalty, ownership, motivation and responsibility are well known. There may be rigid structures and rules to follow but there is much to be gained by demonstrating willingness to learn and move up the ladder.

The acceptance of incentives, motivation and responsibility are benchmarks against which we must measure ourselves. It is common knowledge that the level of people staying on for formal higher education and/or participating in some kind of training is lower in the UK than many other parts of the world. Although statistics do not necessarily reflect the numbers of people involved in training after a break from formal education, MCI, TECs and the CBI have recently conducted broader based surveys on expectations and developments within industry for existing employees.

The idea of training is not to threaten anyone, but rather to maximize individual capabilities and achieve potential. Training will help us compete and win.

All for one and one for all

Cooperation, participation and enthusiasm are needed if training is to succeed. It is not enough just to make the gesture or pay lip service to the latest fad. Managers and employees at all levels need to see the relevance and importance both for themselves and others, not just to make the company look good or be profitable but in their own personal terms and for their own sense of achievement. They must see that they are valued members of the organization whose contribution is both needed and appreciated.

R S Clare was one of the winners of the National Training Awards 1990. Their accomplishments are explained in *Winners 1990*. R S Clare is an old, well-established company which found that increasing competition in their target markets meant that they would have to sell a broad range of products into niche markets. In order to do this, 'the commitment of all employees was crucial to face the challenge of change. It was vital that investment be put into developing the people within the company.' Managers, it was decided, 'had to manage their resources more efficiently and effectively, be able to solve problems and make competent business decisions'.

R S Clare's solution was to organize a series of 'highly participative workshops...to improve their abilities in terms of communication, delegation by counselling, motivation and leadership...Extensive customer-orientated training was also put in place for all employees, based on ownership of standards for Total Quality Management and team building through outdoor-based training.'

Parts of a whole

It is in our own right as individuals that we must participate in addition to our roles as members of a larger organization. The attitude of middle managers towards the value of communication and training must be positive. They must be aware, receptive and enthusiastic. They must not feel threatened or think that training is unnecessary. This cooperation will not take place if managers are forced into things because of 'orders' from above.

Knowing and understanding why we are doing something helps us to achieve our goals. This is true for everyone from assembly line workers whose interest, output and overall performance improved once they understood their role in the whole operation, to junior managers being sent on a training course who needed to understand why and what is expected of them afterwards.

One such manager I know was sent on a course to improve her presentation skills. She enjoyed it enormously, but when asked why she was sent, she wasn't sure. She thought it might be possible that at some later stage in the development of her job she might be asked to make presentations either to the board of directors or sales staff regarding new products or developments and designs.

Training is not necessarily intended to create a society of leaders but to improve skills, increase self-awareness and develop potential so that we can all do as well as possible regardless of our job or social level. If this is not appreciated uniformly throughout the company, or if there is not sufficient support from all levels, then the participation which must be encouraged will actually be discouraged. Acceptance must be active. The line of least resistance, or passive participation, will not provide the necessary incentive.

Leadership training and group dynamics

Like many young people through the years — my contemporaries and my children alike — I enrolled at university without any clear idea of how I wanted my future to develop. I had no career plans and my ambitions centred on 'doing something worthwhile'. I had no notion what, or how this could be accomplished.

My instincts developed into an interest in education and learning in their pure and idealistic sense. I wanted — and believed others should also want — to become an interesting and aware person, able to achieve any realistic target set. I wanted — and believed others should also want — to believe in myself, my strengths, my ability, my initiative and creativity.

My studies began to concentrate on group dynamics and interpersonal relations, approached from an interdisciplinary angle and guided by a professor of philosophy who shared and supported my passion for learning for its own sake. I took courses in sociology, anthropology, psychology, philosophy, communications and education. I attended lectures, seminars, workshops and tutorials, conducted some of my own research and read the results of others' research. I participated in, observed and lead training sessions of all persuasions.

I was the classic example of the academic without any common sense. I had little experience of industry or employment or indeed the world outside what we fondly called our ivory tower. But I knew how to lead and how to interpret what was going on in a group. Understanding group behaviour, and your own behaviour, is one of the skills that can be applied to whatever situation you may find yourself in.

Jane Allan lists a number of steps to becoming a good leader in her book *How to Develop Your Personal Management Skills*. She suggests that a good leader should:

- establish who is in charge;
- know what you want to accomplish;
- know what you want each person in the team to accomplish;
- let people know what you expect;
- find out what others want for themselves;
- find out what others expect of you;
- take being a role model seriously;
- expect others to be self-motivated but don't count on it;
- understand that the quality of leadership is determined by the methods chosen to motivate others.

The acceptance of leadership, and the practice of it, are just as difficult as acquiring it in the first place.

The managing director of one business I know maintains a close relationship with his employees, does not hide in his office, knows each of them and their families. But he expects them to stand up when he enters the room and to demonstrate the respect they feel, or he thinks they should feel, for him.

The managing director of another business I know detests being perceived as a 'boss'. He knows that he is in fact seen in this way but refuses to accept it. He finds asking anyone to do anything for him extremely difficult and although he accepts the principle of delegation, prefers to see himself as an equal rather than an authority figure.

Neither approach is quite right. Neither of them is totally successful as a leader although each has attributes that make others perceive him in that role.

Skills training

David Whitaker, chairman of Whitaker's, publishers of the *Bookseller*, wrote an article for that magazine in April 1991 inviting trade support for those who have lost jobs in the recent round of publishing redundancies and who 'represent a pool of talent it would damage the trade to see dry up'. He also suggested that those who had lost their jobs might like to register their talents, their interest in forming a cooperative base, or acquiring information on freelancing and interviewing techniques — and offered himself as an initial reference point for such activities.

As an exercise in communication to facilitate self help, Mr Whitaker's initiative was both creative and constructive. In a sense, he is advocating pyramid training. By putting people in touch with one another, and forming networks, their experiences are being shared and the skills base widening.

Recruitment advertisements frequently specify interpersonal skills or well-developed communication skills as prerequisite qualifications. Staff are trained to deal with incoming communications, both written and verbal. The impression made on visitors or callers by representatives of an organization has been discussed elsewhere. Such skills are, or should be, high on the list of priorities in training. It is a skill that every employee requires that must be fine tuned and practised to perfection.

In Chapter 5 on Employee Communications I said that it is useful for as many people to have as many skills and as much knowledge of others' skills, roles and responsibilities as possible. I said that it is beneficial for everyone to have an overall understanding of what the company does, and what all its participating staff members do.

Yet there are still prejudices and barriers. There are some executives who consider technology, for instance, to be entertaining when used for electronic diaries or gadgets. This same technology is no longer their department when it comes to keyboard skills however. If more managers were given word processors and trained in keyboard skills, far less management time would be spent in hand writing or dictating correspondence, reports and memoranda, then waiting while they were typed, checked, corrected and checked again before despatching.

Skills training should go right across the board. As should academic training and practical qualifications. Theoretical teaching is fine as far as it goes, but there is nothing like a bit of hands-on experience. Sir Bob Reid, chairman of British Rail and the Management Charter Initiative, strongly believes that no one should begin studying for an MBA before the age of thirty and then only after at least ten years' on-the-job experience.

Stop for a minute and ask yourself if some of the professional people you are dealing with are trained or qualified. Does your bank manager, for example, have any real experience of business?

When hiring or recruiting staff some degree of cross-industrial experience or knowledge is useful for later communication purposes.

The importance of understanding one another, for example through teacher placements, whereby industry communicates its needs to teachers, and teachers see the world outside the classroom that students will have to live in and be prepared for, cannot and should not be underestimated.

Representative training

Frank Keating told the story, in the *Guardian* of June 19 1991, of Sunil Gavaskar, the Indian batsman, and his rejection of honorary membership of the MCC because he had too frequently been 'belittled by the rudeness and hostility of the Lord's gatemen and stewards.' His stand was supported by numerous fans who then began telling tales about these often defensive and offensive guardians.

The result was that two dozen senior stewards were sent on a three-day course with a management consultancy specializing in group training. According to the *Guardian*, the director of the consultancy 'designed a programme for them specifically focused on interpersonal communicating. It featured sequences of practical role-playing in handling potential difficulties and conflicts.' The course was entitled 'Winning Teams That Care' and was run by a specialist in behavioural and motivational skills.

Despite the implication that stewards needed to improve their skills because they were not sufficiently skilful in carrying out their duties, the overall attitude was positive. When the new season opened, both instructor and director attended a match to 'observe, analyze and judge performance under pressure...to maximize any follow-up activity'.

This could be likened to the charm school attended by employees of British Rail and other organizations where staff not only have to do their jobs but deal with the public as well. They are representing their companies, giving out impressions that may be lasting and attributed to the company itself rather than the individual employee who may simply be having a rotten day.

It now seems that the last straw, the incident with Sunil Gavaskar, was brought about by a breakdown in communication. He was apparently the sixth person that day, according to the MCC's secretary, to claim to be Sunil Gavaskar. As he was unable to produce his official pass as evidence, the stewards inevitably refused to believe his claim and would not give him leave to enter the grounds. Other similar incidents emerged in the publicity ensuing on Gavaskar's rejection of membership. Lord's seems to have learned a valuable lesson:

- that the impression made on the audience by a company's employees is all-important;
- that communication skills can be learned and implemented to alleviate and eliminate past problems.

They also learned that training can be the means of creating those changes and teaching those skills. Let's hope that the training was as successful as was intended.

Putting it into practice

How many of us continue doing jobs ourselves that could happily be done by others because we do not have the time to train someone else to take over? Think about it for a minute. Think about what your time is worth and whether it would not be better spent doing things that others cannot do.

If there is any task that can be done just as well by someone else with a little bit of guidance from a good trainer, pass it on. Do not spend your time mending a hole in the dyke when the plumber can do it three times as quickly. You could be earning twice as much in the same amount of time as it would cost you to pay a craftsman. He is trained. Take advantage of that. And if there isn't a trained craftsman available, find someone and train him. Fixing the leaks is not the manager's responsibility; finding someone to fix them is.

IDENTIFYING TRAINING NEEDS

Convenience and effectiveness are high on the list of priorities for training, therefore it frequently needs to be achieved with minimal disruption to the day to day routine of the business. Much training is now brought to the trainee through in-house sessions, open or distance learning, interactive videos and computer based training (CBT).

Mars UK has an open-learning facility used by 50 per cent of its staff. They realize, and demonstrate, that open learning can be combined with industry and careers.

The December/January 1990 edition of *IT Training* carried a feature on the Ford Motor Co which describes the establishment of a courseware library so that training sessions can be suited to staff and not vice versa. Time, location and content are all related to specific needs and individuals. There is no need to book a room in advance, to rely on scheduled courses, residential or transportation factors, conflicts with the job or even the availability of other people who might have similar needs.

Training must be:

* appropriate;
* relevant;
* convenient;
* effective;
* interactive;
* adaptable.

It must be suited to a range of abilities and backgrounds without being either too basic or too advanced. It must be interactive even when using a programme based on distance learning or CBT.

Two of the most essential criteria for training are:

- motivation;
- support.

A case in point

The directors of Smith Co had a discussion one day on business communications within the context of asking employees to give presentations. They decided that their staff were generally not experienced in speaking in front of a group, not confident, did not stand well, needed guidance in elocution and diction. The directors also felt that their staff should have gained that experience at school and although they recognized the need for training to meet that skill, were somewhat resentful that it was necessary.

They then discussed what sort of training would be best, and generally felt that experience of public speaking was needed. They also felt that training was too much of an industry with too much hype and pressure selling. There was concern about the need to evaluate the courses available in order to select the best and most appropriate for their needs. What they wanted was to develop self-confidence in those being trained.

From there, the conversation led incidentally onto the subject of international communications especially telephone conversations. Not all of Smith Co's telephonists were multilingual, and although the directors didn't feel that they needed to be, there was general agreement that they did need to speak English clearly as they often received calls from non-English speakers. Particular problems arose when a telephonist was not in fact a native English speaker. There was an occasion when an Israeli was speaking to a Japanese in English and they both had difficulty in understanding the other.

As the meeting wore on, the directors began to realize the full extent of their training requirements and ended up forming a sub-committee to conduct a communications audit with the specific purpose of devising a suitable programme to meet all of their needs.

The price we pay

Training, or the lack of it in various industries, can have a major impact on those the company does business with. To stick with my example of banks, managers, for example, frequently start their careers behind the till and work their way up through the ranks of the bank.

Any training they receive along the way is within the bank itself. There is no set requirement for secondment to industry, no hard and fast rule about how much time bank employees must spend working in business before reaching the next rung on the ladder.

Banks can provide classic examples of the way in which lack of communication can serve to divide and conquer. Customers generally have only an informal network of friends and colleagues who most likely use a variety of banks. If they are having financial difficulties, and are attempting to negotiate with their bank, they can often feel isolated. Tactics used by the bank are often difficult to counter as individual customers do not usually have precedent or previous experience on which they can rely.

In an effort to remedy this, BUG — Bank Users Group — is currently being set up as a pressure group which will establish links between customers themselves and between groups of customers and the banks. The first of their objectives will be to establish training criteria, possibly determining national standards. The partners of AB Co, the company discussed in Chapter 7 on Negotiations, were the instigators of BUG. In the course of fighting for their own business, they became concerned that the SBM was employing similar tactics on other customers who were perhaps less tenacious than they. Having won their own battle, they then felt that the lessons they learned could be passed on to others.

Quantifying the results

Entrants for the National Training Awards 1990 were asked to demonstrate links between:

- the needs of their organization;
- the identification of training objectives;
- the design of training to meet those objectives;
- the delivery of the training and in particular how effectively resources were used;
- the outcomes of the training;
- an evaluation of the benefits to the organization arising from the training investment.

Assessment of the entries, but more importantly the training initiatives themselves, was a difficult task which required careful criteria. It is not always possible to quantify the results of training. Time is needed for them to take effect, to prove to be lasting and more than superficial. There are not always directly measurable effects. The judges of the training awards believe, however, that 'where organizations relate their training to business objectives and set clear targets, they can normally provide a quantifiable assessment of what has been achieved through the training and what impact it has had on business performance.'

The MCI newletter *Information Exchange* carried an article in its July 1990 edition on establishing management competences. Attempting to devise a 'complete standards framework for managers' was an understandably complicated task and it was decided that, 'as a working proposition, the key purpose of management was to sustain and enhance the performance of the organization to achieve its objectives'. This was, the panel believed, a formula which would be acceptable at all levels from major industrial organizations to small service operations. It was later redrafted to read that management should 'Achieve the organization's objectives and continuously improve its performance.'

One successful programme for measuring the effectiveness of training has been devised by Business Training Services at Thames Valley College. Their Phased Training Outcomes is described as 'a series of highly participative and interactive skill-building courses for personnel at either supervisory or management levels, where the level of improvement in an employee's work performance can be accurately predicted.' The outcome is designed to be 'immediate improvement in the individual's skill and greater job satisfaction through a more efficient use of their time.'

Creating yardsticks to assess and measure the effects of training not only on the individuals concerned, and on their colleagues, but on the organization as a whole, its performance levels, productivity and profitability, is an industry in and of itself. It can be done. Finding and establishing those yardsticks is an integral part of structuring the training programme.

The tactics

Having once recognized that training is a way of life and that it can take a multitude of forms, we need to look at attitudes with regard to specific requirements. Ask yourself what you would do to answer the following questions or deal with the following situations.

- Training for manual or blue collar workers. Are they seen as second rate, and not quite able to make the grade? Do you include in this category technicians and engineers who work with their hands as well as their minds?
- What do you see as the difference between academic and vocational training? Is there a difference between education and training?
- How should leaders, officers and management be trained? Do they just rise naturally to the top and get promoted up the ladder because of their pre-career backgrounds? What about the guy who works his way up from the bottom?
- What help do women who have taken a career break need to get back to work?
- How should training be structured for disabled people to maximize their potential and integrate them into the workforce?
- How can we upgrade people who left school early and want to learn new skills or gain new knowledge and experience?
- What action needs to be taken with regard to training and retraining, as when people are out of work and want new to learn a new career or profession?
- How, in fact, can we upgrade each and every one of us to meet the new requirements of business, industry, technology?

- How can we deal with unemployment caused by new machines or job requirements and specifications changing?
- How can we deal with the present and the future?

The ways and means

Trainers need to be trained. People at different job levels coming from different backgrounds and starting with different knowledge and abilities all need to be catered for. In addition to the constant learning processes that we all undergo every day with varying degrees of awareness, structured training can take the form of every day teaching/training, internal or external training, concentrated or serial training, distance learning, full or part-time training, residential training or a combination of modules of different sorts. Whichever way you treat it, though, the emphasis must be on the entire range of:

- people skills;
- job skills;
- industry-specific skills.

When looking at the entire range of training, there are a number of subject headings appropriate:

- audio-visual training;
- computer-based training;
- education including:
  - post 16 training
  - further education
  - open and distance learning
  - National Vocational Qualifications (NVQ)
  - prior accreditation of learning
  - MBAs
  - technical and vocational qualifications
  - international training
  - retraining
  - language training;
- management and leadership training including:
  - outdoor/activity-based training
  - gaming
  - personal awareness/sensitivity training
  - human development training;
- sales and presentation training.

When seeking to put a training programme in place, the possibilities to evaluate include:

- databases of training courses;

- training styles;
- trainers' qualifications;
- training materials (bespoke and off-the-shelf).

Alternative methods for training courses include:

- educational and private;
- full and part-time;
- residential;
- in-house.

Qualifications

Qualifications can take numerous forms. They can be academic, as with GCSEs, A-levels, International Baccalaureate and an abundance of degrees up to and including MBAs and PhDs. They can be practical, as with BTec, City & Guilds and HNDs. Or they can be experience-based with accreditation of prior learning and certification given for experience.

The Management Charter Initiative wants to develop a national policy, act as a catalyst and facilitator of change, becoming the lead body for management standards, endorsing and encouraging good products. One of their foremost activities is an involvement in the assessment of training materials.

Learning can be applied and thinking can be lateral. Every waking moment does not have to be focused on the job in order to improve performance.

ICI Paints, like Ford and Mars, is one of many large companies encouraging employees to continue learning and training throughout their careers. They hire young people anxious to get out of a formal, full-time learning environment and enable them to continue their education in practical, on-the-job training. They hire people with a range of qualifications who can perform at different levels and continue to achieve and develop at their own pace. They do not expect staff to stand still any more than they expect the world to stand still. The qualification an applicant has when he sends in his curriculum vitae is not necessarily the same qualification he will have six months or six years later.

As John Danzeisen, ICI's Finance Director, told Business Line, ICI believes that 'in the end, it is people who win and keep customers for us'. He believes that preferences for training to lead to job-related certification or qualifications, is broadening to encompass anything that an individual may choose to do to, that is, 'enhance their skill-base, or improve their skills or knowledge, even if it isn't particularly related now to the job they are in'.

Every day training

Weekly departmental or staff meetings have value for day to day functioning, catching up, de-duplication of effort, exchange of information and planning but also for training. They can provide a forum for clearing the air, brainstorming, reacting, analyzing, maintaining and improving relationships, in short a means of communicating. Staff meetings are also valuable for the introduction and orientation of new or recently promoted staff. Among other things, they can be used to demonstrate that staff are included, counted, kept in touch, valued and their participation actively solicited.

On-the-job training

Apprenticeships as a form of on-the-job training shows the historical awareness of the need for training and the sense of hands-on experience.

Likewise, shadowing is a means of communication which involves exchanging information, skills, feelings, changing perceptions and developing understanding. Acceptance of coursework at school, acceptance of experience as qualification, the application of tasks performed on the job to the achievement of formal qualifications, all combine to ensure that credit is given for practical skills and demonstrations of ability.

Off-the-job training

Residential courses, short and concentrated, build relationships and awareness of our own abilities that must then be taken back to every day life. In *She'll be Wearing Pink Pyjamas*, a Julie Walters film about a group of women participating in an outdoor training course, confidence was built through team work. A television sitcom about a group of middle managers facing an assault course made a similar point. Problems have to be solved, tasks completed, teams and relationships built, responses to leadership and responsibility applied and assessed.

Not all residential courses are so active. They can be intense in different ways. Sensitivity training, management training through personal awareness and encounter groups can all be cathartic and purging as participants learn about themselves and others. Awareness leads to development.

All of this occurs to varying degrees depending on the type of group, its size and purpose, its membership and its leader. Task-oriented groups do not capitalize on emotional experiences; sensitivity training groups and encounter groups do. It's a bit like the education debate — education for its own sake, for knowledge and philosophy and learning — or for skills, job and career applications, practical abilities.

Revealing and sharing feelings has an effect on the group present as well as interaction with others outside the group when participants go back to their daily routine. Changes can be permanent or transient and it is up to both the individual and the group to determine which it will be.

The training group

What happens when groups gel? Sometimes something happens, perhaps through instinct, you just know something for no reason that you can explain, and a relationship is born. What the effects of that moment will be cannot be predicted but neither can the moment be denied.

Learning to understand our own and others' behaviour has implications which extend far beyond the training group. A decision to act out a role, whether conscious or not, can radiate out to affect all sorts of situations never anticipated.

I find it difficult, for instance, to keep quiet in a group. No matter how good my intentions about letting others have their say, about trying not to take over, I invariably find it impossible to resist expressing my opinions. Even worse, I always have some suggestion to make on what the group should do. I have to try not to get carried away. When I feel strongly about something it shows. And if I try to keep quiet, that also shows.

This is just the sort of intimidating behaviour that puts off people who are naturally reticent. Some people cannot resist the opportunity to share their views and cannot bear the strain of silence. Others cannot endure the torture of what they consider public speaking and define this as anything that verbalizes their thoughts.

Role playing in training groups provides the opportunity for people to make believe. They can do things, and behave in ways that they would not normally and have a ready made excuse — I was role playing, they say.

Sometimes role playing leads to changes in behaviour that can be applied after the group session is over, though, and achieve change that would not be possible otherwise. The beauty of training groups, according to the skill of the leader, is that such behaviour can be discussed openly, in a relaxed atmosphere, with no value judgements applied. Assessment and feedback — personal and from colleagues — can be accepted and acted on in a way that would not be the norm in the context of real situations. But the response to it can be applied to real situations and adjustments to beliefs, perceptions, behaviour made accordingly.

Who are the trainers

A trainer is not necessarily a leader. He may sometimes be one, within the confines of leading or initiating or guiding a discussion, in terms of stimulating activity and decision making, but does not necessarily have to do so. Trainers may be participants or they may be observers. Their role depends on the function of the group and the response of the group. Knowing what to do, and how and when and why to do it is not straightforward. Trainers need to be trained.

Whatever type of course you join or introduce, be sure that the trainer knows what he is doing and knows what you want him to do.

The type of training, the assessment of training and the conduct of training are the three features which must be understood and satisfied when deciding what suits your individual or corporate needs.

The needs survey

Conducting a needs survey is very similar to conducting a communications audit. It is an ongoing process which should be regularly checked, modified and verified to allow for changes in people and circumstances.

After the ball

Peter Sheal, in his book *How to Develop and Present Staff Training Courses*, stresses the importance of application of learning. 'Changes in behaviour,' he says, 'are not brought about by intellectual comprehension alone. A participant who has always behaved in a certain way cannot be made to behave differently without being given the chance of practising the new behaviour.'

An allowance for following up the training, and applying it to daily activities, is part of what the plan for the training programme should include. After participating in a residential course, we all take the effects on ourselves and take any resolutions to change back into our daily routines. If we work with the same people with whom we went on the course then relationships are built — for better or worse — and then taken to the workplace.

We take what we have learned home with us as well, though, and the reactions from friends and family may well reverberate through our interaction with colleagues. Home and business cannot be separated. If we are learning and training for life, all of our relationships with anyone and everyone we meet, must be considered in seemingly unrelated contexts.

Examining the effects of training includes asking whether change has been sustained after the programme or course is complete. We need to know why or why not and identify means by which we can ensure that it is sustained.

The cost of training

Cost is a large reason for feeling a reluctance to train people despite the increased awareness of the need for training and the agreement in principle that it must be implemented. Investment is long term and the return cannot always be quantified. It is one of those costs that may not have immediately measurable results. It is difficult to decide whether training will give you value for money as you have to invest now and reap the benefits later.

It is not totally unknown that people can be trained out of their jobs. It could be that by raising aspirations and skills, staff decide to look elsewhere and may be lost to other companies. While this could discourage any expenditure of money and manpower it should be accepted as a fact of life in an economy that works on a system of barter. You win some and lose some. You may lose some staff but you may gain others who move on to your company from elsewhere. It is far better to concentrate on encouraging people to stay by increasing motivation and incentive, as discussed in Chapter 5 than to keep them untrained and unqualified in the mistaken belief that ignorance is bliss.

Cost can actually be the hidden agenda in any discussion of responsibility. Is industry truly responsible for training because they know their own needs best? Or are they responsible because they are the ones who will get the profits and should therefore incur the costs? Should the individual pay for his own training on the grounds that it is he, in the final outcome, who will benefit?

All the while the argument goes on, the buck gets passed, no one will pick up the tab. So training gets shelved, or at best, limited to available funds. Who, in the end, will take responsibility?

The cost of not training

Writing this chapter has been an intensely personal experience. More than any other subject, it is the one about which I care most profoundly.

Training, education and learning are, as I have said in one way or another again and again, a constant occurrence in our lives. It is up to us to recognize this and make the most of it, to put that training, education and learning to the test and make the most of it.

If we recognize that we are doing it anyway, we can find ways of doing it better and even best. Ungrammatical as that thought may be, the sentiment cannot be denied. Spend a few minutes thinking about what would happen if we tried.

Think about a world of people who care only for themselves and for the moment, who go through the motions of feeding and clothing themselves, fulfilling only those tasks required to reach minimum standards of comfort. Think about a world full of people who are not interested in the wider picture and allow the few to rule the many.

Think about whether this is what you want for yourself or your children.

And then think about training.

Chapter 7

Negotiations

Before going into the finer points of negotiation, I would like to tell you a story which will illustrate some of those points. After you have read it, we can look at the stages where different reactions could have achieved different, perhaps better, results.

Not so long ago, at a point which was just being openly acknowledged as a time of serious economic recession, I was involved in negotiations between a small business and a large bank. The business had been trading successfully for twelve years but had then had an extremely bad year. This was partly due to the recession but partly due to insufficient management controls and marketing.

The bank remained quiet for a considerable time, neither making demands nor offering advice or help, while the company struggled and got deeper in debt. When the crunch came, and the company reached the limit of the borrowing the bank would allow, crisis management took over. New accountants (of whom the bank approved) were appointed, a marketing strategy to make the business profitable once again was implemented and tight financial controls exercised. The partners re-mortgaged their home and invested the additional capital in the business, thereby reducing the bank's liability.

In this way, the business was able to continue trading, albeit in a hand-to-mouth fashion. The marketing strategy became successful very quickly and, from the partners' point of view, the company looked like it was on the road to recovery. Not so the bank.

Despite the fact that the general economic climate was worsening, the company was signing new contracts and slowly but steadily reducing its bank borrowing further. Within four months, the total debt had been reduced by some 40 per cent. But the bank was not satisfied and handed the company's account over to a newly appointed Small Business

Manager. His brief was, on the surface, to help this company and other small businesses in the area. His (only slightly) hidden agenda was to get back the bank's money.

During the time which had passed between this particular company's difficulties starting and the appointment of the small business manager, most high street banks were suffering from the increased number of bankruptcies throughout the country. What had been suspected, but not openly admitted, in spring 1990 had turned into a widely acknowledged recession by the end of the year. Forecasts of long-term repercussions were in the news daily. Banks were panicking and exacerbating the situation by calling in loans rather than seeing small business through their crises. Thus they perpetuated the cycle and increased the number of business failures still further.

John Banham, Director General of the Confederation of British Industry (CBI) when speaking at the Thames Valley Network launch of the Management Charter Initiative in September 1990, stated his belief that bank lending officers are inadequately trained to make decisions on the possible future of businesses coming to them. He maintained that they are therefore causing the unnecessary demise of many businesses and increasing the number of bankruptcies as well as increasing banks' own losses.

To return to our case study, our small business manager (who I shall call the SBM from here on) commenced negotiations with a smile and an assurance that he wanted to be constructive, reasonable and helpful. He conducted negotiations in a manner which totally contradicted this stated agenda.

The bank's only proposal during the course of the negotiations was that the company should repay its borrowings immediately. To that end, the SBM prevented the company (which I shall call AB Co from here on) spending any of the money deposited by the partners, claiming that the funds had to be used to reduce the borrowings. Salary cheques, telephone bills, stamps, rent, payments to the Inland Revenue were all blocked. The partners were not allowed to draw any funds for themselves, putting their ability to deal with the mortgage on their home and other personal liabilities in jeopardy. So while he agreed verbally that the only solution was for the company to trade out of its difficulties, he created a cash flow situation which made this impossible.

In addition, a period of increased and unexplained charges, and protracted correspondence, ensued. Letters left questions unanswered or provided different and contradictory answers. Facts were omitted or misrepresented. Unilateral agreements and arbitrary deadlines were imposed on the partners. Time which for their mutual benefit should have been spent in marketing the company's services and fulfilling contractual obligations which were bringing in sorely needed income, was instead devoted to dealing with these negotiations. The relationship deteriorated until it became untenable.

The company's approach to negotiation, up until this point, had been win/win. Let us trade out of this, they said, and we will all get our money back. The SBM's approach was win/lose. Pay what you owe us now or we will take legal action.

While this may have achieved a nominal win for the bank, in real terms they, too, would have been losers. The business had no assets and only had the partners been able to sell their home would the bank have received any return at all on their investment. Furthermore, this was not a viable option because the recession, as we all know, had also affected the property market. In view of the excellent progress the company was demonstratively making in increasing its profitability, the bank stood to recover its money much faster by allowing it to continue trading than to force the sale of the house.

The partners were thus compelled to change their negotiating strategy to win/lose and all stops were pulled out. Both sides now had to make the other lose. At this point, when both sides were backed into opposite corners and both were losing, the partners began exercising stalling tactics. They knew, though the SBM still refused to believe, that in a matter of months their situation would improve considerably as a result of other negotiations in which they were involved.

When the SBM rejected their proposals for repayment of the borrowings over a five-year period and announced that he was instituting legal proceedings, they wrote to the chairman of the bank. The matter was passed to the regional director and a delay of three months followed while an investigation took place.

Although the regional director eventually decided the company would have to continue dealing with the SBM, enough time had been gained for the partners to complete some of their other negotiations and make a more reasonable proposal regarding a repayment schedule. They had also reduced the borrowing by a further 20 per cent, making the outstanding debt just 40 per cent of what it had been nine months earlier, when the crisis began. The partners also tried to switch back to win/win negotiations; the SBM stuck with his win/lose strategy.

The partners felt they were in a position of strength by this time. They had repaid a large proportion of their debt in a relatively short period and knew that they could, if necessary, repay a further amount very quickly. This information they kept to themselves as negotiations recommenced. They also believed that, if legal action was taken, their continued willingness to repay the borrowings over an agreed period of time would be considered reasonable and that they could not be forced out of their home or business.

But when the next meeting with the SBM took place, he still had no proposal to offer beyond a suggestion that the full remaining debt be settled immediately. His recommendation on how this could be achieved was that the company should go to another bank to borrow the necessary funds. A threat to take legal action if satisfactory proposals were not offered within seven days was made. The SBM would not move from the corner into which he had backed himself.

After we have looked at this story from the viewpoint of both opponents, I will tell you how it ended. It is not actually either relevant or important, however. The point of the story is the way in which the negotiations were conducted.

There are a number of issues raised by AB Co's negotiations with their bank. It is important to consider the relative value of different types of advice on how the negotiations could have been handled differently if:

- the partners had been frightened by bullying;
- the partners had believed, as the SBM did, that the bank had power;
- the SBM had accepted the partners' belief that things would improve by a mutually agreed time rather than a deadline arbitrarily imposed by the bank;
- the bank had served formal demand papers;
- the bank had agreed to the partners' suggested repayment schedule;
- either side had trusted the other;
- self-preservation had been less important to each of the individuals concerned;
- the issues had been solely business with no personalities or principles involved;
- advice had been offered by different people.

Most of these issues will now be discussed in general principles. As an exercise, once you have read the rest of this chapter, you might find it useful to outline a range of scenarios that might have ensued following some of these options. At the end of the chapter, the actual resolution to the case study will be divulged, and whether it was a successful negotiation for either or both of the parties will be analyzed.

WHAT ARE NEGOTIATIONS?

Life would surely be simpler, less stressful, happier and generally more pleasant if give and take were more honest, open and straightforward. But as soon as two people begin bartering, they go for what they can get. If you ask for something and immediately get it, you begin to wonder whether you might not have got even more had you tried. So the next time you negotiate, you extend the boundaries a little bit. And the other person may begin to feel that he is being taken advantage of, so fights back by either refusing to give or demanding more in his turn. And so it goes on. We are all out for what we can get. That's life. Those are the rules we have chosen to live by. Negotiations are a fact of life.

Successful negotiations must, however, be a process of give and take. Each side has a starting point and a finishing point. The ostensible object of the exercise is for each side to reach its finishing point, giving as little as possible and taking as much as possible, along the way. In reality, this is not likely to happen. A third finishing point, one that each side can live with, has to be agreed. Identifying this point is the real object of negotiation.

Thus we can say that negotiation is:

- an attempt to influence others by exchanging ideas or bartering;
- the process we use to satisfy our needs when someone else controls what we want;
- a process of compromise with each side giving something in order to get something that they want.

Or in other words, negotiation is about effective communication. After the Gulf War, talks were held for the stated purpose of communicating ideas, not negotiating; for informing rather than debating.

In *Winning at Business Negotiations, A Guide to Profitable Deal Making*, Colin Robinson says that 'The essence of negotiation is that it is not about winning or losing — it is about striking a deal which is satisfactory to both sides. Of course, your efforts should be directed towards ensuring that it is more satisfactory to your side than to the other.' Robinson also believes that 'The purpose of commercial negotiation is to create an economic benefit to the negotiator that would not otherwise have been obtained.'

So each side must gain something and, equally important, feel that they have gained something, for negotiations to be successful.

When to negotiate

During the course of our working lives we negotiate with:

- colleagues, employees and/or supervisors;
- union officials;
- sales people;
- financial markets.

about such matters as:

- contracts;
- job performance, benefits and working hours;
- responsibilities, conditions, grievances;
- products or services we want to buy or sell;
- prices or loans;
- when and where to meet.

Colin Robinson's book, *Winning at Business Negotiations*, deals with the practical aspects of many of these points. It is generally more concerned with commercial practices, contracts, supplying goods or services, measuring quality, meeting delivery dates etc than the more philosophical negotiation of issues raised in other books. Robinson discusses far more in the way of specific matters than many other authors and is an especially good source of information regarding commercial activities and aspects of commercial activities which require negotiation. He tends to be concise and to the point on issues where you may find precedents and advice useful.

The finer points of communication, including strategy and tactics, are essential as background reading, however, if you are to be aware of the situations in which you are negotiating and understand what is going on around you. Or, more to the point, if you are to control what is going on around you.

What about the other side?

One of the similarities I came across when researching negotiations was the terminology, which included the frequent use of the word 'opponent'. Perhaps this was for easy reference but there did seem to be an underlying attitude that all negotiations are adversarial, that they are not necessarily amicable and even when they are being used to build a relationship or partnership, there is still a slight feeling of distrust. Each side is there for its own benefit, therefore there is a suspicion that this cannot be achieved without some degree of loss to the other side, hence turning the other side into an opponent. One of my colleagues, an experienced and effective negotiator, makes a point of looking for the down side of every offer. Only by exploring this, can he accept that there may also be an up side and begin to weigh up their respective merits. He never, ever, accepts the existence of an up side without ensuring that it is entirely free of strings and hidden catches.

Each side thus needs to be both defensive and aggressive simultaneously, so no matter where the parties have come from, or where they hope to go, each book assumed an attitude that all negotiations are by definition at least partially negative.

Robinson, for example, says that the approach, attitude and style factors that will influence a negotiation include:

- the personalities of the negotiators;
- the degree of concern over protecting their own rights;
- the determination with which demands are made and countered;
- the firmness with which requests for concessions are handled;
- the amount of flexibility which is available and used.

The entire process of negotiations, and the preparations for them which will be discussed in greater detail later, revolves around knowing and understanding the opposition.

There are good negotiators...

Samfrits le Poole in *Never Take No For An Answer — A Guide to Successful Negotiation*, states that in negotiating hardly anything applies always. An all-round negotiator has to be flexible and able to adjust to the specific requirements of the specific negotiations he is conducting with a specific opponent in specific circumstances. He goes on to list a number of useful traits, saying that a good negotiator should:

- know how to perceive and exploit power;
- notice when the balance shifts and take advantage of it;
- be able to take charge and not be afraid to grasp the initiative;
- have self-awareness and self control;
- be able to distinguish between major and minor issues, discarding or disregarding red herrings;
- be persuasive and flexible;
- be ambitious and set high goals and standards;
- not settle too easily or take the line of least resistance;
- be firm;
- project himself as someone who knows what he wants;
- be reasonable, rational and realistic;
- be courteous, pleasant and tactful;
- know when to stop;

in order to reach agreements that:

- are crystal clear;
- are creative;
- take care of as many interests as possible, long and short term;
- inspire and motivate both sides to be faithful to the agreement;
- anticipate unforeseen problems and provide mechanisms for dealing with them.

There are times when this can result in the creation of lengthy documents to cover any and every possible contingency after the terms of agreement have been negotiated to both sides' mutual satisfaction. So the implementation of the agreement, and the guidelines for the implementation, must also be part of the negotiations. If they do not fulfill the spirit of the agreement then the negotiations themselves are not entirely effective or complete. As le Poole says, in negotiations, nothing is settled until the entire package is settled.

...and bad negotiators

Among the less useful traits le Poole cites are:

- an eagerness to please others;

- being naive and overtrusting;
- being too emotional or temperamental;
- being aggressive, argumentative, belligerent;
- being insecure;
- being unable to cope with uncertainty.

Colin Robinson points out a number of others things to avoid. He advises his readers not to:

- believe that everything is negotiable;
- start negotiating unless you have at least a reasonable expectation of coming out better off than you went in;
- grant concessions without gaining them;
- forget to ensure you have a clear fallback position;
- underestimate either your own, or your opponent's, strengths and weaknesses.

What the experts say

Without writing a full volume on negotiations, a task which has been done exceedingly well by a whole range of authors, it is possible to highlight the points which these authors uniformly emphasize.

Here, then, in no significant order, are the major issues which nearly every author felt were crucial to effective negotiations.

1. Find out how much authority your opponents have. You must know who you are negotiating with and the amount of decision-making authority they have, and whether or not they will have to take any agreement reached back to others for ratification and possible alteration.

2. Prepare your facts. Find out as much as you can about the implications of your own proposals to yourself and the other side. Find out as much as you can about their views and attitudes, what their possible objections might be, how far they might be prepared to go towards meeting your requirements. Find out about their company policy but also find out as much as you can about the individuals with whom you will be negotiating, their own strengths and weaknesses, what they personally stand to gain or lose and what their past experience is of negotiation. Find out what you can about their style.

3. Set the ground rules immediately. Beware of multi-subject agendas which could bury important issues among less important ones so they lose their potency. This tactic is good if you've done it, bad if the other side has done it.

4. Learn what you can about common ploys and techniques, decide which ones you might feel comfortable using and determine both

your objectives and your tactics before you go in. Know which are your primary and secondary objectives, that is, which are negotiable.

5. Be flexible but firm.

6. Work out in advance how to counter someone who has read the same books you have. Plan some scenarios and work out what you would do in each so that you are not caught out. Be alert and aware, allowing for the fact that the opposition is trying to do exactly the same thing you are and that neither of you wants to give away any more than necessary.

7. Be aware of both your own and the opposition's attitude to the negotiations. Are they win/win, with both sides standing to gain or are they win/lose, with one side wanting to come out clearly on top?

8. Be aware of both your own and the opposition's perceptions, messages (verbal and non-verbal) and body language, deliberate or otherwise. Make allowances for misinformation, giving out the messages you want to give out as well as those you would prefer the other side not to notice. Watch others' reactions to what you say and do. Look and listen to what they are saying and doing, making allowances for the fact that they may be feeding you misinformation or trying to cover up attitudes, ideas, beliefs that they do not want you to be aware of.

9. Be polite and patient.

10. Do not make snap decisions or concessions; if caught out, ask for a recess to think things over.

11. Never admit a mistake; agree to investigate, stall, concede that you have learned something but never admit that you were wrong.

12. Establish a timetable. Agreeing a finishing time gives something to work towards. Some negotiators will set their watches out on the table in front of them, making you aware that time is limited, and indicating that they will leave when the time is up regardless of the stage reached at that point. Set deadlines if you think they will help, but again, be aware that the opposition may be doing the same thing. Test others' deadlines in case they are trying to apply undue pressure. Remember that for both sides, deadlines are negotiable. Decide on your own time restraints before beginning negotiations.

13. Consider, before you begin, who you think should go first. If you go first then you can set the tone and style but may have to give away too much. If the opposition goes first, they set the pace but may be forced to tell you more than they want to at an early stage. Decide for yourself whether you would prefer taking the lead or giving the opposition the opportunity to give you some clues. This is also important, incidentally, when preparing any documentation. Whoever submits the first

draft for discussion is able to insert clauses which can safely be conceded later, giving the impression of generosity. The person writing the draft can also word things in certain ways to create an instant advantage and overall put the opposition on the defensive.

14. Know when to stop — when each of you is better off with the agreement being proposed than with no agreement and when one or both of you believe there are no more concessions to follow.

There were also a number of common features to negotiations itemized by almost each and every one of those authors:

- conflicting interests;
- common interests, that is a mutual intention to live up to the deal;
- common purpose;
- mutual dependency — either side can break off at any time therefore each must get some agreement from the other in order to conclude;
- give and take;
- exchange of information;
- play acting, manipulation, misrepresentation — as one author succinctly stated, 'negotiating is not a process of total honesty. Exaggeration, evasion and being incompletely truthful are routine aspects of the game';
- uncertainty;
- risk taking.

HOW TO NEGOTIATE

As with all other communications techniques, including reading and writing, it is essential to go step by step through the whole sequence in order to understand and apply procedures properly. Whether you are writing a speech or document, or reading instructions before following them, it is still worthwhile working through from beginning to end before actually making a start.

Samfrits le Poole in *Never Take No For An Answer* and Robert Maddux in *Successful Negotiation* each list six stages through which negotiations proceed. There is a remarkable similarity between the two, largely because whatever variations exist in individual situations, certain patterns almost always recur.

le Poole	Maddux
orientation	getting to know one another
position-taking	statement of goals and objectives
search for solutions	starting the process
crisis/deadlock	expressions of disagreement and conflict

settlement	reassessment and compromise
finalization	agreement in principle or
	settlement

Taking Maddux's stages in turn, he explains what goes on in each.

- Getting to know one another . . . a process during which you should observe, listen and learn.
- Stating goals and objectives . . . getting feedback from the other person so that you know what common ground exists for goals and objectives . . . and attempting to build an atmosphere of cooperation and mutual trust. (Note that this is also the time when you should listen for any hidden agenda the other side may have.)
- Starting the process by discussing the issues being negotiated one at a time but with an awareness that several issues may be linked and therefore exploring those links. (Note that this leads to the argument of whether negotiations should open with a minor issue, easily resolved, so each side has gained something, or a major issue, bound to be more contentious, because if it isn't resolved, then the minor issues don't matter anyway.)
- Expressing disagreement and conflict . . . a phase which should never be avoided as conflict has a way of bringing out different points of view and crystallizing the real wants and needs of the negotiators. (Note that each side must be clear on the differences between what they want to gain and what they need to gain, having previously established for themselves where the bottom line lies.)
- Reassessing and compromising . . . the stage when concessions are most likely to be made, when a delicate balance is struck between what the other side can offer and does offer, between what you want to accept and can reasonably settle for.
- Agreeing in principle or settling then deciding terms, timetable and ground rules for implementation.

Nearly every book I read, and everyone I spoke to who had ever been involved in any form of negotiations, assumed that anyone entering into any negotiation has left room for manoeuvre. The difficulties lie in:

- gauging how much room the opposition has allowed itself;
- gauging how much room you must leave yourself;
- gauging how much room the opposition believes you have left yourself.

If you don't calculate correctly, or haven't left yourself sufficient space, then you could end up accepting less than you want. Alternatively, you must convince the other party that you mean what you say and that issues are non-negotiable.

One of the other important factors in determining how to conduct negotiations is identifying aspiration levels. These, according to le Poole, vary according to the length of negotiations and whether one or both sides is getting weary. They also vary in proportion to the confidence level of the negotiators and each side's perceptions of the other's confidence level.

An accurate identification of aspiration levels by each side will determine their attitude to the other side. So while you are figuring them out, they are trying to figure you out and each of you is trying to prevent the other one from figuring anything out.

Preparing to negotiate

Roger Bennett in *Personal Effectiveness* offers suggestions on the procedures leading up to the actual negotiations. Some of them revolve around fact finding, others around assessing and forming conclusions regarding:

- the opposition's attitudes towards the issue;
- the strengths and weaknesses of their case;
- the abilities of their representatives;
- their background knowledge of you and the issue;
- the extent of their opposition to your proposals.

As a means of structuring your approach to the negotiations, Bennett suggests preparing:

- a list of the arguments the opposition are likely to put forward;
- a list of their likely objections to your own position.

In order to prepare and rehearse tactics, he recommends:

- delivering the opening statement enthusiastically and with conviction;
- dealing with the more obvious objections to your statements during the introduction;
- stating the facts as you see them, quoting examples and precedents (blinding them with science) and emphasizing the strongest aspects of your case;
- predicting in advance questions likely to arise from your opening statement;
- providing answers to those questions before they are asked.

He further points out that preparations do not end when negotiations begin. Throughout sessions, and particularly during breaks between sessions, the process must continue.

In summary, Bennett says that

As a negotiator, you need to collect and analyze all the facts available on the disputed issue, to list your objectives and study the objectives of the other side. Highlight points of agreement and differences between the two positions and how disagreements might be resolved. Write out the feasible solutions that you would least and most like to see imposed. Try empathizing with the other side.

Robert Maddux offers useful advice on factfinding. He recommends investigating the opposition's communications network and conducting a mini audit to find out:

- who has dealt with them before;
- what their opinions are;
- how they behaved during previous negotiations;
- how they resolved and implemented previous negotiations.

Maddux also suggests talking to the opposition's employees and colleagues, customers and neighbours, as well as reading press cuttings and annual reports to see what the opposition say about themselves and what others say about them. In common with most other experts on negotiations, Maddux suggests using the negotiations to get a better idea of needs, preferences, expectations, perceptions, feelings, strengths and weaknesses. Like Bennett, he believes that preparation is an ongoing process and although the negotiations may have commenced, you must still continue to think and plan ahead.

Forward planning also indicates the need to make allowances for planted misinformation. Never underestimate an opponent or believe that he does not know that you are investigating him. Beware of what Samfrits le Poole terms 'information from heaven'. If he leaves behind a document, do not believe that it was done accidentally. In order to verify the results of your own factfinding and preparation, it is advisable to take a few precautions:

- Do not rely solely on opinions given by others.
- Gather facts and opinions and then form your own judgement both prior to and during negotiations.
- Use what you have learned to put your own observations and perceptions into context.
- Make some allowance for others' biases.
- Prevent misinterpretation and inaccuracy by ensuring that evidence is available on which you can form opinions.
- Do not jump to conclusions.

Tactics and Strategy

Robert Maddux defines strategy as the overall plan of action employed in a negotiation. Tactics are the step by step method used to implement the strategy. Or, as le Poole puts it, 'Strategy determines where you want to go, tactics how you get there.'

Win/win or win/lose

Unless your negotiations are absolutely, definitely the only time you will ever do business with the other side, you must make allowances for the future. If either side comes out unhappy, it does not bode well for any later encounter. A decision as to whether you should employ win/win tactics or win/lose tactics, must be made before negotiations begin.

Are you out to develop a working relationship, one in which whatever agreement is reached can be implemented to everyone's satisfaction? Or can your needs and wants only be satisfactorily achieved if you come out demonstratively better off than the opposition? What is their view on this? Are you both following the same pattern or, as with AB Co v THE BANK, are you on different wavelengths?

Priorities

Setting objectives during the preparation stage will help to clarify the structure of the negotiations. As Colin Robinson says, you must establish what both your own side and the opposition need, want and desire from the negotiations. He describes the sequence of moves during the negotiations as:

- identifying major issues to be discussed
- identifying those issues on which full or partial agreement is to be sought;
- assessing those issues on which discussion will throw light on subsequent issues or reveal valuable data;
- assessing those issues on which debate will give you psychological or other advantage;
- classifying the respective size of those advantages;
- ascertaining those issues on which debate is likely to put you at a disadvantage;
- classifying the respective size of those disadvantages.

It is just as important to understand the opposition's priorities. Points that you feel are important and cannot possibly be conceded may not coincide with theirs. Conversely, points that you feel are relatively unimportant may have far more significance for them.

Colin Robinson suggests testing the opposition's resolve by introducing issues just to get a reaction. If you are then able to drop them because they aren't really important, you have at least gained some information and gone some way towards establishing their needs, wants and desires. The odd bit of role playing can also contribute to your understanding and countering of their perceptions.

Robert Maddux refers to a similar technique which he calls feinting. In this, you give the impression that something is more important to you than it actually is so that you can afford to concede it and look as if you are making a sacrifice. It can also divert attention from some other issue which is actually of major importance to you.

Concessions

One point on which almost every negotiator is agreed is that you must determine, in advance, what you are willing and able to concede. How much are you able to give in order to get what you want; how much extra should you ask for to give yourself sufficient room to manoeuvre? Everyone knows that the other side is asking for more than they expect to get. Gauging the boundaries of the 'extras' or 'desires' is the secret to successful negotiations.

Of equal importance is the timing of concessions. General advice culled from the experts includes:

- Never accept a first offer.
- Never offer more than you can afford.
- Always appear to offer more than you can afford.
- Do not act on impulse.
- Consider all the possible implications before giving or accepting a concession — be sure you know what it will cost you.
- Always give in gracefully.

Counter ploys

So now you know all this, and most likely your opponent knows all this, you're both sitting at the table practising on each other and the negotiations are going nowhere. What do you do?

There are a number of options. You can:

- confront one another and agree to deal with issues rather than tactics;
- keep fencing and try to deal with the issues along the way;
- walk out.

And this is where your skill, judgement and ability to be flexible is put to work because there is no hard and fast answer. Just as you have to assess your own needs and the opposition's needs, you must also assess the best way of achieving them. Different situations call for different actions and reactions. If you are responsible enough to negotiate, you must be responsible enough to make decisions. For all the preparation you have put in, the final confrontation has to be down to your perception of the situation.

After the ball

In the immortal words of that great American detective, Lieutenant Columbo of the Los Angeles Police Department, 'Just one more thing, sir...' Columbo invariably stopped after exiting, turned back just when he seemed to be leaving his victim to think he had got away with murder, and delivered the sting.

'One more thing, sir' can actually take several different forms. What they all have in common is that they come at the end of what seem to be satisfactory negotiations. Everyone is happy, packing up their papers, ready to go home when someone utters those sinister words. There are of course several alternative ways of handling such a situation. You can:

- concede because everything else is settled and it is generally only a small point that is being added;
- start all over again;
- say you have changed your mind and decided that the price/terms agreed to are too stringent/binding/high;
- say you were happy with the deal as it stood but cannot possibly concede anything further.

There are a number of reasons why anyone uses this tactic. If you are going to try it, you must believe:

- the opposition will give in because what is being asked is relatively small;
- the opposition will not want to endanger the deal.

A decision to add a last-minute point can be perceived as greediness or an attempt to achieve the last word and assert your superiority. It could therefore push the opposition to the wall and jeopardize everything that you have all been working for. You may assume, or hope, that the opposition will not walk away for the sake of such a small extra concession but they may believe that you will not walk away for the sake of such a small concession either. If they believe you are simply trying it on, then all the goodwill which may have been built during the negotiations could be lost regardless of who makes that last concession.

Take it or leave it

This works both ways and follows that extra demand. Either side can look at the agreement that has been reached, consider the new 'afterthought' and decide that they have had enough.

If the person making the final demand believes it is sufficiently important to jeopardize the entire agreement, then he can stamp his foot and say, 'You must agree this final point or the entire deal is null and void.'

If the person being confronted with the final demand believes:

- the other side is bluffing;
- the new demand is being made on principle to gain some advantage through having the last word;
- the new demand is one demand too many;

he can opt to leave it. But if he feels that the point is:

- small enough to concede without losing more than he comfortably can;
- the entire contract is too important to jeopardize;
- life would be easier and a long-term relationship firmer if he concedes;

then the final demand can be accepted.

Take it or leave it is also used frequently to get an adjustment in price. Once terms have been agreed, the buyer can reduce his offer or the seller can increase his price. It isn't a pleasant way to do business, and certainly should never be used if you intend to do business with the person again, but it is one of those frustrating facts of life that we have all encountered at one time or another.

Reaching a conclusion

Finalization and implementation are a vital part of the negotiating process. Parties can always agree terms at the table but if implementation isn't complete or efficient then any resolution is incomplete. As Samfrits le Poole points out, negotiators can sometimes afford to be reasonable and rational just because they know that implementation can and will be blocked by others.

Colin Robinson believes that conclusions should be amicable in order to facilitate implementation. He suggests helping the opposition save face by implying that you have given away more than you intended and gained less than you intended.

Roger Bennett points out the need to balance the costs and benefits of different outcomes. Whatever is agreed, he says, will be regarded as a precedent. You should therefore not give away more than you can afford or live with.

The logical conclusion to be drawn from all of this is, do not let your opponents wear you down by agreeing a small thing here and a small thing there just for the sake of reaching a conclusion. But once agreement has been reached, presumably to everyone's benefit, leave graciously, with dignity, as the first step towards the next round of negotiations in your career.

The mistakes we make

Robert Maddux lists eight critical mistakes frequently made during negotiations:

- inadequate preparation;
- ignoring the principle of give/get;
- using intimidating behaviour;
- impatience;
- loss of temper;

- talking too much and listening too little;
- arguing instead of influencing;
- ignoring conflict.

Team negotiations

The most well known of all team techniques is the ubiquitous good guy/ bad guy. As a tactic it frequently works, unless of course the opposition spots what you are up to. If it is employed on you, it can either be turned to your own advantage or acknowledged and discarded.

Team negotiations can also create a philosophy of divide and conquer, with alliances and secret agreements being formed, balance of power being shifted and some people knowing more than others. This can culminate in a general atmosphere of distrust along with a win/lose result.

Teams can and should be comprised of a number of people with different specialities and skills to contribute. Although this tactic can always be used to advantage during the preparation stage, when it comes to sitting around the table, blinding the opposition with science (or statistics) can be both impressive and, simultaneously, intimidating. Decide in advance if this is one of the objectives you want to achieve.

Colin Robinson does see both sides of the coin and lists both the pros and cons of team negotiations.

Pros	Cons
• more knowledge and experience available	• more breaks needed for consolidation and planning
• wider range of topics can be covered knowledgeably	• opponents can take advantage of differences of opinion
• one negotiator can think while another is speaking	• limitations of members may become unclear
• different perceptions and opinions can be pooled	• more difficult to ask for discussion to be held over until the right person is available
• different styles can be accommodated	• timescales can become extended in order to suit everyone
	• team may disagree within itself, indicating weakness

AB Co v THE BANK

And now, as promised, a practical application of all this information and advice. How was the battle between AB Co's partners and their SBM resolved?

In a sense, it was all very anti-climactic. AB's partners received a range of advice from people with a range of backgrounds and perspectives. They spoke to their accountant who had been introduced to them by the bank, they spoke to their solicitor whose firm was overwhelmed at the time with *cris de coeur* from others in similar situations, and they spoke to friends who also ran their own businesses. Some of these advised caution and reason, others advised fighting and helped formulate tactics.

AB's partners went on the offensive and refused to let the SBM defeat either them or, if they could influence the situation in any way, other customers who may have been having similar dealings with him.

It was their own perceptions that got them through though. They knew other people who owned businesses and dealt with more cooperative bank managers. They believed that they were being reasonable and the SBM unreasonable. They believed that if the SBM issued his formal demand papers then they would have their day in court and be found by others to be in the right. They believed they could reach a structured solution if they had someone more responsible to deal with. Who can say whether those perceptions were right? Certainly the SBM believed, or purported to believe, that he had been reasonable and helpful in every way, that he had done no wrong and had bent over backwards to be fair and patient.

In the end, the partners remortgaged their home again and found sufficient cash to reduce their borrowings to a level the bank could agree to collect over a three year period. A loan form was drawn up along those lines. The partners were able to concentrate on rebuilding their business in order to service the loan, the bank agreed to accept their investment back in instalments and life went on.

Each side emerged better off in that the business continued and there was a good chance that both the partners and the bank would eventually recover their investment. So in a sense the negotiations were effective.

But if these negotiations had to be categorized, they would be called lose/lose. The partners lost time and money and confidence in the bank. The bank lost customers because the partners had moved down the high street and would not return. They lost credibility and respect. In real terms, nobody won a thing.

Chapter 8

Selling Techniques

As you will no doubt have gathered by now, this *Handbook of Communications Skills* is not an instruction manual. Rather, it will help point you in the right direction, and provide the raw material for you to build upon.

So here, I am about to raise some issues that you should examine for yourself. Your responses, I hope, will encourage you to develop your communication skills so that you can see for yourself ways in which to improve your sales technique, and therefore increase sales targets.

THE CUSTOMER KNOWS BEST

Before going any further into the subject, I have to admit that my own knowledge of sales techniques has led to a certain scepticism. I always go to at least two suppliers, checking on claims for a specific brand or product before I purchase it.

I do not take kindly to salesmen who cannot, or will not, answer my questions. I am not afraid to cut short their pitch and refuse to be drawn by leading questions. Salesmen who appear without an appointment are shown the door. I rarely call them back or buy from their company.

The best response they can expect is permission to leave sales material for future reference. Maybe I lose occasionally by not allowing them to demonstrate some revolutionary and/or cost effective and/or time saving product or service. I tend to doubt it.

When I need a product or service I call a salesman. I do not appreciate being called and 'persuaded' that I need something unless I have decided for myself that I do in fact need it. And when I do need it, I expect to get the information I want, when I want it, accurately and without justifications and excuses and endless attempts to escalate my order into something larger or more expensive than I had originally intended.

I am a firm believer in the authority of the customer. If I want advice I will ask for it and expect to get it. And I do mean informed advice, not just sales technique. If I know what I want, I do not expect to be coaxed into believing I want something else.

The point I am making is that I'm too often on the receiving end of bad pitches: I **can** be sold to, but it has to be done properly.

Making friends with your customers

One of the best and most successful advertising sales teams I know represent a certain number of clients with whom they have built a relationship over a long period of time. They work on continuous long term projects as well as one-off and new projects for these clients, researching new publications or media. They offer advice as well as producing revenue.

They realize that it is not to their advantage to snow the client. If it doesn't look as if an idea will work, they say so. It is not worth spending their time trying to sell space if there is no demand for a particular publication. Even if the client can be persuaded to let them have a go, if they are unsuccessful then both the sales team and the client lose out.

They are great believers not only in communicating with the client to whom they are selling advertising space but also in communicating with their own clients, old and new. Three times a year they circulate a newsletter about the projects on which they are engaged. They send this to people they may not have been in touch with directly for some time. They also send it to potential advertisers and potential clients.

TT Partners are great believers in knowing what they are getting into before they get into it. They keep clients apprised of developments on a regular basis. Their network is open-ended. They never write anyone off.

Not every project is successful and they are not always correct in their assessment of what will work and what will not. No one could be. What they are successful at, though, is selling themselves and their services so that even when things don't go as well as they would like, they are not written off by their client for ever more. There is always another day and another sale. And they are almost always given another opportunity because they have sustained the lines of communication throughout each and every transaction.

SALES TECHNIQUES AND COMMUNICATION

Selling is about persuasion and persuasion is communication. Both salesman and customer need a clear idea of whether the item for sale is:

- a product;
- a service;
- an idea;
- a person.

Both salesman and customer must have a clear idea of why the item is for sale and the way in which it will benefit the customer. The only way that idea will be shared is by communicating.

Built-in obsolescence

When calling for a repairman, or ordering a replacement part, the delay can be indefinite. The same person never answers the telephone twice, papers get mislaid, deliveries forgotten.

One business I know has stopped leasing its photocopiers, for example, because of poor service. The final straw was when their copier was taken away for repair because it needed so much attention that it had to go into the workshop. A replacement, which was not particularly efficient, was left and several weeks elapsed. After chasing the repair department several times, the company was finally told that it was actually on the workbench. Later the same day, a salesman from the leasing company called to offer a 'special rate', only 'slightly more expensive each month' for a new, improved model. The customer began to suspect that there was a plot afoot to pressure him into replacing his frequently broken down machine with one that required less attention from the leasing company.

Built-in obsolescence is often used as an excuse for not being able to repair machines or get essential parts and therefore encourage the purchase of a replacement. When my own computer system recently needed to be enlarged, my supplier took what I considered to be an unacceptable length of time to do the job. They insisted that the reason for their difficulties was that we were using old software which was therefore incompatible with what was currently available. The software had in fact come from this very supplier just two years earlier.

Whatever the speed with which technology is changing at the moment, there is no excuse for not creating models that follow on from one another — rather than forcing replacements prematurely. Upgrades for software, for example, come out at increasingly frequent intervals, offering additional features without which we are told we cannot survive. There is such terror of being out of date that many of us are being encouraged by salesmen to purchase far more than we ever imagined we would need or use.

All of this applies to much of industry whether manufacturing domestic appliances or business machinery. It can be seen as an indication of a need for better training across all levels of competence as well as specifications. Convincing a customer that they need to buy more than they actually do, or that something cannot be repaired, is a sales technique that may succeed but has longer term implications when the customer realizes that they have been taken advantage of. Resentment builds and later communications and sales are negatively affected.

Getting a hearing

Stephan Schiffman in *Cold Calling Techniques* summarizes the steps a salesman should take in making an appointment and convincing a prospective customer to allow him to make a presentation. He advises that when the salesman calls to make the appointment he should:

- Never give out too much information.
- Never try to turn around an objection by engaging in a full conversation.
- Never try to sell on the phone.
- Always plan the call by using a script.
- Always listen for the most common objections.
- Always turn the objection around by repeating, reassuring and resuming.
- Always be positive.
- Always be firm.
- Always be one step ahead.
- Always hang up first to avoid rejection.

The objections to which Schiffman refers are:

- stalling and stringing the salesman along when there is really little chance that an appointment will ever be made;
- blocking the salesman by having more information than he does;
- blocking the salesman by admitting a need for his product or service but preferring to deal with someone else;
- denying the authority to make the decision;
- requesting additional information before making a decision;
- agreeing with the need but refusing to make an appointment or explain any reluctance to consider the pitch.

Not all salesmen will agree with Schiffman's advice, particularly his recommendation not to sell over the telephone. Telesales, as we all know from being on either end of the line, can be highly successful. It is up to a good salesman to decide whether a face to face presentation is necessary or not.

To persist or not to persist

Every salesman is familiar with rejection. Sometimes this is a reflection on his technique. He may have a perfectly good product and may have approached just the right potential customer but failed to communicate the link between the two to the customer. There is a definite ratio between approaches and sales. A certain number of calls must be made in order to get one live lead, making each and every call a valuable one. The smaller the number of calls made, the smaller the chances of getting a live lead. Both the salesman and his product need to be put in front of the maximum number of customers. This precept, incidentally, applies to all forms of selling, including advertising, public relations and corporate communications.

Salesmen must by all means be persistent but they must also be aware of the customer's response to their persistence and know when to stop short of causing irritation. Each and every salesman, on each and every call, must identify the border between being an effective communicator and being a nuisance.

For every tip given to a salesman during training, there is a counter tip for the customer not interested in being wooed. Salesmen cannot succeed without making a certain number of cold calls but they must accept that a certain number of prospects will refuse to accept those calls. Salesmen can prepare their presentations by working to scripts but customers can be put off by a lack of flexibility.

Support material

Stephan Schiffman is not an advocate of sending out sales literature, on the grounds that it often ends up in the bin and is a common ploy by a customer brushing off the salesman. But some people, myself included, prefer to read the literature in order to discuss the product knowledgeably. Even if I keep it on file for several months before agreeing to an appointment, it serves as a useful reminder of the product and its potential value to me.

Sales literature gives me the opportunity to learn more about the product or service before deciding whether or not I am interested. The preparation of sales materials is covered in Chapter 14 on Corporate Communications. The way in which it should be written, designed and presented is quite separate to the issue of whether it should be widely circulated or saved for likely candidates only.

One indirect negative response to receiving sales material is the number of copies received. When a second, third or even fourth copy of the same leaflet is delivered I lose confidence in the communication skills of the company sending it. They have obviously not cleaned their mailing list for some considerable time and have allowed minor differences in name or address to result in unnecessary duplication. This type of carelessness and lack of attention to detail generally tells me that they are more interested in flooding the market with their material than concentrating on the potential customer's actual needs.

Negotiating a sale

Salesmen have to be willing to negotiate as customers will inevitably insist on negotiating any price or estimate they are given. Chapter 7 on Negotiations goes into the various techniques. All that needs to be added here is that all sales should include an element of give and take, with both salesman and customer willing to concede various points on price or specification in order to achieve a successful conclusion for each of them.

The salesman wants his commission or profit, the customer wants the product or service. Both should come away happy and will if they follow the precepts of negotiation and communication, considering each other's needs and finding a way to meet them without sacrificing their own.

Sales training

There are fine lines differentiating telesales, telemarketing and cold calling. Representatives who spend their time on the road are different again, as are shop assistants in retail outlets who wait for customers to come to them. Salespeople need different training and techniques.

The Bradford and Bingley Building Society were one of the 1990 winners of the National Training Awards for their success in training front-line staff to generate new business. The Society wanted to ensure its share of the highly competitive mortgage market and felt that counter staff needed sales training in order to go beyond their stated job descriptions. Each contact that a customer made with the Society should, in effect, become a potential sale. A sophisticated training course was devised and all new and established staff were encouraged to participate.

According to the case study of the Society published in *Winners 1990*, a synopsis and report of what were considered to be success stories, staff were evaluated throughout their course and required to reach 'measurable specified standards'. Furthermore, 'Underperformance was identified and remedied through individual training plans.'

The results achieved not only won an award for the Society but also increased their lending beyond expectations.

Some people would see this as a success story. The Society increased its profits and won an award. The staff were trained to exercise new skills. Customers were able to buy more houses. Somehow, though, the story makes me feel slightly uneasy.

The pressure applied to customers entering the Society's portals in order to make simple transactions could potentially be taken to extremes. I do not mean to imply in any way that this was actually the case, simply that in some instances it might have been or could have been. Banks, too, are increasing the 'services' they offer to customers. Bank managers have had their job descriptions broadened to include the selling of pensions and insurance policies. Meetings that may have had totally different agendas have been known to include a sales pitch. Again, this is not always the case. But sometimes it is.

Managers who may be seen by customers as financial advisers are now seen as salesmen. Their objective opinions may be coloured by their own desire for commissions or pressure from above to meet targets. Developing an awareness of customers' financial needs and the skills to match them with a bank or building society's services is indisputably helpful. But changing the role of the counter staff or manager to enable them to pressure customers, even occasionally harass them, could result in declining confidence, annoyance and resentment.

The implications of identifying underperformance and having individual remedies applied has undertones which could conceivably be interpreted as sinister or threatening to staff. While the offer of incentives or commissions is a positive approach to encouraging loyalty and high performance, offering a carrot for achievement and success, the other side of the coin causes stress and nervousness to say the least.

Yes, indeed, we can all benefit from constructive criticism. The effect of sales training on the customer, and the application of that training, must be monitored. There is such a thing as too much of a good thing. Training, particularly where selling is involved, should not be misused. Guidelines are essential and must be communicated to the trainee as part of their course.

PART III

COMMUNICATION THROUGH AN INTERMEDIARY

INTRODUCTION

In addition to face-to-face communications, there is a wider audience that is only occasionally seen. Not every meeting can be face to face, or indeed needs to be face to face. Time and distance frequently dominate communications. The ability to rely on telephone, fax machine and the media through press releases, advertising and marketing drives should be used to the full.

Managers have to communicate up and down the ladder within their companies. They have to deal with many of the target audiences discussed in The Communications Audit. Managing, by definition, includes delegation of responsibility. Rather than addressing a target audience himself, a manager will often:

- brief his human resources development director on interviewing and hiring staff;
- brief his finance director on communicating with financial markets;
- brief his sales director on communicating with representatives going on the road;
- brief his marketing director on new products and changes to brands;
- brief his public relations director on information to be circulated among the media and the community.

Managers often don't supervise shopfloor staff. They make their objectives, needs and wants clear to departmental managers and expect them to communicate directly with employees. While they may spend time walking around the factory or arranging meetings with staff as described in the section on Employee Communications, on a day to day level they have little direct contact with the running of the company.

What they must achieve, however, if the day to day running is to proceed smoothly, is that their instructions do not lose anything in the translation. Unlike the game of Chinese Whispers described in Chapter 9 on Telephone Techniques, managers must ensure that they transmit their own message so clearly that it is then passed on accurately through their intermediaries.

Obviously companies of different sizes have different communications needs. The number of levels of employee, the relative position of the manager and the range of people with whom he needs to communicate varies enormously. An overall understanding of the company's structure, including the politics of who speaks to who, is one of the responsibilities of the manager.

Communications with external target audiences are one of the key areas where intermediaries are active. Market research companies, financial markets and the media all take information from the company and pass it on in turn to their audiences. You will have little direct control over this and if you are to get your message across to the end user, must find suitable ways of communicating with the intermediary who will be interpreting and re-presenting it.

The powers that be, government and bureaucrats, are an unavoidable part of the manager's business life. The more responsibility you have, the more obstacles you may find in the way. Charles Dickens' book *Little Dorrit* contains a wonderful, funny and sad story of a man trying to register a patent. He is sent from one office to another, down an endless series of corridors, searching for the one civil servant whose stamp must finally be put on the plans. He makes one appointment after another, spends days and weeks in waiting rooms, finding one bored, giddy bureaucrat after another sitting in dusty rooms surrounded by mountains of plans working their way through the system while the bureaucrats themselves eat their dinners, play their games and patiently await the day they can retire.

Who among us has never felt the frustration of dealing with bureaucrats or chafed at the length of time things take? Think about what they are communicating to you regarding the importance or urgency of your requirements. Why, after all, do proposals and requests have to go through quite so many channels?

When the Training Enterprise Councils were established, they were intended to link people. In fact, they have created a bureaucracy of their own, often serving as an extra level for people to go through in their search for assistance and information. Although their intention was to direct people to one another, to act as one-stop shopping to provide information and to help people find what they're after, in fact what they often do is act as a buffer.

Civil servants and secretaries 'protect' those on the level above them from communicating directly with unwanted callers. We go through screening procedures and must communicate with the intermediary before being permitted to communicate with the person we are seeking to contact. The message communicated by the intermediary is that the caller has to prove their importance or value or right to speak to the top man. Callers, particularly salesmen, are well aware that you must submit to this procedure and work your way through the right channels if you are ever going to get anywhere.

No matter what anyone may say about this being a small world, deep in our hearts we really know that it is nothing of the kind. Telecommunications and technology may facilitate long distance communications but they do not change the fact that we literally cannot speak directly to every person we would like to speak to during the course of our lives. We must rely on intermediaries. And if we are to communicate effectively, we must learn to communicate through intermediaries.

Chapter 9

Telephone Techniques

This chapter is not about telemarketing or telesales. It is about speaking on the telephone, communicating your message effectively, which sometimes includes persuading someone to listen to you. It also includes listening to callers. It even covers terminating calls. It may help you avoid telemarketing or telesalespeople.

Having said this, some of the techniques will be similar to those used by sales people for one very good reason — that they are basic skills which everyone using a telephone ought to master. If as a result of reading this chapter you become a better sales person or conclude a negotiation more successfully, then that's good, but it will be a fringe benefit, not a specified objective.

This chapter will deal with telemarketing, however, in the sense that you may learn how to counter a salesperson's ploys. If the salesperson's main aim is to prevent you hanging up before he has made his point, or an appointment, or at least before gaining some minimal sign of interest from you, and you definitely do not want to be bothered, then read on. Some of the skills you should learn in order to make and receive telephone calls will stand you in good stead when being caught by someone to whom you absolutely do not wish to speak.

Telephones can facilitate all sorts of business communications. They can also be an instrument of torture. Some days the telephone is essential for giving, gaining and clarifying information, for making or maintaining an important contact, for obtaining a product or service in a hurry. Other days, it causes interruption and irritation, distraction and disruption. It can be the direct cause of lengthy deviations from matters you may have in hand.

PLACING A TELEPHONE CALL

Why do people use the telphone? Because speaking directly to people, is the best way to communicate effectively.

So why do so many people have difficulty using the telephone? A great deal of time and trouble could be saved in the every day conduct of business if people had better telephone skills and manners. These can be developed and improved very simply with remarkable results.

Preparation

I recently observed a marketing executive getting ready to start his day. He was planning to make a number of telephone calls, some cold and some follow-ups to letters or previous conversations. Before picking up the handset he followed what I can only describe as a ritual. Before making that first call, he cleared his desk completely. He then set out, in an obviously practised pattern, his notebook and pen, telephone book, diary, a box of index cards containing information on people he planned to call and the telephone itself. There was a stack of company literature to hand and a list summarizing the points he felt need to be emphasized. He did not actually have a script, but he did have reminders to himself on the way he felt the conversation should go and the facts he wanted to cover. It was neatly printed, widely spaced and easy to read at a glance.

Apart from that, the desk was clear. There were no extraneous bits of paper lying around, no post, no empty coffee cups, no clutter.

He then checked the telephone, ensuring that the cord was not twisted. He removed his jacket and hung it up neatly, took a few deep breaths, consulted his card index and picked up the telephone, now ready to start.

We joked about all of this. We exchanged comments about the value of reading the textbooks, going on training courses, about the importance of time management, of using common sense and generally being well organized in order to be successful.

In fact, it wasn't all that funny. He had psyched himself into the mood to start making calls. He was prepared for a few difficult encounters but he was excited at the prospect of speaking to interesting people about a subject that was important to him.

As telephone marketing goes, this particular executive is fairly successful. By the end of the day, he had made three appointments, agreed to send information to a number of people and arranged to call still others again after a set period of time just to keep in touch. After each call was completed, he made a notation on the relevant index card as a reminder. He knew exactly who he had spoken to and when, the gist of the conversation and had made a note of what action he was taking to maintain the contact.

Organization

The marketing executive followed a number of rules and proved that they were successful:

- prepare yourself;
- prepare your material;
- keep track of your calls;
- pave the way for further contact.

In short, he was well organized. He did not have to search his desk or, worse, leave it to get information to answer possible questions. All of his reference material was at his fingertips.

His own notes were also completely up to date. Whether you use an index card system, a diary, a computer or some other means of keeping records, the important thing is to keep them. Whether you are making sales or marketing calls, or seeing through a project, it is impossible to remember every conversation or every detail discussed without making notes. And once you have made those notes, they need to be accessible so that you can go back to them, review them and act upon them.

Speaking to a script may often be advised during training courses and the degree to which you rely on a script depends on your own level of confidence. What is important, however, is to have an idea of what you want to say before starting the conversation. If you have also mentally rehearsed the approach you want to take and the course you would like the conversation to take, all the better.

Another acquaintance of mine is managing editor for a publishing company and is currently working on a series of 100 books. The series has a distinct identity and, even with allowances for individual titles being self-contained, there is a clear set of house rules which must be followed. Many of the books have illustrations. So my acquaintance has to keep track of the progress of each book through its various stages of design, illustration, typesetting, proofreading and production. She spends a large part of each day on the telephone, speaking to others involved in getting those books printed and ready for distribution to the shops.

There is no way that she can keep track of such a diverse and complex project without a telephone. There are so many people working from so many locations making contributions needed at different times that face to face communication would be impossible. Nor is there any way she could remember each and every conversation about each and every title without making extensive notes and filing them in such a way that she can retrieve them instantly.

Both the marketing executive and the managing editor illustrate a similar point. The telephone can be used as a successful tool only if it is supported by other forms of communication. Organization, preparation and follow-up are just as much a part of the communication as the call itself.

Keeping in touch

Given that not many people want to spend a great part of their day in small talk, just gossiping or chatting, the telephone is still an effective means of keeping in touch with colleagues. You may not have a specific query or point to make, but contacts and relationships should always be maintained. This sort of call does not have to be lengthy or frequent but should not be neglected. A mutual exchange of information, 'touching base', reminding someone of your existence, can often pay off in unexpected ways.

Having had that chat, though, it is always a good idea to confirm anything that may have been said and to provide the other person with a reminder of your conversation. Particularly if you have discussed something that may be of importance in a later encounter, or reached agreement on something of import to both of you, the telephone call should be followed up with a letter of confirmation. If you have introduced yourself or your product for the first time, sales or support material that can be kept on file for future reference can also prove helpful.

RECEIVING A TELEPHONE CALL

Most of the time you will be unable to prepare for receiving a telephone call, giving the caller the advantage. He will have all his reference material to hand, and will have decided what the conversation should concern. In that way he will stand a better chance than you of steering the conversation and controlling it.

It is also possible to be put off-guard by an unexpected caller. Some people, as I shall describe later, never give their name when answering the telephone. They do not want the caller to know who has answered the telephone just in case they do not want to accept the call.

The person answering the telephone gives the caller a first impression of your company. It is important that that first impression should be a good one. Good manners and the ability to sound informed and to deal with messages, is essential regardless of who is calling and who is answering the call.

Answering a call

There are several standard ways of answering the telephone —

- 'Hello' (which all by itself can be deep and husky, cheerful and friendly, questioning, flat and abrupt).
- 'Hello, Jane Smith speaking, can I help you?' or 'How can I help you?'
- '234 3456' (which tells the caller that the number they have dialled is correct or incorrect but does not actually tell them who they have reached, which may of course be your intention).
- 'AB Co, Jane Smith speaking.'
- 'AB Co, can I help you?' or 'How can I help you?'
- 'AB Co, good afternoon', followed by a pause in which the speaker has to say who or what he wants.

- 'AB Co, who's calling please?' (So you can decide whether or not this is a person who ought to be put through to whoever he is asking for.)

There are some calls that you know, when you answer the phone, need to be stonewalled.

Leaving a message

In the United Kingdom, children play a game called Chinese Whispers. In the United States, the game has a more interesting name from a communications point of view — Telephone. As the children grow up and go out to work, many of them rising to positions of responsibility in their jobs, they continue playing the game. But what was amusing to the children, that is the growing inaccuracy of the message the more intermediaries it passed through, is far from a joke in business communications.

There are no hard and fast rules about messages other than common sense and politeness. It is always difficult to decide how long to hold on if the person you are calling is busy. At what point do you leave a message? And if you leave a message, should you simply leave your name or explain what you wanted in detail? Should you say that you will call back or ask the other person to return your call?

The first, and most straightforward approach, is to see if anyone else is available who might be able to help. If not, it does not serve much purpose to spend your time waiting while the person you are calling completes another conversation. The longer you hold on, the more of your own time is wasted and the more short-tempered you are likely to become, starting the eventual conversation on the wrong foot, perhaps, because you were not pleased about having been kept waiting.

At that point you have several alternatives. Is it preferable to arouse the other person's curiosity by not saying who you are or what you want? Are they:

- more likely to return your call because they are intrigued or
- less likely to return your call on the grounds that if you had anything important to discuss you would call back in any case?

The decision should be based on whether or not the other person knows you and is likely to want to talk to you. If you are selling something, or asking for information, it is common courtesy to call again. On the other hand, if you are the customer, or you are calling a colleague with whom you work on an equal footing, it is not unreasonable to ask them to return the call when they are free.

Just remember that messages can get lost or distorted. As in the children's game, they may be inaccurate when delivered and bear little resemblance to the message you actually wanted conveyed. British Telecom Business News quoted a report by the CBI which claimed that:

- Nine out of ten messages are taken down wrongly or create the need for another call to find out what the original call was about.
- Making calls to answer messages can account for up to 40 per cent of a company's telephone bills.
- Approximately half of all business calls fail to reach the right person.

Messages that are not delivered, or are delivered belatedly or inaccurately, can cause confusion, misunderstanding and even arguments. Antagonism and mistrust, anger and prejudice which will affect later communications, can result and may be difficult to resolve.

Taking a message

Answering a call and taking a message is a test of your listening skills. If you are not to pass on a Chinese Whisper, you need to pay attention to what the caller is saying. If the person asked for isn't available, find out if anyone else can help. Make sure that you get certain basic information every time:

- the caller's name;
- the caller's telephone number;
- the name of the caller's company;
- the reason for the call.

Finally, be straight. If you are making a cold call and trying to get through to someone who you are perfectly aware may not want to speak to you, do not try to coerce them into calling back by leaving a misleading message. Do not dangle a carrot such as:

- Ask Mrs Black to call me please, it's about CD Co, her competition.

Do give her a clue, an indication of why she should call you back, such as:

- Ask Mrs Black to call me please, it's about her free listing in our annual yearbook and I want to ensure that the information we have is accurate.

When noting the message, be sure to add the date and time to provide a point of reference and put the call into context.

If you are leaving a message, always find out who you are talking to or leaving the message with and agree on who will call who in response. Try to find out when the person you are calling will be available so you have some indication of when to call again or expect to hear from them if they are calling you.

It is also important to maintain frequent voice contact if the person calling decides to hold on and wait for a few minutes. Make certain they know you haven't forgotten about them, or been cut off. And when you do go back to them, don't just apologize for keeping them waiting. Give them a chance to change their mind, to say that they won't wait after all and to leave a message. If they seem to have been waiting a long time, be helpful.

Offer to take the message, promise it will be delivered and ensure that it is. You may not be able to guarantee that the call will be returned but you can do your best to move things in that direction.

Special types of calls

The telephone is used for a range of special purposes beyond maintaining contact and achieving rapid communication. It is frequently used as a means of complaining, for example. If you are not satisfied with a product or service, there is no faster way of making your dissatisfaction known. No matter where you are, it is a simple matter to pick up the telephone and make your displeasure felt. It may be necessary to make several telephone calls and to deliberately make a nuisance of yourself but voluble complaints almost always result in having your complaint dealt with.

If you happen to be the recipient of a complaint call, tact and diplomacy are often needed to defuse an irate caller and this is yet another skill which anyone using the telephone regularly must develop.

Remember, though, that it is also a wonderful way of saying thank you and expressing your appreciation or approval for a job well done. It is a way of establishing a positive contact that will give pleasure to both caller and receiver.

In the past year or two the telephone has become an increasingly popular means of chasing outstanding accounts. So popular, in fact, that there are a number of training courses you can attend if your job definition includes debt collection.

Learning to use the telephone

Training in telephone skills is one of the subjects offered in those leaflets that land on my desk at least once a week. You can learn how to:

- reach the person you want to speak to when they have retreated behind a wall of colleagues;
- persuade them that they want to speak to you and, better, make an appointment with you;
- obtain information;
- sell your services or product;
- respond to the euphemisms explained in the Appendix on Jargon;
- listen;
- speak clearly.

In short, you can learn how to use the telephone as an effective tool for your purposes and hopefully, simultaneously, to use it to its best advantage without exerting undue pressure on the person at the other end.

Market research companies use the telephone constantly to get people's views on all sorts of subjects. List brokers and directory compilers use it to verify and update information on their databases. The special task they have is to ask the same questions over and over again of people responding with varying degrees of interest, enthusiasm and willingness.

Obtaining information

I recently received a telephone call from a market research company conducting a study on industry and training, a subject dear to my heart. The interviewer politely asked if I would answer a few questions and, when I agreed, worked his way through a well-prepared script. Before he began, he introduced himself and his company, explained the purpose of the study and the way in which it would be used. After he finished, he asked permission to fax me samples of various advertisements which he would call me again to discuss. Later in the day I duly received the fax which was accompanied by a covering letter, again explaining the purpose of the survey and who it was being conducted for, along with an explanation of why the ads were being sent. The interviewer then called a second time to find out whether or not I had ever seen the ads before and check my recollection of them.

Granted, he had an advantage in finding someone who was interested in the subject of his survey. It was his approach, however, that convinced me to take time out to speak to him because he:

- explained why he was calling;
- explained why my help was being sought and would be valuable;
- explained just what I would be asked to do and how long it would take;
- was polite but not pushy or aggressive;
- was organized and efficient;
- conducted the interview carefully and smoothly.

I felt, afterwards, that my contribution had been useful. I did not feel that my time had been wasted. So the interviewer was successful and gained data from a cooperative interviewee. And I gained because I felt that my views were important and were being transmitted to a source I was anxious to reach. We both felt a sense of satisfaction at having communicated effectively.

SKILLS AND TECHNIQUES

Julie Freestone and Janet Brusse in *Telemarketing Basics*, list ten requirements which anyone using the telephone should aim to fulfil, not just the salespeople at whom their book is aimed:

1. Have a positive attitude.
2. Establish goals.
3. Know your product.
4. Organize your work area.
5. Organize your records.
6. Practise your message.

7. Ask the right questions.
8. Listen carefully.
9. Learn how to handle objections.
10 Think success.

Whether you are getting an opinion or selling a product, your goal should be the same — effective communication. And it is that at which you should aim to be successful.

Stephan Schiffman in *Cold Calling Techniques* also has a list with applications beyond selling:
1. Limit your own talking.
2. Empathize — think like the person at the other end of the line.
3. Ask questions to clarify, not to confront.
4. Don't interrupt.
5. Concentrate on what's being said.
6. Take notes.
7. Listen for ideas, not words.
8. Don't jump to conclusions.
9. Listen for overtones and clues.
10. Smile.

Speaking to an intermediary

Although this entire section is devoted to communicating through an intermediary, there is one very important intermediary who needs particular attention. The secretary, or personal assistant, to an executive frequently receives and places his calls. Part of her job definition is to screen the manager from unnecessary and time-wasting callers, both on the telephone and in the office. Which means that if you are calling to make an appointment, she is the first person you must persuade that your subject or contact is important. This can, of course, cause inconvenience and annoyance to the caller. If the secretary is new, or insufficiently briefed, she may not know whose calls should be passed on immediately.

Before anyone is likely to speak to some unknown person calling them for the first time there is a wall of suspicion to break down. You may have to persuade a telephonist or secretary or assistant that you are of sufficient importance to be permitted to speak to Mr Smith. As sales calls have a negative connotation, this is an immediate obstacle which must be overcome.

It can also be irritating, and even offensive, if you are called by a secretary who then passes you to the boss: if he cannot take the time to call you himself, then why should you take the time to talk to him?

Secretaries or assistants can be used to protect you from calls you don't want to take, but remember not to use them to the extent of putting off people whose calls you do want to take. Do not use them as a status symbol, attempting to prove to the other person that you are too important or too busy to make your own telephone calls or speak to them without preliminary screening. Be sure that your secretary or assistant is formal if need be, but not forbidding. She is still the person who makes a first impression on callers; she should make sure that that impression is a positive one.

Small talk

When making a call you need to decide how far you want to establish contact with the intermediary. There are definite advantages to making friends with assistants and secretaries. Abruptness, rudeness, ignoring their existence, are not only silly and unnecessary but can cause offence and make them reluctant to help you reach the person you are actually calling. Particularly if you speak to the same assistant or secretary regularly, it helps to find out her name and tell her who you are. Giving a friendly greeting directly to her and establishing yourself as someone who takes notice of her goes beyond simple courtesy — it ensures that your call or message is passed on rapidly and accurately. People quickly learn to recognize voices and resent being ignored if you call over and over again, asking to speak to the same person, and treat the person answering the company phone as a robot.

There is a limit to this of course. Going too far and spending time chatting, exchanging meaningless pleasantries or going overboard in exuding charm can do more harm than good. Again, a measure of your success will be knowing where to draw the line and not ooze a disproportionate amount of interest or sincerity.

One executive I know always asks the name of the person who answers the telephone. He states his name and job title immediately, hoping to impress them with his own status and therefore getting better and faster service. He then enlists their assistance by asking for their help or advice in contacting Mr Green. Although people invariably realize that he is not the least bit interested in them personally, they also realize that he is aware that they can be helpful to him and tend to cooperate.

His own assistant, however, not only asks the name of the person who answers the telephone but goes on to ask, how are you today? Very few people believe that he is the least bit interested in the answer and he, in fact, gets far less cooperation than does his boss.

No one, not a secretary or telephonist or even a temporary clerk answering the telephone, wants to waste time on chitchat with a total stranger. They do not want to spend their time talking to someone who is patently going through the motions of getting them on his side in case they prove useful at some time in the future. Sincerity is something that shows clearly in the voice; so too is insincerity. When you have to rely on making an impression with your voice on the telephone, it is of the utmost importance to know what message your voice is conveying. It is not just what you say that counts but how you say it.

Hiding behind the telephone

The telephone has distinct advantages as an intermediary. You can choose not to admit who you are when answering the phone until know who is calling. Similarly, not admitting that someone is in is a common ruse. Even answering machines can be used as intermediaries. You can leave them switched on until the caller begins leaving his message at which point you can decide whether or not to take the call. This is all especially helpful if you are trying to avoid contact with sales people and/or accounts departments chasing money.

The telephone can be used as a disguise. The Appendix on Jargon offers a range of excuses that you can get away with simply because you can't be seen. Signals to colleagues telling them that you are unavailable are invisible. There is also some benefit in not being able to use body language, although you must be aware that the same applies to the person on the other end. You each have to guess what the other is doing. Most of us have seen the old sitcom or film routine where one person is being extremely rude to another person who doesn't understand his language. His broad smile deceives the person addressed so that he doesn't know he's being insulted. The telephone works in much the same way. As long as there is a smile in your voice and your tone is acceptable you can give a friendly, polite message. You may be thinking something totally different which your eyes, for example, might give away in a face to face encounter. Just remember that this ploy may be used just as readily on you, however, and listen very carefully to the combination of words, tone and silence to ensure that the message you receive coincides with the message transmitted.

Good manners

One of the most basic skills needed when using the telephone is patience. It can be incredibly frustrating, when calling someone, to go through channels, repeating your purpose each time. If you are unfortunate enough to pick up your telephone and get someone who has been passed through umpteen stages before reaching you and is not very patient or calm or happy and not anxious to tell you what he has already told all those other people, then your first task is to calm him down, assure him you can help and either say you will get his requirements from someone else and call him back or persuade him to tell you what he is after. Such a call is challenging to those on both ends of the line.

Judgement is required, during any conversation, as to how friendly, jokey or informal you should be. When speaking to someone for the first time, reactions have to be gauged. Does a casual approach loosen them up or make them feel you are moving too fast? As usual, I cannot give you an answer to that question. Every conversation is an individual one. An awareness of the need to handle each call differently, however, can make you listen harder to what the other person is saying — or not saying — and decide the best way of proceeding for each call.

Hearing, listening and speaking

You can convey all sorts of moods and attitudes just by the tone of your voice. You can be:

- happy to hear from someone;
- not at all pleased to hear from someone;
- brisk and businesslike;
- calm and unruffled;
- harassed;
- friendly yet firm;
- mildly annoyed;
- impatient;
- stiff, cold and formal;
- suspicious or sceptical;
- charming and solicitous.

It is a simple matter to ensure that you know what you sound like when you are conveying each of those, and other, moods and attitudes. Pick a few sample phrases and speak into a cassette recorder using different inflections. See how many ways you can find of saying the same phrases. Write a few sample scripts to fit different occasions, types of call and reaction to different callers. Record them and listen to what you sound like. Think about how you ought to change your intonation and speech then try again. Assume that in some of the calls you are the instigator and in others that you are the receiver.

If you know how you sound then you can choose how you want to sound at any given time. We all know that different interpretations can be put on word or phrase depending on the tone of voice used. Listen to the way in which you pronounce different words or expressions. And listen carefully to the intonation of your callers so that you can try to understand the feelings behind their words.

Body language

Body language is invisible when using the telephone. Which does not mean that it should not be used. If it makes you feel more comfortable and relaxed to wave your hands about or gesticulate or make faces, by all means do. It would be difficult, in fact, to refrain. There are certain advantages to not being seen. Your voice may sound patient and restrained while you are scribbling furiously or playing with worry beads or an executive toy in order to release your tension.

According to British Telecom, posture is also important. Standing, they say, helps create a sense of authority. Clenching your fists, curling your toes or flattening your stomach can relieve tension. Using the same gestures you would when speaking face to face helps you speak more naturally.

Without being able to see the other person's nonverbal signals, we are forced to concentrate on words, silences and intonation. There are no visual cues, for example appearance, to establish either credibility or prejudices.

It is often easier to make your feelings known than it might be when facing the person to whom you are speaking. It is also easier to conceal your feelings than it might be when facing the person to whom you are speaking. Invisibility gives you those options.

The sound of silence

Pauses in conversations, silences on the telephone, generally make people uncomfortable. They rush to speak and fill the gap. You can use silence but should be aware that the person at the other end may be using it on you. Silence can cause stalemate. Each person is waiting for the other to speak, trying to oblige them to respond. You can try asking questions to prompt a response or you can let it lie. Do not feel pressured by silence. Instigate pauses by all means. And only succomb to them if you feel you should.

Hearing and being heard

A voice can often be recognized from one word and, knowing this, people often change their tone to avoid recognition. I do it myself. Even colleagues with whom I speak often rarely know when I have answered my own telephone. Several of them try to guess who has answered the phone, anxious to appear clever and sufficiently familiar with everyone in the office to make an appropriate greeting. Some of the errors they make when they think they are talking to a particular person but have guessed incorrectly can be both amusing and embarrassing. When I hired a Spanish assistant, a number of colleagues began calling with increasing frequency, trying to identify her accent. They refused to ask, just kept chatting with her until they managed to work it out. One believed she was Irish, another American. It was all friendly and jolly but proved that they were all hearing different things.

Listening

There is only one thing to say on this subject — do it. You never know what you might be missing and cannot maintain your share of a conversation if you do not listen. It doesn't matter what you say if you do not listen to what the other person is saying.

Making sure you are listened to

Chapter 2 on Speaking and Listening goes into voice control in greater depth but there are certain tips given there that are particularly important to telephone techniques. Modulating your voice, avoiding extreme volumes of speech or extreme speeds are particularly important on the telephone. You need to make sure that people can both hear and understand what you are saying. Clear and precise enunciation are vital.

International calls

We all have accents. To anyone hearing us speak, no matter where we come from, we each have an individual way of pronouncing our words. The difficulty lies in understanding that pronunciation. The difficulty increases if we are trying to pronounce words that are not in our mother tongue or if we are speaking to someone who does not speak our language as their first language.

Without exaggerating our speech or resorting to a version of Pidgin that implies the listener is ignorant rather than unfamiliar with the language, enunciation should be as clear as possible to facilitate understanding. Trying to guess what someone means works on occasion but it is often preferable to ask them to repeat, or for you to repeat, the words used until they are comprehended.

While difficulties of vocabulary may compound the problems, recognition that international communications are going to increase over coming years means that it is incumbent on all of us to make the effort to communicate clearly. Even people who ostensibly speak the same language, for example the Americans and British, often find that they are talking at cross purposes because words have different meanings to each of them.

Dealing with international calls is another growth area in telephone skills training. If you are calling someone who may not understand you, you need to be able to explain who you are and what you want so that you are connected with someone who can help you. If you are answering the telephone and cannot understand what the caller wants, you must be able to find out enough to pass them on to someone who will be able to understand. Recognizing accents and languages, remaining polite and helpful, are the crucial elements in speaking to people who do not share your familiarity with your own language.

Communicating with a blunt instrument

The telephone can facilitate the fulfilment of purchase orders by sorting out specifications with suppliers. It can also be used by the supplier to escalate the customer's requirement, however. A businessman of my acquaintance had two encounters recently with different computer equipment companies. Neither is atypical.

On the first occasion, my colleague discovered that his business had grown to such an extent that his computer system could no longer cope with the amount of data being input. He needed to increase its capacity. At the same time, he was short of office space and one keyboard operator agreed to work from home. This meant that an additional terminal was needed, one that would stand alone in the employee's home. It would have the same software as the system in the office so that she could send data back in the form of a disk and it could then be copied into the central system.

So what he needed was memory expansion for the central system and an additional terminal. Sounds simple? Jack phoned his supplier, one he had dealt with for three years and who had set up his system in the first place. He deliberately went back to this supplier because he was familiar with the system. So there was no need to let his fingers walk through the Yellow Pages or to shop around or to check references. He went directly to someone he knew and was ready to place an order.

No problem, said the supplier, I'll send you some information and prices. Several days and telephone calls later the information duly appeared. It was not complete and did not answer Jack's questions. He called the supplier yet again and explained his requirements again and asked a number of pertinent questions about what the equipment recommended could and could not do.

Eventually more information was despatched, more telephone calls clarified the precise specification and the order was placed.

Time passed, but the equipment was not delivered. Jack phoned the supplier. He was told that the equipment had arrived and was being tested. Several days later he phoned again to enquire as to when he could expect to have his order filled. He was told that the hardware and software had turned out not to be quite compatible and that the supplier was phoning his supplier, chasing a replacement. Jack lost count of how many more calls were made while the equipment was located and tested.

At last it was supplied and installed and the engineer departed. Jack turned on his computer and was faced with a blank screen. He picked up the telephone and called his supplier. Between them, with the supplier reading the manuals and sitting at his own keyboard, and Jack sitting at his computer following instructions, they got the system operative.

Then the next stage began. The supplier's accounts department decided that as Jack had used the telephone so effectively to get what he wanted, they should make use of this excellent tool to insist that their invoice be paid immediately. Not surprisingly, Jack felt that their service did not warrant prompt payment and the telephone became a weapon in a new battle.

Jack had used the telephone to pressure the supplier into filling his order with all due haste. The supplier used the telephone to pressure Jack into settling his account. During the course of this transaction, the telephone served as little more than a blunt instrument.

Having sorted it all out however, some months later Jack decided that he needed still more equipment and space. An office became available nearby and he decided to move some of his staff into it. Guess what — he needed more computers.

The computers to be installed in the new office would need to be linked to one another so that two or three operators could work on the same software simultaneously. Needless to say, Jack decided to use a new supplier. This time he did browse through the Yellow Pages and he selected a dealer who seemed to be reputable. He called them and explained his requirements.

Yes sir, they said, no problem. We'll send you some information and prices. This they did. Jack read the specifications, called the supplier for clarification and then asked when they thought they could fill the order. We'll make some calls, they said, and let you know. This they did. We can't locate the equipment we quoted on, they said, but we've found something better. It will only cost a little bit extra but we can get hold of it immediately. They had used the telephone to find what they needed but they were also using it to blackmail Jack into paying a higher price than he had originally agreed. He went back to the Yellow Pages, back to the telephone and stuck to it until he found both supplier and equipment able to fill his order, within his budget, in what he felt was a reasonable amount of time.

Telecommunications equipment

Not long ago I attended a conference held at a very large company with several hundred employees working in the same building. Halfway through the day there was an emergency and the building had to be evacuated at great speed. This was done with great efficiency and we all assembled in the car park while the police dealt with the incident.

We were in that car park for one full hour during which time the telephones did not stop ringing — because the one thing which at least a dozen different executives grabbed on their way out the door was their mobile telephones. So there they were, shivering in the drizzle, still talking as if they were sitting comfortably ensconced behind their desks, with the person at the other end of the line none the wiser.

Whether travelling by car or train these days it is rare not to see at least a handful of people carrying on telephone conversations. On more than one occasion I have received a call to tell me that someone was stuck in a traffic jam and would be delayed. No more worries about people not knowing where you are or why you're late — you can call and give them a minute by minute account. Speaker phones mean that they don't even have to take their hands off the steering wheel to conduct their business. Drivers who may seem to be talking to themselves are doing no such thing. Travel need not interrupt business any longer.

We cannot escape telephones. For better or worse we can always reach people or be reached. It is not only doctors who carry pagers in their pockets. One building firm I know counts several volunteer firemen among its employees; there they are hammering or sawing away, mixing cement, tiling a roof and when their bleeper goes, they're off like a shot.

Minutes later you hear the siren and watch the engine go past, manned by the same people who were just a minute ago building your new office.

Answering machines, as we all know, are both a boon and a bone of contention. Lengthy psychological studies have been conducted on the number of people who refuse to speak to machines, on the obscene messages they leave if they cannot speak to a live person, on the best wording for messages to encourage callers to leave their names.

Distance is no longer an obstacle to immediate communication. Transatlantic cables and satellites long ago made direct dialling a simple matter. Delays are rarely encountered. Conference links mean that people in different cities can speak to one another simultaneously, solving problems that previously had to rely on scheduling a time to meet.

The British Telecom Business Catalogue on my bookshelf is 128 pages long, full of information on telephone systems, call management systems, fax, telex and electronic mail details, mobile phones, pagers, message services, network services, teleconferencing, security... I have no doubt that this, and more, is available in virtually every developed country. Nor do I have any doubt that one morning my telephone will ring with a wake-up call and hand me a cup of tea at the same time.

SUMMARY

The telephone can:

- facilitate negotiations and transactions regardless of distance;
- provide information;
- build and maintain contacts and good relations.

But it can also:

- invade your privacy;
- disrupt your working day.

The telephone should be accepted for what it is — a tool for achieving effective communication — but should be used rather than abused. Advertisements for diet food products point out that they can only be successful when treated as part of a calorie controlled diet. Likewise the telephone should be treated as one of a range of instruments and techniques only.

Chapter 10

Communicating with the Media

REACHING THE AUDIENCE

Media coverage can be either purchased or solicited. It can be supportive or combative. Either way, it is a means of communicating a message to the maximum number of people at any given time.

The old expression that the best defence is a good offence is a perfect definition of advertising. The media is perpetually used to communicate the benefits of a product or service and build a customer base.

The audience, however, is selective. Not everyone reads a particular publication or listens to a particular radio station or watches a particular television channel. In order to reach the widest audience, the message must be transmitted through a number of different sources, each with their own share of the audience. This can lead to varying interpretations of the message and a varying degree of support. Not all media coverage is fair and unbiased.

Seeing is believing

Press coverage must be evaluated by the individual. There are undeniably instances when the camera is on the spot and we have all heard the adage, the camera doesn't lie. This is not in fact true.

My first experience of being disillusioned with the media came when I was at university. A group of students staged a peaceful demonstration, a sit-in in the administration building. Several other universities had experienced more violent demonstrations in recent weeks, including shootings in one instance, and the president was understandably nervous.

He called the police who marched onto campus kitted out in riot gear, carrying large sticks and shields.

The police positioned themselves at arms length along the paths leading to the administration building. They stood there quietly for several days until the sit-in dispersed. There was no riot, no confrontation. I was there and I saw this at first hand.

However, when I went home on the first evening, the television news showed the police marching through the gates and taking up their positions outside the administration building.

Film showed the students inside the building and concentrated on the size of the crowd, which in this instance consisted of approximately a dozen people in a room that measured some 400 square feet. Not a dense crowd by any means. Anyone who has ever seen a room containing people translated onto film knows that the size of the room and the size of the crowd can be made to look more impressive than it actually is by the angle of the shot.

The reporter did not actually say that a riot had taken place, but implied through words and pictures that this was the case. Tension was built through the true statement that the demonstration was continuing. It was truthfully stated that no one could yet predict the outcome and that anything could happen.

Friends, neighbours and family who saw the film believed that there had in fact been a riot. Imagine what other viewers, who did not know someone who had been at the university and had viewed the situation, must have believed.

The power of the press

Of course, not all media coverage is harmful. The press has always been associated with campaigns, taking the side of the underdog and investigating wrongdoings. Causes championed by the media have lead to legislation and compensation in instances far too numerous to mention.

But there are always two sides in any campaign, one of which is bound to feel maligned and misunderstood. There is a dichotomy, for example, between the image projected in advertisements in the media of friendly, helpful, knowledgeable and experienced advisers (bankers) and the descriptions written by editorial and feature writers (not to mention cartoonists) of wolves dressed in sheep's clothing. The way the media, sees and presents bank staff, when left to their own devices, is not the same as the way in which bank staff present themselves to the public via the media. A great deal gets lost in the translation.

Is it not the role of the press to present this opposing view, to allow the audience to decide for itself which image is more realistic?

Who, what, where, when, why and how

Any student of journalism learns to ask those questions in the very first lesson. Anyone attempting to communicate with an audience through the media would be well advised to ask themselves those same questions before attempting to present their message.

The relationship between business and the media is mutually dependent. The media needs things to report. They have pages and air time to fill. There is an ever-expanding demand for people with views and ideas to express, so it is worthwhile remembering that the media needs you as much as you need them. They need an endless supply of stories and information. If they can't find news then they will create it — and the opportunity is there for you to be one of those pointing them in the right direction.

Businesses, for their part, want the best possible coverage for the least possible expense. Whatever brands and products they may choose to promote through purchasing space in the media, it is to their advantage to have as much favourable editorial coverage as possible. Businesses need the media for support and promotion, to communicate and publicize their message, intentions, (including future plans and reasoning as well as historical policies) and, perhaps most important, their philosophy.

The media provides an opportunity for communicating with the entire spectrum of audiences. Do remember that different audiences are reached through different media and that both the media and the audience need to be addressed in different ways.

HANDLING THE PRESS

Before writing a press release, or calling a press conference, you not only need to know what you want to say and why, but who you want to say it to and how it should be said. There are a variety of different media to use including:

- consumer newspapers and magazines;
- trade publications;
- radio;
- televison.

Each requires a very specific type of approach. Before planning a press campaign, you must decide what is important and interesting in order to decide what is likely to get coverage.

Contact between media and industry includes handling queries, giving interviews, press conferences and launches, news releases and advertising. It is only by communicating effectively with the media that your message will be accurately transmitted to your target audiences.

The media industry, like any other, is highly competitive and jealous. *The Sunday Times*, taking credit for launching the recent campaign to investigate banking policies, devoted several column inches to an examination of how other publications had jumped on their bandwagon.

Some, they said, started out by deriding *The Sunday Times* until they realized the extent to which readers were supporting the campaign. They then switched tacks and joined in the attack, but without attributing the material they published to its original source. The reporter's conclusion was that 'Newspapers make the news, televison reacts and magazines comment'.

Stepping stones to success

When communicating with the media you should always try to:

- Check who is asking the questions and why — this particularly applies to press conferences, either planned or impromptu but also to telephone interviews.
- Be familiar with your company's policies and views on media contact.
- Know your facts and do not make statements that you cannot back up.
- Listen carefully to questions.
- Give a straight answer, explaining your reasoning clearly.
- Ensure press releases are authorized by senior managers before circulation.
- Maintain contact with relevant local and trade publications and press and build long-term friendly relations.
- Prepare for the interview or press conference, considering facts, opinions, presentation style and appearance according to the circumstances.
- Think about the audience to which the media will be reporting — your presentation must be tailored to both the interviewer and the reader/listener/viewer.
- Appear friendly and co-operative even if you are not saying anything new or important and especially if you are trying not to say anything new or important.
- Keep to the issue at hand and not go off on a tangent.
- Make your point in a variety of ways to ensure that your message gets across but try to be subtle; do not hit the interviewer or audience over the head with a sledgehammer.

When communicating with the media you should always try not to:

- Answer questions that you do not know the answers to or give facts of which you are not sure.
- Allow your personal opinions to be confused with company policy.
- 'Leak' information which senior management might not be ready to release (unless you are prepared for possible repercussions).
- Refuse to make a statement or comment.
- Avoid answering the interviewer's questions.
- Start a public argument and make statements without due consideration that you may regret later (or, to put it more simply, try not to put your foot in your mouth).

- Lose your temper or raise your voice.
- Appear flustered.
- Use jargon or terminology that your audience will not understand.
- Show doubt or hesitation.
- Seem self-conscious or appear to lack confidence.
- Take a negative attitude towards either the media, the audience or the competition — try to ensure that your point of view is seen as reasonable rather than argumentative or combative.
- Talk too much or repeat yourself.

Espousing the party line

Any business likely to have contact with the media should have someone with specific responsibility for building and maintaining such contacts. A press officer or spokesperson needs to be appointed and briefed. Employees need to know company policy if they are likely to speak to the press so that any individual opinions are either clearly stated to be just that or to ensure that they reflect the official policy. It is important for the company to have a consistent policy and communicate it to employees so that the media are not given conflicting information.

Anyone likely to be asked questions about company policy should also be able to deal with impromptu, unprepared confrontations with media.

When a spokesperson is put on the spot by a reporter, they are generally expected by their company to stick to official policy no matter what questions are asked. The spokesperson is expected never to concede responsibility or liability but will either:

- make excuses;
- give an irrelevant answer showing the company's strengths rather than discussing their perceived weaknesses;
- say the matter is being looked into.

So while the spokesperson might show up in a bad light, he is not actually admitting anything that will have to be retracted later.

Press conferences and visits

The most important reason for holding a press conference or hosting a visit from the press is to provide an opportunity for interaction. Otherwise a press release would do the job just as well and would, in addition, guarantee wide circulation. There is no guarantee that having sent out invitations, enough people will accept to make the event worthwhile. Nor can you be sure that those you especially want to turn up will be there on the day.

Before deciding to hold a press conference, you should consider:

- why it is a good idea;

- what you want to announce;
- what sort of coverage you hope to achieve;
- when to have it;
- where to have it;
- how to structure it;
- who to invite.

Unless you are new to dealing with the media, you will have built up your contacts and relationships over a period of time. You and your contacts will have mutual interests and you will have a core list of people to invite, knowing that they will pick up your story and give it favourable coverage. If you have an event or product of major significance to announce, you can broaden your list by referring to one of the publications listing trade and consumer, local, regional and national press.

In order to attract their interest in the first instance, and maintain it once they have arrived, you must make sure that what you have to say is relevant to those you are inviting and, of course, to their audience.

The usual format for a press conference is:

- reception;
- presentation;
- questions;
- informal discussion.

Refreshments can be served during the opening and closing sections. Press packs can be distributed at either point.

Press conferences should be prepared just as any other presentation. That is, you should have all possible relevant material ready to hand or, better, committed to memory. You should not answer questions you cannot answer and you should be sure to know company policy on any and all issues which may be covered. No matter how well you plan, there is always the stray question that can catch you off guard.

Among the skills required for successful press conferences are presentation, speaking and chairing. If this is the route you decide to follow, make sure that the team preparing the event, and running it on the day, can offer between them each of those requisite skills.

How to make a point

Following through, or not following through, on a promise to the press can have long-term effects. At the height of the BSE (the so-called Mad Cow Disease) scares a year or so back, I attended a press conference held by the Meat and Livestock Commission. Not surprisingly, the theme of the conference was to reassure the press and the public that British beef was safe. Not surprisingly, there were some sceptics in the audience. Afterwards, a colleague and I suggested that if the MLC was doing such thorough testing of meat and meat products, they would perhaps welcome the opportunity to invite a group to tour their laboratories and kitchens. The chairman himself agreed emphatically. He took our business cards and assured us that an invitation would be forthcoming. I am still waiting.

Not long afterwards, at the height of the listeria scares and the early debate on food irradiation, Sainsburys decided that they needed better press coverage. They invited a group of food writers to a press conference at their head office, made a presentation, answered a number of questions and, as the meeting ran into lunch time, promised that if anyone submitted a question in writing, a report containing full replies would be circulated. The chairman and several top executives then circulated for two hours over a buffet lunch and those who wanted still more specific information were taken on a tour of the testing facilities before departing some five hours after the press conference started. Some three weeks later the minutes duly arrived, with, as promised, full answers to all questions not dealt with on the day. There was even a covering letter which, when presented to the manager of any Sainsbury branch, resulted in delivery of a parcel of sample products.

This did not result, I hasten to say, in uniformly positive coverage for the supermarket but at least friendly relations had been established and good intentions proved. Sainsburys were willing to demonstrate that their products and executives could communicate a caring, considerate philosophy. Perhaps the MLC has a similar philosophy but their communication of it was somewhat less effective.

Planning the press pack

Press releases provide information to an invisible audience. You must make your point without being able to see an instant reaction when you are addressing 'the public' rather than individuals or a finite audience. Presentation of both bad news and good news must be as straightforward as possible, with as few excuses and as little dressing up as you can manage. Although blows do need to be softened, camouflaging bad news and burying it amongst justifications is never advisable. Press and public are so apt to interpret such an approach as a cover-up that it is far better to brazen things out than try to slip them past what is no longer an unsuspecting — or unsuspicious if such a word exists — audience.

Press packs should be composed of:

- a simple release outlining the facts of the main news item;
- a background piece containing information including statistics, company details and biographies if relevant;
- a statement from the chief executive or similarly placed officer of the company.

They should all be presented as separate documents, clearly labelled, so that the press can select whichever bits they need to use.

Interviewing techniques

Being interviewed is a little bit like playing chess. You must consider all possible moves or questions, consider the consequences of each and then decide which way to move. The key to successful interviews is saying what you mean and meaning what you say. You must never say anything you cannot support with evidence. If you are not sure of your facts, do not be trapped into making suppositions. If you give opinions, make sure that they are clearly labelled as your own and not your company's.

Planning your moves

When asked for an interview, try to find out:

- the subject and perspective of the interview;
- what programme it will be on;
- whether your interview is related to a news item, occasion or event;
- whether it is a news piece or a feature;
- why you have been selected;
- whether anyone else is being interviewed about the same or a related subject and if so;
  - whether your interview will be before or after the other person's;
  - who the other people are ie rivals or supporters;
- what format it will take eg interview, panel discussion, chat show;
- whether there will be an audience who may be allowed to ask questions;
- whether it will be live or recorded;
- who will conduct the interview;
- what areas will be covered;
- how long it will be ie is this an in-brief interview or an in-depth interview.

It is also advisable to watch or listen to the interviewer and the programme before being interviewed so you have a better idea of what to expect in terms of style and presentation.

If you are going to be fully prepared, you need to know:

- what the media want;
- what type of questions to expect;
- how your answers are likely to be interpreted;
- how to get your message across.

As far as possible, try to work out in advance all the questions you are likely to be asked, especially those you would prefer not to be asked, and then work out your answers. Depending on when and where you are going to be interviewed, try to take your notes with you. If this is not possible, practise before the interview to ensure that you know how you want to respond. Try not to be caught off guard; if you are, try not to let it show and do not answer if you do not feel able to.

Honesty is the best policy

Wordy statements deliberately designed to camouflage facts or bad news can be interpreted as an attempt to hide something, or even to misinform. Audiences are very likely to lose confidence in the speaker, believing instead that where there is smoke, there must be fire. Covering up an event or a fact that you would prefer not to have widely discussed in the media is one of the best ways of backing yourself into a corner.

After all, look at what happened to Richard Nixon. Had he not resorted to destroying evidence, had he admitted that he was aware of his associates' activities and publicly apologized rather than trying to deny the entire Watergate affair, he may not have been forced out of office. There is nothing the media loves more than an opportunity to expose someone — and the truth, if it comes out after you have tried to hide it, looks all the worse than if it had been admitted in the first place.

Every reporter's goal is to win a prize for investigative journalism. If you are in a position to represent your organization and its policies, do not put yourself in a position to encourage investigation. Communicating fairly and honestly will generally result in your message being interpreted — and transmitted — in the same way.

Too little communication can also lead to speculation which could be detrimental to your business. A lack of hard facts has been known to cause the press to jump to conclusions that are not always accurate. Poor relationships can result in poor coverage or, when you are looking for coverage, no coverage at all.

Tricks of the trade

During the interview itself there are a number of tips that will help you feel more relaxed and help the audience to find you more credible:

- Always listen carefully to questions.
- Do not give monosyllabic replies unless you want to cut the answer short and move onto the next question.
- Use body language but do not exaggerate it.
- Try to look relaxed even if you do not feel it, but do try to feel relaxed if at all possible. (At the very least, taking a few deep breaths will help you keep calm).
- Speak slowly and calmly but avoid being monotonous. Take some time to rehearse at home before the interview to get your tone and speed right.
- Don't speak either too loudly or too softly — modulate your voice and enunciate your words.

- Don't speak to the camera but do not glue your eyes to the interviewer, you are allowed to move a bit.
- Consider your appearance. Be sure to look neat and tidy, if filming. Check which colours are best/worst under the lights. Wear something that suits you and that feels comfortable.

Chapters 2 and 9 on speaking and phone techniques offer advice on training and controlling your voice. If you are being interviewed on the radio then it is particularly important to bear in mind that as the audience cannot see you, you cannot rely on body language.

If you are being interviewed on television, you will quickly become aware that this is an artificial setting. Backgrounds are dictated by the director who may decide that a film should open with someone typing or talking on the telephone to make them look busy and as if they were interrupted to speak to the interviewer off the cuff rather than having been rehearsed. This so-called 'fly-on-the-wall' approach can seem annoying to the viewer because it is so obviously contrived and it is incumbent on you to overcome it by being all the more interesting and informative.

It is also incumbent on you, no matter what the medium, to keep the audience's attention. Although you will have less control over opening statements in written or pre-recorded interviews, you should still make an attempt to start with a strong statement. The bottom line should always come first, your opinion should precede the reasons for formulating that opinion. I'm sure that I am not the only person to read the end of a story first to know whether or not I want to know how the author reached that point. You do not have to be controversial to deal successfully with the media but you do need to be firm, clear and concise. You have to give the press a reason for interviewing you and the audience a reason for being interested in the interview. It is up to you to communicate your message effectively to the interviewer so that he interprets it correctly and transmits it to his, or your, final audience.

Live versus recorded

Live interviews involve giving your message directly to your audience and not allowing the media any opportunity to interpret or edit your statements. It also means, though, that you will be held to anything you say and may find it difficult to retract later. So it is all the more important that you are fully prepared and not likely to get tied up in knots or say anything you may regret later.

Chapter 2 on Speaking and Listening, Chapter 3 on Presentations and Chapter 11 on Hi-tech Communications cover the important subject of voice control. As radio and television interviews are quite frequently conducted down the telephone line, you must view the relative advantages and disadvantages of being transmitted live alongside the importance of making your speech patterns and voice tone appropriate. All of the comments in Chapters 2, 3 and 11 relating to controlling your voice and the impressions made on listeners who cannot see you should be reviewed if you are ever contemplating such an interview technique.

As with everything else, there are both advantages and disadvantages to recorded interviews. Although it is conceivable that editing can cut out some of the sequences you consider to be most effective, and can occasionally result in comments being taken out of context, recording does at least give you the chance to correct anything that goes wrong.

Recording what will eventually be a one- or two-minute slot almost invariably requires several hours of taping or filming, the vast majority of which will inevitably end up on the cutting room floor. This is true regardless of whether the interview is for a radio or television programme or a promotional video for your own company. In order to get the best material, any director will record far more than he needs so that he has the maximum amount from which to select.

You may also like the idea of having a rehearsal so that you know what to expect. But many people find that having gone through the entire interview in a rehearsal, during the actual interview they forget that what they have already said was practice only and miss out vital statements during the take. Thinking you have already said something and worrying about repeating it can result in leaving out a vital point entirely.

Rehearsals can take the edge off the actual performance. You may speak too quickly the second time around, for example. Or you may be pleased with what you said in rehearsal and so anxious to repeat it that you concentrate too hard on remembering and thus fail to respond correctly during the actual interview.

It is true that rehearsals can sometimes calm you down and help prepare you but they can also make the actual interview seem repetitious and leave you feeling uneasy. It is important, if you are rehearsing and recording, not to let the final recorded version lack spontaneity.

Attribution and verification

Many people speak to reporters 'off the record'. They are cited as unidentified sources, a source close to someone of importance or relevance to the subject being covered. Their statements cannot be attributed or officially traced back to them yet the reporter still has an obligation to verify any information obtained in this way. Games of semantics are played and stories that some people would prefer never to see the light of day are published or recorded for mass consumption.

There have been a number of television programmes and films in the last few years on just this subject. *Yes, Minister* took an entertaining approach but gave the distinct impression that there was a large dose of accuracy in the tales. *House of Cards* and *All the President's Men* examined media and political ethics more seriously. One real-life Press Secretary, Bernard Ingham, wrote his memoirs and chose to publicize his disclosures with a series of television interviews and documentaries. The scandalous story behind *The Hitler Diaries* and their alleged verification is now common knowledge.

If you are going to follow this route and communicate with the media anonymously, you will be taking some risks. You need to be sure, when speaking to someone from the press, that your statements are not taken out of context.

It is as well to remember though that once a statement is published, even if it is retracted later, the memory remains with the reader, listener or viewer. Thus apologies often appear as single paragraphs on an inside page while the original story may have been splashed across the front page.

Any reporter agreeing to maintain the anonymity of his source will want to be sure that he is not reporting inaccuracies or untruths so must check what you say with another, alternative source. Only after material is confirmed should it be used.

Communication of information which is in some way confidential requires evidence and commitment. If the information is true, and there is good reason for preventing its continuing secrecy, then you must be prepared to back up your statements. If the information is not true or there is a good reason for keeping it within the confines of the business then you must be prepared to take the consequences should the 'leak' be traced.

Repercussions

Press coverage, for better or worse, means that more people know more about one another than ever before. There is a much greater public awareness and understanding, for instance, of takeovers and share offers, privatizations and flotations. The affairs of large corporations are public knowledge and most people, whether they are shareholders or not, have their own views on such subjects as directors' salaries, profit levels, price controls and quality controls.

The public, therefore, expects and demands information. They have little patience with statements that are not entirely accurate. Even if they are retracted later or an apology is forthcoming, harm may have been done to their perceptions of you and your business that will make recovery long and slow in coming. Similarly, the unsatisfactory 'no comment' implies that all is not above board and there is in fact some comment that should be made.

The media has a role to play in establishing lines of communication between businesses and their target audiences. Its role can be positive or negative but its existence should never be ignored or denied.

Chapter 11

Hi-tech Communications

Technology evolves *very* quickly — just think of the advances which have been made in even the past 20 – 30 years. The ways and means of communicating and exchanging information through machinery have developed to such a degree that the shelf-life of any given piece of equipment is becoming progressively shorter. Data needs constant updating in order to maintain accuracy. Perhaps this is proof in itself that communication is a living creature — if it is left untouched, it stagnates and becomes obsolete. Is hi-tech communication therefore a contradiction in terms?

COMMUNICATING THROUGH AN INTERMEDIARY

Not so very long ago I attended an exhibition of on-line information. There were several hundred stands, each with a range of computers, modems, cd-roms and slick executives begging to demonstrate how easily they could access information on companies all over the world. As I walked around, I could hear conversations being conducted in a dozen different languages. This was state-of-the-art, hi-tech communications, bewildering in its versatility and almost frightening in its implications.

Hi-speed transmissions

There are days when I wonder how we ever managed without telephones and fax machines. Speed and economy are both served by these offerings to the god of communications. Letters, contracts and designs can all be transmitted in a matter of seconds, discussed knowledgeably with both parties having copies in front of them, revisions made and approved without taking the risk of postal service or couriers losing them, or eating into precious time at a much higher cost than a few minutes of connection time.

Questions can be answered, problems discussed and negotiations completed in less than the time it used to take for a draft document to reach its destination for the first time around.

Interactive transmissions

Entire transactions can be conducted without any of the interested parties meeting one another. Everything from design specifications to payment can be transmitted electronically with people speaking through their machines. They may hear each other's voices on the telephone if discussion or clarification is needed but then again, they may prefer to 'speak' through their computers and fax machines. Calculations and drawings, forecasts and spreadsheets must be seen to be understood.

This is communication through an intermediary taken to the nth degree. Only delivery of the finished product needs to be three-dimensional.

Far-flung communications

As for dealing with alterations and corrections, desk-top computers and word processors make short work of such details. No more laborious retyping or rewriting, just a few key strokes and whole chunks of text can be revised, rearranged or removed altogether. Drafts can come from a number of different sources, in locations worldwide, to be incorporated in the basic document. Internal newsletters and magazines can incorporate contributions from staff in every office the company or its customers may have.

Authors, whether of books or letters, can check their own work and edit at such an early stage that later proofreading and correction time can be kept to the minimum. Spread sheets, figures, diagrams can all be incorporated at the outset and alternative page layouts and type styles experimented with in order to achieve the most suitable presentation.

The personal touch

Mail/merge software, which allows names and addresses held on a database to be pulled into a letter, has widened the use of personalization. This, in turn, creates an impression of interest and caring which the more traditional 'Dear Sir or Madam' approach has been unable to achieve. How much higher is the response rate to a mailshot where the recipient feels he is being personally addressed than one sent to a nameless individual from a company too busy to find the right name?

Hi-tech design

Although more sophisticated endeavours, such as newsletters and magazines, require the skill and talent of a trained designer, they too can be produced by a single operator in a fraction of the time previously required. Desk-top publishing offers standards of quality, flexibility and production speed that would be unthinkable with traditional methods and although amateurs should avoid getting carried away, certain standards are achievable virtually from the outset.

The reduction of corrections through having fewer people handling each project, and the facility for redesigning presentations, has made desk-top publishing an internal task for staff in many large corporations.

Those companies using contract design consultants to produce their corporate communications are often happily surprised at the ability to produce alternatives within a much shorter turnaround time than has ever been achieved before. Specialist contract publishers can create a layout grid and appear monthly or quarterly to collect copy which is then tailored to fit the grid. More control can be exercised, and a satisfactory result achieved more easily, than ever before.

Laser printers can output near-perfect quality almost instantly so that where appearance is a prime concern, everyone involved can see exactly how a design or document will look in its finished form.

And now for the bad news

There is a down side to hi-tech communications. Not everyone knows how, is able to learn how, or even wants to get to grips with it. How many times have you made a telephone call, been answered by a machine and hung up without leaving a message? How many times have you turned on your own answering machine to hear messages and found that your callers preferred not to leave any — waiting to speak to you directly? Do you understand all of the features on all of your office equipment? And of those you understand, how many do you actually use?

Business Week recently published a report detailing customer difficulties in using hi-tech equipment and the manufacturers' responses. Ricoh, Xerox and Philips were all aware of customer complaints regarding the complexity of their products. Design features that had been made into selling points were frequently neither understood nor used. As a result, users were rebelling, refusing to buy their products and sales were falling.

The intelligent machine

The only solution has been to simplify and clarify. Customers have communicated their needs; manufacturers must now communicate the purpose and instructions for equipment more clearly. They must be more straightforward to use, facilitating rather than hindering communication.

Machines are only as intelligent as their masters. If the people operating them do not understand them then they cannot fulfill the functions for which they were created.

Machines who need people

Cleaning of mail lists is one of those tasks for which real, live people are needed. Computers often cannot identify names or addresses with minor differences, resulting in a waste of both time and money when multiple copies of the same mailshot are sent to one person. It can also cause irritation at the receiver's end and make them less susceptible to the information being sent them. Manual de-duplication is needed to locate minor deviations if you are not to send out far more copies of a given mailshot than are actually necessary.

Similarly, spellchecks on computers will tell you if you have typed a non-existent word. What they will not tell you is that you have used the wrong word in the wrong place or if your typing mistake has simply substituted another legitimate word for the one you actually intended to use.

Winning and losing

Listing the pros and cons of technology could fill another book. The important thing is to take advantage of it and make best use of it while not letting it run away with you. Hi-tech equipment is sensitive and expensive, it needs to be protected and may raise questions of security you never dreamed of.

Like every other aspect of communication, you must consider not only your own needs but the responses and perceptions of others. Is their equipment compatible? Are you moving too quickly for them or vice versa? Is installing a fax machine going to give salesmen an additional means of sending you junk mail?

The Data Protection Act was designed to prevent the kind of scenario George Orwell predicted in *1984*. Now that we have gone beyond that, in every sense, we must consider the ramifications of buying and selling information. The availability of detailed information is well and good if you are the one who needs it but could be potentially disastrous if you are on the receiving end. Not every item of data that can be found or transmitted is suitable for disclosure.

Technology opens doors and facilitates communication. There is no question of that. What is questionable is, as usual, the human element. Communication can break down or be distorted, misused or abused, whenever people are involved. The relationship of man to machine is one that needs to be considered and resolved within the context of hi-tech communications.

Creating a specification

It is incumbent on any business intending to increase its usage of technology to conduct an audit of its needs and potential applications. You must know:

- how the equipment is going to be used;
- why equipment should be used rather than people;

- who will be using the equipment;
- what training needs to be provided by yourself and by the suppliers of the equipment;
- what you expect the equipment to achieve;
- where the equipment is going to be located;
- what other equipment your equipment will have to communicate with;
- how the data stored or obtained from your equipment will be applied to your overall business objectives.

Specifying technology, whether it be hardware or software, is definitely a case of *caveat emptor* — let the buyer beware. Anyone who has ever had to complete an audit or specify hi-tech equipment will tell you tales of horror. There is a complete dependence on communication in the form of specification and training. There is a direct correlation between the successful use of technology and:

- accuracy of the specification;
- clarity of the specification;
- degree of completeness of the specification, that is, does it cover every one of your requirements and contingencies;
- depth and success of the training for users.

Knowing what you know and knowing what you want

To illustrate, I will give you an example of my own learning curve with hi-tech equipment.

In the early eighties we used BBC Microcomputers, among the first non-mainframe computers available to businesses. We thought we were very progressive people.

Come the late eighties we woke up to the fact that our computers were out of date. They had 32k of memory, they did not have hard disks so every file had to be copied and then copied again in case the first copy went wrong, and the computers could not talk to one another. We used them for words and text only. They had no capacity for dealing with data, either storing it, manipulating it or retrieving it. They had little facility for graphics or spreadsheets.

We realized that we needed more powerful, faster, computers. We were introduced by someone we knew to a consultancy who came to talk to us about our needs. After explaining in depth what we wanted to do, they went away to look for the right equipment. They came back and presented us with a list of hard and software that they believed would satisfy our requirements and provide a system that would last us for a long time into the future. So far so good.

We were sent along by these consultants to another consultant who would demonstrate the software to us and show us all the wonderful things it could do. We were duly impressed. Everything we asked the demonstrator to do, he did. In minutes he created a window to show the information we wanted, keyed in some sample records then sorted them and created reports that extracted all sorts of combinations of data from what he had input. We were sold.

I still have nightmares, three years later, when I think about how innocent we were. We had no idea how little we knew. We did not know what questions to ask. We did ask about cost, however, and were given an estimate. It seemed like a great deal of money but when we considered what we were getting and how we were going to use it, we convinced ourselves that it was a necessary investment. We signed the purchase order.

The computers were delivered and the software installed. We were left with two boxes of manuals. We switched on and did not know what to do.

'Don't worry,' said our suppliers, 'the software consultant will be here in a day or so to find out how you want it configured.'

'Configured?' we exclaimed. 'What does that mean?'

'Well,' he replied patiently, 'you have to customize the software to your requirements. You have to tell George what you want the software to do and he will make sure it does it.'

'Why?' we asked innocently. 'Why do we need George and why does he have to tell the software anything? Why doesn't it do all the things he showed us it would do when he demonstrated it? Why, we cried, doesn't it *work*?'

He remained patient and explained to us that you cannot simply switch on a computer and expect it to work. You cannot buy software off the shelf and use it. You need expert assistance. You need to specify your requirements and have the program programmed to fulfill them. (Surprise number one.)

Along came George. We told him, as we had told the first consultant at our very first meeting, what we wanted to use the computers for. He advised us to think carefully and make sure we planned as far ahead as we possibly could because once he tailored the software it would be very difficult to change it later. He frightened the life out of us.

He also told us, for the first time, that the clock was ticking and of course there was a charge for writing up our requirements into a detailed specification for our approval and then doing the work itself. We began to get the first inkling that all was not as straightforward as it seemed.

To cut a long story short, several weeks and many pounds later, we began to use our computers. George spent a full day showing us how to do things and two of us stood over him frantically scribbling notes, writing down every word he uttered so that we would be able to cope when he left.

We began inputing data and learned some simple exercises in manipulating and retrieving it. It took months to come to grips with it and each week we learned more and more about how little we understood the system. We called George frequently and found that he spent most of his time on the road doing unto others what he had done unto us. Through the grapevine we made contact with some of those others and discovered that they knew even less than we did. As we became familiar with the machine we got braver and managed to extract little favours from it. Every new procedure we learned was a cause for celebration.

The moral of the story

Apart from mastering the machine, we learned a number of lessons about communication. We had to communicate with our computer and it had to communicate with us. The only way that was going to work was if we communicated successfully with our consultant and he translated our message into a format we could use and understand. Furthermore, he had to communicate the procedures for using the format back to us.

What we established with George in the end was a complete lack of trust. We began to suspect that he was deliberately withholding information, programming 'bugs' that would force us to call him for help — at a cost — and that he was deliberately misunderstanding our needs so that we would be tied to him inextricably. When he suggested installing a modem so that he could help us long distance, we refused. We did not trust him not to interfere with the system. We believed, in the end, that he had created our need for support. He was encouraging our dependency in order to keep himself in business.

The lessons we learned regarding procedures can usefully be passed on:

- Be sure that anything you order comes complete with an agreed amount of time to be spent in training.
- Do not rush the training — repeat exercises until everyone understands them.
- Ensure that the training includes hands-on, staff participation — watching an expert demonstrate can be misleading and you will not begin to know what you don't know until you begin using the system.
- Do not rush your specification — think carefully about all the items listed earlier in the chapter regarding who will be using what and why.
- Do not be persuaded that you cannot amend your system at a later date — insist on developing it in stages so that you have time for use and assessment before moving on to the next stage.
- Look at the manuals while you are sitting at the computer — they will make no sense at all otherwise.

A few of the pitfalls to watch out for are:

- failure to find out all of the costs, including those that are hidden and come after the purchase is complete;
- delays in getting service or help — it's no good having a helpline available for the first three or six months if it takes a week to get a response each time you call;

- consultants and developers who do not tell you, before you purchase, what is included and excluded;
- consultants and developers who let you do the talking — you do not want to be persuaded into more than you need by a hyperactive salesman but you do need to feel that you are being well advised.

Not all consultants are like George. Since parting company with him we have met a number of others who have been far more obliging, taking a different approach and accepting that their responsibilities as consultants include asking hard questions. They have formed a clear picture of the uses the equipment would have so that they could make informed, correct and accurate recommendations. They have also tried to ensure that it would not be outgrown or become out of date too quickly.

It is also possible to write a clear and useful computer manual. We recently bought a new piece of software, installed it ourselves and handed the manual to our seventeen-year-old trainee. After experimenting with it for a day or two, we sat down and talked about the specification and how we wanted to use the software. He has now designed a window, created reports and begun inputing data for a new project. He has written up his procedures into a house manual and trained the rest of us.

We have a system that understands plain English and with which we are all happily communicating.

Security

Computers not only have their own language for communication, they have their own language for the problems that may be encountered. There are bugs and viruses, hackers who create the need for security and passwords. Electronic data exchange, global networks, and on-line transmissions increase the incidence of all of these and the need for protection to prevent them. Anyone using hi-tech equipment who does not recognize or understand these terms had better learn them PDQ.

Fear of flying

Training is needed not only to learn how to use technology but also to overcome fear. People who are used to manual or electric typewriters, or even BBC microcomputers, can easily be worried about having more sophisticated equipment introduced.

In-house manuals, which translate suppliers' manuals into relevant terms, can be invaluable. As users begin to use the equipment, and to realize why they are using it and how they can use it, they become increasingly adept. Fear goes out the window. Most people find it difficult to resist the challenge and the excitement that technology can generate. The sense of achievement is a great incentive for coming to grips with what may have appeared a daunting innovation when it was first mooted.

None of this will happen with the next generation, of course, as children start learning about computers and getting used to them from such a young age. Our trainee has become a trainer in next to no time at all. His own age and education have made him far more amenable towards machines than the rest of us in the office. He has learned more quickly and is far less hesitant about experimenting. While we stood in terror in the early days, convinced that we could not make any changes to what George had told the computer in case we caused any permanent damage, Steven sits there adding and deleting to his heart's delight. He sees the computer almost as a toy and there are days when it strikes me that I should get him to pay us for the privilege of employment.

Resistance

Resistance to decimalization, metrication and technology are all linked. After all, to a certain degree most of us adhere to the principle that if God had meant us to fly he'd have given us wings. But they are all attempts to improve the quality of communication. Trying to find words and structures that are mutually understood is one of the chief prerequisites of effective communication. Even EMS, the Ecu and the Channel tunnel have applications to communication. They are all designed to facilitate our dealings with one another.

If the use of hi-tech equipment is to be successfully implemented within a business however, the resistance of managers must be overcome as well as any resistance from the operators themselves. Executives who do not have their own typewriters or word processors, who have clung to more traditional methods and the status of having a secretary to do their paperwork for them, need to be shown the gains in time management and costs which can be achieved by technology. The time needed to read and correct a secretary's output is often wasted.

Perhaps part of management training should include self sufficiency and keyboard skills. Investment in equipment on each desk and the cost of training middle managers and those above them in the company hierarchy would more than pay off in time and effort saved waiting for a secretary whose services may be shared with several others.

At least two companies that I know of refuse to move into the 1990s in this aspect. Their communications must go through channels. One of them has been known to send out letters dated seven days prior to receipt. The date on the letter is almost certainly the day on which it was dictated to a secretary. It took that length of time to get typed, processed in the mailroom and delivered, second class, by the Post Office.

Effective and efficient communications

Communications Week International, which refers to itself as the newspaper of global networking, is distributed free to qualified management and professional personnel at companies involved in the communications industry outside of the United States. It is distributed to paid subscribers within the United States. In a June 1991 issue, the magazine had an insert called 'Communications Close-Up' which gave case studies of what it called 'progressive users'.

The writer defined a progressive user as someone who 'incorporates technology with a realistic eye to his needs, integrates the human and technological elements of his business, sees the benefits of technology without losing sight of what his business does best'. He points out that 'It doesn't take a progressive user to acquire that latest piece of equipment, to be the fastest, the first. It does take a progressive user to understand how that equipment might fit into the larger scheme, to be flexible enough to get the most out of the equipment while still meeting his original goals.' In short, to make use of technology without letting it rule his life.

The case studies were of companies in different industries who had realized the importance of information technology and devised creative, effective ways of using it. I have used the word 'realized' here in two different ways. The companies described had realized, that is, understood and appreciated, the importance of information technology. They had also realized its importance in the sense of making it happen and making use of it.

EQUIPMENT

The following section offers an overview of some of the equipment available and the facilities they offer for communicating with real people as well as transmitting and receiving information from other people's hardware. This is not the place to go into detail about any of the hard or software but will hopefully provide a summary of how it works and a little bit of information about what technology can and cannot do.

In the olden days

Some of the most obvious changes in office environments are in telephone systems. We have moved away from old-fashioned switchboards, needing several operators to plug in a complex set of leads, often creating confusion and crossed lines and now the most complicated board can sit on a conventional desk and one person can coordinate dozens of lines.

Direct dialling can go all over the world without requiring operator assistance. Calls can be transmitted via satellites and transatlantic cable, from car, ship or train to shore. Even from Earth to spaceship. Old films depicting telegraph operators tapping out coded messages are regarded as history. Newshounds standing over a hot ticker tape machine getting the news as it happens are no longer novelties. Words and pictures can be transmitted by virtually any and every business instantly. We all have access to information and the ability to communicate, should we wish to, as never before.

Telephones

Apart from the wide range of handsets and systems that are in use within the confines of your home or office, speaker phones, cordless phones and mobile and cellular phones enable us to make and receive calls from any location you can think of. Whether this is always a good thing is a debatable point and one which must be determined by individual circumstances and conscience.

Answering machines

These can give your recorded message to callers so that they know you will call them back and can also serve as a screen so that you can hear who is calling before deciding whether or not to answer the call at that time or return it later. Many answering machines have a remote control device that you can use to call your machine and get your messages while you are still away from home.

Voice mail

One step beyond the answering machine. Callers still get connected with a machine and hear your pre-recorded message to which they must respond, but you are then bleeped and informed that the message is waiting.

Pagers

In their simplest form, pagers will send out a signal, or bleep, to let the person called know that he is wanted. He must then get to the nearest phone, or use his mobile phone, to call in and collect his message. In their more sophisticated form, pagers can offer a range of different toned bleeps so that you know exactly who is calling. Some models will also display the telephone number of the caller so that you can get back to them directly rather than checking first to find out who you have to call. Other features can include displaying a brief message in words or numbers or storing messages until you are ready for them if they arrive at an awkward moment.

Messages

Written messages can be left on a computer terminal linked to a telephone network so that you can 'post' your letter through an electronic mailbox at any time and it can be there waiting for the recipient to pick it up and print it at his convenience. The message can be transmitted to several mailboxes simultaneously, is delivered as quickly as the telephone takes to work and, unlike a fax, is totally private. Networks can be set up internally for individual companies or a system such as Telecom Gold subscribed to. Telecom Gold also holds a library of business information which can be used by subscribers at any time.

Call forwarding/diversion

This is a service for those who do not want their callers to be confronted with a machine. Before setting out, you key a pre-set code into your telephone along with the number where you can be reached and calls are automatically diverted.

Queuing

A call waiting service allows for your conversation to be interrupted with a beep to let you know that someone else is trying to get in touch with you. You then have the option of putting the first call on hold while you respond to the waiting call. With some telephone systems, those on hold are kept in strict sequential order ensuring that calls are answered in the same order in which they were received.

Instant communication

Telex

Telex machines were perhaps the first mechanical means of transmitting written words by means of telephone lines. Messages are typed onto a special keyboard at the sending end, and retyped automatically by the keyboard at the receiving end. Each machine has its own code number, similar to a telephone number, thus needing to be dialled to begin transmission. Many telex machines can be linked to computers and message switching systems to increase and simplify their facilities.

Facscimile machines

Faxes, as they are familiarly called, transmit documents via telephone lines. The length of time the transmission takes depends on the density of the copy on the page. Unlike telex, illustrations and graphics can be transmitted in addition to words.

Networks

These can be internal or worldwide, linking equipment through cables, radios, satellites or telephone lines. Internal networks, linked by cables running within one room or building, are known as local area networks. Networks connecting your office with other locations on a permanent basis are known as wide area networks.

Whether internal or external, however, networks enable people to access information from multiple sources as well as from a shared information bank. When computers communicate directly with one another by using a telephone line they are on-line. The alternative is to exchange information in the form of disks or tapes which take data off one system and are then read into a terminal on a different system. In some cases data can only be read, while in others it can be edited and amended. When you see the abbreviation CD-ROM, (compact disk) read only media, you will know that this is what you are getting.

Private circuits

These are exclusive lines which can link all of your communications technology to other branches regardless of distance. They are expensive to install and are generally cost-effective only for the largest companies with heavy traffic in verbal, written and mechanical communication.

Prestel

This and other interactive media are used to access information that you need to read but not to manipulate. They allow you to ask questions and offer multiple answers leading to other questions and answers until you have tracked down the item that you want. Financial information, travel information, details of leisure and entertainment events, weather, news and even directory enquiries can be obtained in this way. There is also an electronic mailbox facility.

Conference calls

These can be made from your own office — and others' offices — making all of your own documents available during the call. They can also be recorded and transcribed to ensure accurate minutes are available.

Videoconferences

These can be held by sending the individuals involved to special studios convenient to them. A satellite hook-up with individuals in other studios then permits you to see as well as speak to colleagues.

Computers

Mainframe computers are massive pieces of equipment requiring special rooms, temperature control and highly trained expert users. Their use is not likely to be eliminated entirely, but they are now restricted to the largest of companies only. Small- and medium-sized businesses, as well as individuals running their own business, can now share the benefits of computerization in a way unprecedented just a few years ago.

There is a flaw in the use of computers, however. One of the so-called advantages promoted by suppliers is the philosophy that you can work anywhere, at any time. The result is inevitably an increase in expectations pressuring us all to work everywhere, all the time. Desktops, laptops notebooks, handheld computers, personal organizers, electronic diaries may make life easier but they also make life harder. I recently gave electronic pocket organizers as gifts to two executive friends who like to manage their time efficiently and make the best use of the latest in gadgetry. Neither of them has actually mastered the thing and they are both mouldering away in desk drawers. They found that it took so long to figure out the instructions and input the basic information that they gave up trying. The amount of time that would have been saved in accessing the information was far exceeded by the amount of time they needed to feed it in in the first place.

Speaking the same language

Computer languages, including the so-called BASIC which is a misnomer if ever there was one, is now supplemented in many instances by plain English. It is generally necessary to get the syntax right though and tell the computer exactly what data you want and how a report should be structured or presented. As I may have mentioned before, the computer is only as intelligent as its operator. It will work things out for you if you program it to, or teach it how in the first place. It will not do anything it is not told to do unless you tell it how and when to do it. Even computer aided design (CAD), which can produce two- or three-dimensional models of plans for engineers and architects, requires a skilled operator. If you do not know the basic techniques of engineering or design, if you are not familiar with the tools and formulas needed, then it doesn't matter how much you know about computers. You will not be able to get the computer to do the job for you.

Audio visual equipment

The range of cassettes, slides, films and videos available, and the varying degrees of expertise needed to operate them and edit the results, is vast. If you are interested in using audio-visual equipment, consider the purposes for which you will use it and decide first whether it is a one-off need or an on-going need. Decide whether you need an expert on a consultancy basis or can justify purchasing equipment and setting up your own in-house facility. Study the market and, once again, conduct an audit. As with all other forms of communication, audio visual equipment has its place. Treat it as a tool and decide whether or not it is the right tool for the job.

Flexibility

Technology can help people to work from different locations and to pool information. We can work from home when it suits us or run our businesses from the back bedroom with no one the wiser. With no one to see you, you can reduce overheads and manage more flexible hours.

This has proved particularly advantageous in recent years when more women, for example, want to continue their careers while having a break to raise their families. Working from home is also a way to make best use of people moving into consultancy because their services are no longer required on a full time basis by individual companies.

One of the effects of redundancy and one of the reasons why there has been an increase in the number of small businesses and start ups than ever before is that people are unable to find new jobs. As a result, they frequently have to remain unemployed or become self-employed. This has proved a bonus to many larger companies. It enables them to cut overheads and only use consultants when the need for a service arises rather than keeping people on the payroll when their skills may not be utilized to maximum capacity.

It has proved a blessing in disguise to many of those making an unplanned change of direction in their careers by giving them freedom, independence and flexibility if they feel able to cope with a new set of pressures. It may have been technology that put them out of a job in the first place by making internal systems more efficient but it can be technology that provides them with an alternative form of livelihood.

Chapter 12

Marketing and Public Relations

Marketing requires communication between a business and its external audiences in order to:

- introduce the product or service to potential new users;
- introduce a new product or service to existing users;
- research the potential for new products or services;
- test the reaction to new products or services.

Perception is therefore all-important. The audience must be presented with the product or service and its uses and motivations. If any of their perceptions regarding these do not coincide with the company's then the company's message has not been adequately communicated. If the audience has decided not to accept the product or service for some reason then they have decided not to accept the message. The message received may have been a negative one, convincing them that the product or service was not what was promised.

Communication and marketing

Poor communication leads to poor marketing and a lack of sales. If customers do not believe that a company cares about them then they are not likely to go to that company on a second occasion. The customer or user has to have demonstrated a policy of 'the customer is always right' both before and after the decision or sale is made.

If aftersales service is not satisfactory, or the customer is not continually wooed with a view to the next transaction, then interest and cooperation will disappear. One of the roles of the marketing department, and the public relations department, which I'll discuss later in this chapter, is to maintain a relationship and a friendship towards the company. They should be building loyalty.

Customers speak to one another and pass on bad experiences as well as good ones. Customer support is a method of communication which it is incumbent on marketing executives to cultivate.

Awareness and appreciation

Aubrey Wilson, in *Practice Development for Professional Firms*, cites the stages through which marketing can be used to make audiences aware of a company and its products or services. Each audience moves from:

- unawareness;
- to awareness;
- to comprehension (understanding what the business does, what products and services it provides);
- to relevancy (appreciation of the benefits);
- to conviction (belief in the accuracy and value of those benefits);
- to favourable decisions (to use the company or purchase its products or services).

The onus is on the marketing department to seek opportunities to provide additional services. There is much truth in the cliché that the best advertisement is a satisfied customer. Theoretically, marketing should encourage re-orders and keep old customers while simultaneously looking for ways to increase the market and expand or broaden target audiences.

Objectives

Marketing must make the product or service seem relevant to the potential user. Its value and the benefit to the recipient must be communicated in order to move through the stages specified by Aubrey Wilson. Motivating the audience must be counted as one of the prime objectives of marketing.

One of the first lessons taught to those interested in marketing is that the marketing mix consists of:

- people
- product;
- promotion;
- price;
- place.

Each of those elements is interrelated and none of them can be achieved without being identified and targeted. It is up to the marketing department to ensure that its plans are structured in such a way as to meet the needs of the company and its audiences in terms of each and every element of the marketing mix.

Marketing or selling?

There is a very thin line differentiating marketing from sales, and from public relations. Money may not change hands between the marketing executive and the potential user. There may not be a straight barter or cash transaction in exchange for the product or service but the ground should have been set for the sale which will hopefully follow.

Marketing is actually indirect selling, introducing the product or service and the target audience to one another, promoting the value of the product or service and stopping short of closing the deal.

John Frain, in his book *Introduction to Marketing*, describes marketing as 'identifying and satisfying user preference'. He accepts, however, that the term is generally used as a verb equivalent to or associated with selling.

Frain sees marketing as an 'exchange process' because consumers and producers are willing partners and therefore both sides gain. He explains that:

- the market for a product or service consists of a 'population', that is individuals or business organizations or industries with the means and propensity to buy;
- salesmen are 'creative agents of exchange';
- sellers are mass producers who must be brought into contact with mass consumers by mass (or marketing) communication.

Frain also describes marketing techniques as mass selling, as opposed to individual selling. He sees the exchange process as a transfer of information and 'education' to the user or dealer from the seller.

It behoves the marketing executive therefore to find a way to reach mass consumers through a combination of advertising, promotion, publicity and introduction to representatives who will finalize the process with face to face selling.

Marketing identity and loyalty

Just as companies have multiple audiences, so they have multiple images. The company needs to be aware of this and also to find ways of taking advantage of it.

Internal perceptions

Chapter 5 on Employee Communications, as well as the first section of this book on the Communications Audit, discusses the importance of knowing what employees think of management and company policy. It is their perceptions of the company's image which they transmit to others. Their perceptions also determine their own behaviour and their behaviour, in turn, transmits further messages to the company's various other audiences.

If employees are not thinking or acting in tandem with management, then they can convey a poor image and create a detrimental effect on marketing. Sales may suffer if the message the company is officially trying to communicate gets lost or misinterpreted before reaching its audience. Employees can also convey contradictory messages if the marketing or public relations departments say one thing but employees and products demonstrate something different. Communication with employees must be truthful and accurate, not committing the sin of omission any more than the sin of *commission* in letting them know what is going on.

If a satisfied customer is, as said earlier, the best advertisement for a product, a satisfied employee is the likeliest person to demonstrate and promote loyalty to the firm.

Employees must also be one of the marketing and public relations departments' target audiences. They act as intermediaries, representing the company to the various people they meet both officially and unofficially. If they do not understand the company's message, or do not feel willing to transmit it, conflict can arise.

An example of a middle manager following company policy but taking it too literally, recently occurred with a local branch of a High Street clearing bank. A young customer who had held an account in a different branch of the same bank for some years, applied to open a new account in the branch nearest to his home. He duly filled in the forms and waited. Some time later he received a letter turning down his application, with no explanation given other than that the bank had investigated his circumstances and did not feel that they could extend their facilities to him.

The applicant had not requested either a loan or an overdraft, and he had been one of those attracted by the bank's marketing initiatives aimed at children who would one day grow into adults putting business and profit in the way of the bank. Yet here he was, grown up at last, and being rejected without explanation. Both the image and attitude conveyed were in conflict with long-standing marketing and advertising themes.

Packaging

Design consultancies may not grow rich by creating new or altered packaging for clients but some of them come pretty close to it. What the package communicates, and what the manufacturer wants it to communicate, need to coincide. There must be a high perceived value if sales are to follow marketing as night follows day.

First time buyers particularly are attracted by packaging. They have not sampled the product and will not know whether it is indeed all it is cracked up to be unless they try it.

This applies to services as much as products. An assortment of beautifully designed and printed full-colour brochures of clients, accompanied by other photographs and brochures of the company's own facilities, is simply a further example of marketing a package.

You do not necessarily see what you get or get what you see with packaging. There are times when we pay more for packaging than we do for the contents, which may be mediocre or inadequate in their own right.

There is a strong similarity between packaging and corporate identity. As discussed in 'The Communications Audit', companies have to determine their identity and then acquaint their audiences with it. The image that each company decides to project is wrapped up in packaging.

It is not unknown for people to buy clothes or apparatus with labels as a way of advertising their own affluence. Those labels may well communicate reliability and quality. It is up to the company to ensure that this is the case and that the labels are not simply communicating that the purchaser has enough money in the kitty to afford top of the range. The most expensive is not necessarily the best.

Changing a package to change an image is a controversial step which should be taken with care. If the contents remain the same, or are only being modified slightly, alterations may backfire.

Remember the famous soft drinks company that altered its recipe slightly because it felt that it had been too long since there had been any change? There was no need to change such a successful product. Change for its own sake is unnecessary and in this particular instance it did indeed backfire. Customers preferred the original product and the new product was hastily discontinued.

The Communications Audit discusses in some detail the reasons for 'tweaking' a company logo. If packaging is going to be altered, audiences must know why. The company should be very concerned about the audience's perception of new packaging. Do they believe that the contents have changed or not? If they have, then is the change for better or worse?

Pricing

Pricing can make or break the customer's loyalty to a company. The questions of value for money, consistency of quality, reliability and comparison with the competition must be pre-empted by the marketing department before the salesman makes his pitch.

British Telecom's Business Catalogue is a perfect example of this edict. Much of their equipment is available from office suppliers and high street shops at a considerably lower price than one may pay when dealing directly with BT. This is common knowledge. BT accepts it, although they may not admit it openly.

They do admit it tacitly however when, as a means of combating it, they clearly stress, again and again in their catalogue the quality of their service. British Telecom promote their reputation, their expertise, their reliability as much as their products. They promote support services and an entire package. They deflect exclamations of surprise at their prices by introducing a degree of value which they maintain cannot be beaten by other outlets.

Pricing must convey value for money. Perceived value is one of the factors affecting purchase therefore a clear message is conveyed through price. Businesses and audiences must look at the value of a product or service, its price and what is on offer by the competition. Does their higher price ensure better quality or service or provide some extra feature? We can always find something cheaper but have to decide how long it will last, whether it will need replacement sooner, whether or not it does everything we want and need it to do. Businesses must ensure that their products or services live up to their (that is the company's and the product or service's) image and packaging.

Look at those well-known companies Marks & Spencer and John Lewis. Each has a longstanding reputation of quality. Their brands and packaging are immediately recognizable. They have loyal customers who come back time and time again. Prices would have to increase dramatically for those loyal customers to be driven elsewhere as the general perception is one of value for money.

High price is not always a guarantee of quality however. Some people instinctively believe that if a price is low, there must be something wrong with the product. They are influenced by price in a reverse way and this, too, the marketing department must take into account.

According to Aubrey Wilson, 'Because fees are not broken down to reveal professional and support staff salaries and overheads, the global figure will be interpreted as an indication of quality, high or low, 'value for money', 'over charging', 'fair', 'bargain' and a host of other image perceptions.' Prices do not necessarily communicate what has gone into producing the end result, they simply reflect the demand for the product.

Branding and differentiation

There are several reasons why companies introduce brands. There needs to be clear differentiation between their own products and the competition's. There also needs to be clear differentiation between the products within a company's own range. No manufacturer can survive with a single product. When looking at new cars recently, I was taken aback to realize that one particular company had a dozen or more brands, and up to fifty different models. By the time I left the showroom I was totally confused about the differences between them. The same applies to computers, photocopiers, anything you would care to mention. Branding separates and identifies the variations.

Branding can also inspire recognition and loyalty. When speaking to the export director of a large food conglomerate recently I enquired about the disappearance of a brand with which I was familiar. This particular brand was originally introduced by a smaller manufacturer and later absorbed into the conglomerate. I wondered about all the customers who went to their supermarkets looking for the brand and unable to find it. How would they know, I asked, that it was still there but under a different name? He replied, matter of factly, that they would not. Loyalty for the smaller brand was far outweighed by loyalty for the conglomerate's brand which was now benefiting from an additional product. Adding value to the more well-known brand through the introduction of a new product would serve to increase its market share by improving its benefits and quality. Customers were delighted at the improvement in a range they already liked and showed their approval at the cash till.

The last few years have brought about a proliferation of own brands fighting for their share of the market with better known brands. Their introduction has been a reflection of market trends. One retail outlet boasted that they were 'never knowingly undersold'. Other retail outlets soon followed suit, promising to refund the difference between their own price and the competition's if the customer could find the same item selling for less somewhere else.

The catch was that the item had to be identical. By introducing their own brand, sometimes at a higher price and sometimes at a lower price, they were negating the offer and preventing a price war. By promoting their own brand and its quality, by marketing, like British Telecom, their own integrity and reliability, customers began moving away from the name brands and started to establish a loyalty to the company's own brand. Supermarkets and DIY shops began increasing their ranges in order to offer something extra to customers and prove that they did not need to shop around or go to a multitude of shops when all their needs could be filled under one roof.

There was a twofold reason for introducing own brands. To add to the product range and offer that little bit extra. Books, for example, were introduced into chain outlets to show customers ways of using their products. Thus a dual message was conveyed:

- Our products are good and useful and we'll show you how to make the most of them.
- We are a caring company, offering you these support services to supplement our traditional products and services.

Logos, design and packaging can also be used to link brands with their parent thereby communicating ownership, stability, credibility and their position as part of whole unit with a high professional standing.

Loyalty

Most of us will incline towards loyalty given half a chance. Part of what a marketing executive must do is build and maintain that loyalty. The other part of what he does is to chisel away at loyalty to the competition. Communication can be cut-throat when it comes to competition but it is only by communicating that marketing, like every other form of business transaction, will be successful.

Presenting an image

When using image as a marketing tool, we need to find the best way of making a positive impression on the audience with regard to corporate ability as well as the quality and reliability of our products or services. The marketing department utilizes the corporate image after first identifying what it should be and ensuring that it is what management wants. Primary stages in planning a marketing campaign include:

- identifying the image most suitable to the company's message;
- creating the image;
- communicating the image;
- assessing and adjusting the image.

Marketing is an ongoing process, relying on feedback. It must allow for change and be flexible. Referring once again to The Communications Audit, the establishment of a corporate identity and its accoutrements is a preliminary to any exercise conducted by the marketing department.

Advertising is often used to convey corporate image. It can just as frequently be used to support a particular brand. The difference between the two is that advertising a brand is intended to make customers buy the product while corporate advertising is intended to build trust and confidence. By establishing loyalty and support, by developing a relationship, the results of the advertising are seen as more long term than brand advertising may be.

Whatever methods are selected, however, the implementation of corporate identity needs to be consistent.

First impressions

This may well be stating the obvious, but it is worth repeating that first impressions are often lasting ones and are difficult to change. Premises and personnel greeting visitors can communicate messages that no end of marketing can change. No one says that it is fair. It is a fact of life, business or otherwise. Impressions that, whether justifiably or not, affect decisions on whether to do business with a company can include:

- location of premises;
- size of premises;
- decor of premises;
- condition of equipment;
- dress of receptionist;
- hospitality;
- general atmosphere of busyness;
- mood and attitude of employees.

Projecting the right image is all important. Sometimes it should be so; at other times physical environment is not an accurate representation of standards and qualifications. This does not change the fact that visitors want to be impressed and a favourable impression will do a great deal more for your marketing efforts than a negative impression.

Lasting impressions

Images conveyed through an intermediary are harder to correct than those conveyed directly from you to the audience. When there is little or no direct contact with the audience, control is diluted and it is that much more difficult to ensure that your message is adequately communicated.

Among the factors contributing to the establishment of a lasting impression are:

- word of mouth communications via the grapevine;
- official corporate communications;
- image presented by staff, premises, marketing, advertising and promotional materials;
- quality, quantity and effectiveness of communications;
- quality and reliability of products and services;
- belief in value of products or services and agreement with price structure.

Logos, graphics and design, or the visual image conveyed by the company, are all discussed in The Communications Audit. They are a means of keeping your image in front of the target audience and creating an impression that will stay with them for a long time.

Image is conveyed by individuals as well as corporations. Chapter 10 on Communicating with the Media refers to people giving information on behalf of the company; Chapter 9 on Telephone Techniques, covers people answering and placing calls; Chapter 5 explains the ramifications of Employee Communications. If you look at it, in fact, nearly every single chapter refers to some aspect of corporate image and the ways in which it is communicated.

Perceptions

Customers buy beliefs and expectations communicated to them and instilled in them by a combination of public relations, marketing and sales. These processes can be deliberate or not. The image a company, its employees, its products or services, convey is made up of all the contact the customer has with the company. Every message is stored and influences the decision on whether or not to do business with you.

Marketing must take this into account down to the appearance of the office and the building, the location, corporate identity, uniforms and dress. If, for example, employees meet visitors, they must be neat and tidy whether they wear a uniform or not. Written communication, especially brochures and reports but also letters and stationery, represent the company.

All of the marketing and public relations departments' efforts are aimed at improving the audience's perceptions of the company. Loss leaders may have to be introduced and incentives offered, but more often than not some tangential service can be found to satisfy this requirement. J Sainsbury, for example, sells children's books to please their family audience. As the majority of their shoppers are mothers, providing products specifically aimed at children helps encourage the perception of them as an aware, caring company. They can think of their profits and their customers' needs simultaneously. And gain Brownie points at the same time.

Less successful at improving audience perceptions are advertisements from clearing banks which are intended to communicate confidence yet instead communicate a patronizing, unrealistic attitude which antagonizes customers and deepens their anger and bitterness in a distressing and explosive economic situation. Many feel that our economy has a long way to go to recover and small businesses especially feel that they are being penalized for errors the banks made in financing big businesses which have in fact gone down with much bigger debts than they are ever likely to incur.

MARKETING TECHNIQUES

Aubrey Wilson in *Practice Development for Professional Firms* discusses marketing and communication techniques for professional practices. Much of what he says has a broader application to marketing skills which businesses in general must demonstrate in order to successfully establish a two-way communication with their target audiences. Those that can stand reiteration although they have been dealt with elsewhere include:

- advertising as a means of conscious and subliminal reiteration of product's benefits;
- public relations as a means of establishing the company's images and policies;
- exhibitions as a way of waving the flag, showing goods and services but also having staff available to convey image and practice some first hand communications;
- media through free coverage, theoretically less biased than paid advertising;
- merchandising and point of sale packs in retail outlets;
- packaging to catch the eye and attract potential customers to enquire further and sample products or services;
- logos, uniforms, emblems on delivery vans, all immediately recognizable symbols of the company and what it stands for;
- brochures, sales materials, newsletters, house journals and all corporate communications as a means of communicating with internal and external audiences;

- business gifts and corporate hospitality are a form of public relations and can also be branded with your name as a permanent reminder of where the gift came from;
- directories and yearbooks as a means of publicizing products or services, as well as personnel, generally free of charge but with the option for glitzy advertising to emphasize your message;
- financial incentives and aids to employees and trainees;
- support services — those which strengthen the core product or service and build brand/company loyalty;
- direct mail as a means of keeping your company name, product and service in front of the target audience, ensuring that they have the information that you want them to have and which they might otherwise miss if they do not follow the right media, advertising or other promotions;
- sponsorships of books, events and academics;
- competitions and incentives to employees to encourage quantity and quality of production;
- financial incentives, prizes, discounts to customers to encourage them to use your product/service; offering a free or reduced price gift with a high perceived value implies that you are increasing the value of your own product or service with the gift on offer;
- educational campaigns or secondments to provide links between business and educational institutions;
- inward visits to let people see first hand what you do and how, how employees work together.

John Frain in his *Introduction to Marketing* advises using the mass media as a marketing tool. The media, he contends, has grown up as a result of the increase in population and mass production from the time of the Industrial Revolution. As living standards and purchasing power has increased, so has the need for new means of reaching audiences hence the development of mass media communication. Outdoor advertising, poster sites and cinemas have become a routine way of reaching the public, particularly those who don't buy newspapers or magazines. Visual impact, especially with subliminal messages in association with logos, symbols and colours attached to certain products are widely exploited in the quest for audience awareness.

Frain describes the stages of marketing as follows:

Stage 1 Manufacturer to product distribution
Stage 2 Distribution point to wholesaler
Stage 3 Wholesaler to retailer
Stage 4 Retailer to consumer

He diagrams the relationship (Figure 12.1), indicating advertising as a tool to support the second and third stages as well as being a way of reaching the consumer directly in case the message loses something in translation. As those on the second and third stages are dividing their attention between several manufacturers, this is quite likely to happen every so often.

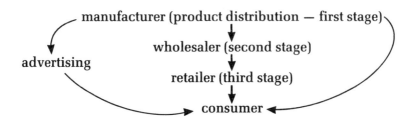

Fig 12.1: The four stages of marketing

Finally, the support materials used in marketing must be assessed and specified. Sales materials, advertisement copy, marketing materials, press releases and corporate brochures all have a role to play. They do not appear by themselves and it is one of the marketing executive's responsibilities to either devise or commission them.

Decision making

Aubrey Wilson used a diagram to illustrate the communication process involved in decision-making which he adapted from A H Colley. Mr Colley's article 'Squeezing the waste out of advertising' was published in the *Harvard Business Review*. The diagram illustrates the forces which drive an audience towards making a decision and further illustrates those forces which drive the audience away from making a decision.

Referring to the stages listed on page 206 showing the progress of an audience's awareness, Wilson and Colley say that the communications techniques which drive audiences towards accepting a company's precepts include:

- public relations;
- personal contact;
- the interpersonal network;
- educational campaigns;
- conferences;
- direct mail.

To these I would suggest adding advertising and corporate communications, which comes as much under the auspices of the public relations department as it does under the marketing department.

Those types of communication or, rather, communication failures, which drive an audience away from accepting the company's precepts include:

- memory lapse;
- competition;
- loss of confidence.

To these I would suggest adding lack of understanding of the company's message and the failure of marketing techniques.

Decisions are made based on the perception of marketing, advertising and public relations efforts. They are also influenced by all the other factors discussed in this chapter. Those individuals influencing and making the decision can include:

- consultants;
- users;
- negotiators;
- buyers.

The person instigating the decision making process and the person making the final decision do not have to be one and the same. Nor do either of them have to belong to any of the groups listed above.

The various marketing techniques which are used influence the decision makers at different stages. The instigator, for example, may be influenced by an advertisement, the consultant by market research, the user by a conference, the negotiator by price, the buyer by delivery schedule. As some audiences are affected indirectly, there is often no control over what they see and hear, or over the opinions and recommendations given to them. All of this the marketing executive must consider when he is planning which tools to use and which ones to take account of when making his own decisions.

Market research

The other side of the marketing coin is knowing what the audience wants, needs and thinks. This falls under the broad heading of market research. If the marketing department is going to see its products, services or ideas accepted then it must receive messages transmitted by the audience.

The law of supply and demand necessitates communication through marketing to:

- Find out what demand exists.
- Create demand.
- Make sure that you are the one to supply the demand.
- Make sure your supply does not exceed or differ from demand.

- Monitor change in demand and maintain a balance with supply.

Market research requires an accurate understanding of the audience. Its needs must be assessed in order to find the best means of data collection and interpretation. Views and perceptions have to be gathered, assessed and acted on.

The accuracy of perceptions must be checked, and adjusted if necessary. This is done through a process of feedback which is of itself a form of two-way communications with the company giving out a message and the audience receiving it. But the audience is also giving out a message concerning its appreciation, or lack of appreciation of the company's message. The company should ensure receipt of that message.

Market research should be conducted before and after a product or service is introduced. It can include a combination of questionnaires, discussions and interviews to provide the necessary feedback. Whichever method, or methods, are used, interviewing key audiences as explained in The Communications Audit is the only way in which a company can judge itself and improve its communications.

Marketing creates change but also reacts to it. It is a method which must be flexible. Many influences combine to increase or decrease sales, making the results and impact difficult to isolate and quantify. Perhaps your sales would have gone up or down anyway. The ways in which marketing campaigns interact with other aspects of communication which target audiences experience can only be identified and an attempt at assessment made. Some assessment is necessary to all forms of communication in order to make adjustments and improvements. Market research is one way of getting the feedback which will facilitate those improvements.

Public relations

According to the Institute of Public Relations, 'public relations is concerned with the deliberate, planned and sustained effort to establish and maintain mutual understanding between an organization and its public'.

Public relations should be an ongoing process, not just reactive or to promote a specific product, innovation or development, or to highlight change. It should keep the company in front of its audiences at all times, maintaining its positive image in the best of times as well as the worst of times.

It is the public relations executive who must deal with complaints, defusing situations and smoothing ruffled feathers as well as preventing and pre-empting possible difficult situations. Any problems within the company that are not visible to audiences, or the effects of which are not explained to them, can create a negative image and this is another situation which the public relations executive must strive to prevent.

The connotation of public relations is one of hype. It is rarely taken as entirely open, honest, unbiased but rather is seen as exaggerated, meant to charm and persuade, to sell gently. It is not a field for the hard sell salesperson. Public relations executives create an impression, woo their audiences, make friends and lay the ground for their colleagues.

Aubrey Wilson's checklist for public relations for law firms can readily be adapted to most other businesses. There are numerous possible assets of which the public relations department should be aware and take advantage. They should be sure to:

- Analyze any special expertise of the firm or its employees who might be useful for external communications.
- Audit non work-related activities of employees, in order to publicize and promote their good deeds especially with relation to the community and including charity work.
- Publish articles in trade press or academic publications, publicizing any research that may be underway or developments, discoveries of note, new procedures, processes that can be used by others to help them whether business or otherwise.
- Arrange speeches by and the presence of senior personnel and/or experts or boffins at dinners, or other special events in order to promote the image of the company and obtain favourable publicity.
- Encourage participation in seminars and exhibitions, ensuring high visibility of employees at all levels.
- Promote involvement in education training links, providing advisers and/or materials and developing joint projects.
- Maintain press contacts through press releases and visits, publicizing any honours or special activities of individual employees as well as the company as a whole.
- Make sure employees at all levels are made the most of.

Taken literally, public relations are relations with the public, that public being defined as any and all of the company's target audiences. It is a difficult job, not often appreciated, as the necessary exercise of charm tends to attract cries of 'Insincere!'

Both marketing and public relations are, none the less, essential aspects of business communications that most businesses cannot afford to ignore.

PART IV

WRITTEN COMMUNICATIONS

INTRODUCTION

Written communication is a skill which can be acquired, developed and improved. There are no prizes in business for creative writing. Imagination is only useful to make documents look interesting — business communications and flights of fancy do not mix, and adjectives should be to the point and used only when essential.

Each and every form of written document is judged according to its structure, format and design. Preparation, presentation, production, distribution and assessment are what matters. I am not going to give examples and case studies, analyzing errors and suggesting ways of improving specific points. That has been done more than adequately in dozens of textbooks which you can consult if you need lessons and guidance. What I am going to cover is the principle and technique of written communications. The rules that must be followed and the little extras that make all the difference.

The cardinal rules which must *never* be omitted if you wish to be seen as sensible and credible are:

- Correct all typing errors.
- Check the boring bits — punctuation, grammar, capitalization, spelling.
- Enclose the enclosures.

The next most important rule is to know what you are doing. Before setting pen to paper, determine:

- the purpose of the document;
- who it is aimed at;
- who will actually use or read it;
- how *you* would like it to be used;
- how it is *actually* likely to be used;
- what you want to achieve, how and why.

Then ask yourself:

- Is it necessary?
- Am I adding paper to a mountain that will not be read or remembered?
- Am I writing for my own sake or for that of the reader?
- Is writing the best way to achieve my purpose or would it be better to speak?

It is possible, after all, to have too much of a good thing. Selection is important; none of us enjoys being flooded with paperwork. The time taken to write and read something is invariably far longer than the time required to speak to someone. The time and space required for filing for future reference often creates another job vacancy. Think about whether writing is really necessary or relevant to the situation.

Words of wisdom

It is quality that counts rather than quantity unless, of course, you anticipate posterity demanding evidence of your thoughts and actions. A recent article in the *Guardian* concerned the number of people and the amount of money required to build libraries and museums to house the millions of documents written by American presidents. Apparently every sheet of paper from every administration — with the exception of those shredded for security reasons — is kept and archives made available for study. The sorting, filing, upkeep and servicing have become quite an industry.

One of my colleagues, who does not anticipate anyone in her organization writing anything that will be of museum value, persistently attempts to reduce what she terms '13-page A4 men' to 'two-page A4 men'. She is not trying to cut them down to size but to improve management of their time and her own. Her argument is that editing documents on grounds of length reduces the amount of unnecessary peripheral detail and time it takes to both to write and read thereby getting directly to the essentials.

Preparation

Michael Stevens, in *Improving Your Presentation Skills* emphasizes that you must know your audience and consider who you are writing to, or for, as a first step to determining the best approach to take. He recommends ascertaining the reader's:

- level of education;
- first language — is it English or not?
- profession;
- level of authority;
- knowledge of the subject;
- interest in the subject;
- professional and personal needs;
- organization's character eg conservative or go-ahead.

To this I would add their attitude and the way in which they are likely to receive what you are saying. Are there, for example, any personal prejudices or fears to take into consideration?

Based on the above information, you must then determine:

- whether to take a formal or informal approach;
- whether to write a letter, a memorandum or a report.

And regardless of the answer, you must then produce a logical, informative document that is reader friendly if nothing else. It must have an introduction, a body with clear and specific headings, and a summary. It must be presentable and it must be clear. All of these factors will be discussed in greater detail throughout the remainder of the chapters in this section.

Organization

Logic is the main rule to follow for structure. When preparing to write this book, I first read all the others I planned to use for reference, covering sheets of paper with notes in order to identify the main subject areas.

My notes were headed, by sentence or paragraph, with key words or the names of the authors to whom I wanted to refer when I began writing. The key words and authors' names were then used to alphabetize the notes so that I could keep adding and shuffling. Finding points and thoughts to assemble and cross-reference later was then a very straightforward procedure. I was able to go back over them one at a time in depth, without forgetting anything. Overlaps meant that concentration on one subject could still stimulate ideas on other subjects. I was therefore able to use constant cross-referencing, refer to sections that I had previously written and pull them together in a sensible order. Bits were often moved from one section to another or jotted down and a decision made later about where they belonged.

Checking

Every document you write should always be read and checked for:

- typing errors;
- spelling;
- punctuation and grammar;
- enclosures.

If it is convenient, ask someone else to read lengthy documents as you may be too close to them from having worked on them for a period of time, and see what you think you should see rather than what is actually there. If the document is complicated, then read it aloud with someone else. Proofreading is not an art form. Anyone can do it and everyone should do it.

This cardinal rule may have been overlooked by a publisher whose leaflet was distributed at a human resources development exhibition. The leaflet advertised a range of training titles including books about management strategies and sales techniques as well as a management development library on audio cassettes comprised of both books and cassettes. Those attending the exhibition, receiving the leaflet and most likely to be interested in the products, were middle and senior managers. All of whom you would assume were relatively intelligent and literate. Yet the very first page of the four page leaflet had as its banner headline the words 'Acheiving Excellence'. Was this a deliberate spelling error or an example of poor proofreading? If the former, it certainly came across as the latter. And considering who was distributing the leaflet and who it was being distributed to, it was one of the biggest blunders I have seen for a very long time.

Yet again, there are exceptions to the rule. We all need to know how to write grammatically and punctuate correctly but once we have learned, there are occasions when we can break the rules. We do not have to follow them blindly and there are indeed circumstances when they should not be followed.

The first time I examined a legal document, I automatically picked up my pen, put on my editor's hat and began inserting punctuation all over the place. The document seemed to have been drafted with a deliberate omission of all commas, semi-colons and full stops, making each paragraph a web of words requiring reading, re-reading and re-reading again. My solicitor threw up his hands in horror when he saw what I had done.

Of course it's deliberate, he declared, shocked at my ignorance. Punctuation allows for misinterpretation.

Litigation directly resulting from a lack of communication between two parties to a contract had put a stop to the use of punctuation in legal documents.

Chapter 13

One-to-One Communications

There are any number of documents which are written for the attention of a specific individual only. They are not intended for wider consumption to either internal or external audiences but are purely to communicate certain items of information to a particular person.

Correspondence can be generally limited to two categories. Within those categories there are countless variations but the principles which apply can be adapted to meet virtually any and all requirements.

LETTERS

Anyone who has ever either written or received a business letter will know that it should make its point in the most direct manner possible.

It needs to be neatly set out in paragraphs which each cover one of the items you want to convey in the shortest and most straightforward way you can find. If the letter is only two paragraphs long, all the better. Say what you've got to say and call it quits.

Standard information

There is certain basic information which must be included in every letter you write, specifically:

- your own name and title (both job title and the title by which you prefer to be addressed, eg Ms, Miss, Mrs, Mr, Sir...);
- your company's name;
- your address, telephone, extension and fax number;
- if relevant or necessary, a reference number.

This may seem obvious, but I have received a letter — and not so very long ago — from a major organization which requested a response to various questions contained in the body of the letter but had no address on its letterheading. The organization's name was printed beautifully and impressively, the stationery was obviously quality, but there was no address or telephone number.

As it happened, I did have their address and when I replied I pointed out my assumption that they preferred responses only from those with sufficient initiative to track them down. Obviously if people were unable or unwilling to take the time to find them they were not interested in hearing from them anyway.

Perhaps they felt that they were so well known that everyone had the correct address instantly to hand without being told. Apart from members of Parliament and the royal family, I do not believe this is the case, no matter how large the organization.

In this particular case, their embarrassment was justified. There had been a basic oversight in checking the copy for the stationery before it was printed and for some reason no-one had noticed when the letters were sent out. So the organization failed on a number of counts and, in my case at least, lost a great deal of credibility.

Getting it read

Here I go again — Keep It Short and Simple (KISS). Catch the reader's attention in the first sentence or paragraph. Make sure they know what the letter is about and why it is important for them to read it. If you are taking the trouble to write a letter, you obviously want it read. So make sure the recipient agrees with you and make sure they read it.

Presentation is another element that will determine whether or not your letter is read. Check that there are no typing mistakes, space it out and lay it out so that it is visually attractive, clear and easy on the eye.

The quality of your stationery and letterhead will make an impression on the reader. Take some care over them and ensure that you control the impression you are making.

Precautions

It is difficult to retract something that is in writing. Letters can be taken as legal and binding contracts. It is difficult afterwards to assert that you did not actually mean what you said. Think carefully and phrase your letter carefully.

Do not make an undertaking you may not be willing or able to fulfil. If you are making a complaint, include the phrase 'without prejudice' to ensure that your own words are not used against you at a later date.

Letters are often written to confirm conversations and cover the writer from any possible misunderstanding. They can include either accidental or deliberate misunderstandings, however, and these must be corrected immediately. If you have had a meeting or conversation and receive a letter inaccurately summarizing the content and agreements regarding action, do not let it ride. Respond. Get your own version on record.

Signing off

The way you sign your letter will give the person receiving it some indication of your friendliness or the degree of formality you prefer. You can sign:

- first name only;
- first name and surname, leaving the choice for response up to the other person;
- initials and surname only indicating that you prefer to be addressed more formally.

Direct mail

Although I have also discussed direct mail in Chapter 14 on Corporate Communications, I am mentioning it here in relation to the perception that the recipient is intended to have of receiving a personalized letter.

The combination of word processors, mail/merge software and laser printers enable companies to churn out literally millions of identical letters containing the name and address of the individual for whom they are intended.

The days of Dear Sir or Madam have long since passed. Companies sending out mailshots keep form letters on their word processors to be personalized and printed out *en masse*. Basic text is re-used with the name and address of the recipient inserted through a combination of codes which take information from a list and insert it in the relevant parts of the letter. We are expected to believe that we are the only one in our road who is being contacted or that the company cares enough to write just to us.

Courtesy demands that we find out the name of the person to whom we are writing. Whether you are sending out one letter or one million letters, it is generally acknowledged that there is a better chance of the letter being read and receiving a response if it is addressed to a named individual.

Readymade letters

Not all of us write well. Nor do we always have time to work out what needs to be said. Although many letters have a purpose or content which refer to specific circumstances, there are also certain standard occasions when similar sentiments can be expressed and originality is not called for. There are ways of dealing with this however. Help is at hand.

Jim Denning, in *Readymade Business Letters*, offers examples suitable for every conceivable occasion. He has pleasant letters and abusive letters, letters making complaints and letters responding to complaints, letters asking for something and letters offering something. As well as letters responding to requests and offers. You name it, he has it.

WEKA Publishing offers *Successful Model Letters for Every Business and Private Occasion* in a ring-binder designed to be added to several times a year. The basic version contains no less than 600 pages, offers ideas and suggestions for coping with awkward situations and has recently introduced a section on international correspondence. It is intended to be used as either a model or as complete units without deviation if there is a suitable occasion.

There are other, similar, publications available. Some offer more guidance than others for tailoring model letters to suit your particular requirements and some are more expensive than others. But they are there if you need them and can occasionally serve as useful sources of reference.

Specifications and quotations

The converse of one another, specifications are given by the buyer to the seller, defining what he wants to buy while quotations are given by the seller to the buyer telling him what it will cost.

Colin Robinson identifies, in *Winning at Business Negotiations*, the objectives that buyer and seller are trying to achieve. According to Robinson, the buyer wants to:

- identify the most suitable suppliers for quotations;
- indicate the importance of competitive pricing;
- demonstrate what concessions may be given, but only against substantial cost savings;
- emphasize the importance of guaranteed delivery against financial penalties;
- illustrate the value of dealing with his organization;
- ensure that vendors fully understand the bid evaluation criteria to be used.

The seller, according to Robinson, wants to:

- be the sole tenderer if possible or to obtain a place on the list of tenderers;
- feed in the view that his is the only truly satisfactory product;
- illustrate the advantages of dealing with his company and using his products;
- indicate why his product is worth a higher price;
- have the delivery time adjusted to suit his delivery schedule;
- assess the price that the buyer has in mind and any technical concessions that might be available.

The two other factors, which Robinson points out, of mutual interest, are:

- the likelihood of arranging future longer term trading relationships;
- opportunities for the vendor to provide other goods or services, or to supply other parts of the same organization.

All of these factors must be identified before either the specification or the quotation can be prepared. It is in light of the answers to these questions that buyer and seller know how to construct their proposal and response.

Time management

Two extremely large companies I spoke to about their procedures told similar tales of delays encountered in producing letters, reports, proposals, specifications and other documents.

A number of senior managers complained about the number of colleagues who shared the same secretary and were therefore subjected to lengthy delays while she made time to type their correspondence. Each of them submit handwritten sheets of paper, painstakingly inscribed as neatly and legibly as possible so that the secretary can read them easily, then grumble about the length of time it takes to get them typed. It is particularly difficult to read various styles of writing and the writer has to take pains to be as neat and legible as possible.

The solution, they uniformly felt, was to increase the number of secretaries available. It did not occur to them, or if it did, was not acceptable, that they should each type their own correspondence. In the same time it took them to handwrite each page they could just as easily use a typewriter or word processor and save everyone's time. If alterations or amendments were necessary when using a secretary, then still more time and delay ensued while the manager waited for the secretary to correct things which he then had to check yet again.

On reflection, I must add a proviso here. Not everyone is computer literate or quick at the keyboard or interested enough to learn how to cope with a word processor. The technicalities of using a typewriter or word processor can be so daunting that far more time is wasted in learning how to use it than actually using it. In such instances there is no point even trying. Resistance to learning will prevent learning every time and there is no point in even trying to teach someone who refuses to absorb the information. There are some people who do not feel comfortable without a pen or dictaphone in their hand and could not, under any except the most dire circumstances, put words to paper with hi-tech equipment being used as an intermediary.

Nor do I mean to suggest that secretaries are an unnecessary feature of the manager's life. Their administrative skills and abilities — which include turning their boss's thoughts into comprehensive communiqués — are often indispensable. When I mentioned earlier that it is preferable to use a craftsman to do a task than to spend the time of someone who is more skilled at a different task struggling to do the job, I should have specifically included secretaries. There is no point at all in a manager spending time slaving over a keyboard when his secretary can produce the same document in a fraction of the time. So long as his words or thoughts are transmitted accurately to the secretary, this is a form of communicating through an intermediary which is far more efficient than either doing it yourself or trying to deal with technology.

Chapter 14

Corporate Communications

The form that corporate communications take must depend largely on:

- the target audience;
- the message;
- the reason for the message.

Answering some of the questions raised in the Introduction to Part IV will enable you to determine the best approach for each given situation. The way in which a report, business plan or brochure is presented must be influenced by where it is going and why.

WAY TO GO

Language and its use, when to use or not use jargon, when to use simple words and sentence structures is a pretty volatile issue. Some people will tell you that you should:

- always stick to Plain English;
- use words of one syllable;
- use single words rather than phrases.

They will advise that:

- sentences should generally contain no more than 20 words;
- paragraphs should generally contain no more than three to four sentences.

Other people will insist that this smacks of patronizing the reader — which is where knowing who you are writing for comes into the issue. Oversimplification may occasionally be necessary if you are explaining a complex technological point to an audience of lay people. As a rule there is an argument for assuming some basic minimal level of intelligence in the reader.

John Fletcher and David Gowing do not agree with this view. They are strong advocates of the audience-as-simpleton theory of writing, going so far as to give the example that the word 'write' can be a better choice than the word 'communicate'. Try this example and see if you agree. Do you think that the phrase

I am writing to you because....

is better, or clearer, than the phrase

I need to communicate with you because...?

Fletcher and Gowing follow the advice of H W Fowler and Sir Ernest Gowers, long recognized as authority figures in the field of clear speaking (or writing). They further maintain, in their book *The Business Guide to Effective Writing*, that accusations of patronizing the reader are unjust. They say that 'this fear must be responsible for much of the long-winded language written today. But ask yourself how often in the past you have read documents that you felt were written in such simple language that you felt insulted; if the answer is 'never', forget about the risk of "talking down".'

They may be right and they may be wrong. Context, as I have said before, quoting my Latin teacher of old, will tell.

Business plans

Business plans can be used internally and externally. When used for internal purposes, they can identify and describe what the business is doing, how, why and where it is going. When used for external purposes, they generally identify the same information but with the intention of selling the business to someone else. Either literally or figuratively. Business plans are, as Brian Jenks of Touche Ross says, a *sine qua non* when seeking to expand and obtain additional finance. He explained in an article for the *Observer* in May 1991 that business plans:

- review products, services and markets to confirm the essentials of the business;
- assess whether or not there is a case for consolidating production lines or reducing the number of locations or offices;
- assess whether or not there is a case for cutting down on the number of products or departing from certain markets or subcontracting fewer functions;
- can identify how changes should be made and by whom as well as what the consequences will be in terms of cash flow, profit and confidence in the business.

The golden rule of communication applies to business plans. Keep It Short and Simple. Do not waffle. Present the facts and do not embellish or camouflage them.

It is widely known that most business plans, particularly those presented in the hopes of raising finance, are tossed aside and never read. They are first weighed and if they are too heavy or too unwieldy, immediately discarded. Here, more than anywhere else, it is quality that counts rather than quantity.

Business plans should be as short as possible with the bones, that is hard facts, alone forming the body. They should then be fleshed out with support material in appendices.

Do not put anything that is essential into the appendices. Make sure that they contain useful but supplementary information and that the reader doesn't actually have to refer to them in order to get the gist of what you are proposing.

Do not force the reader to rifle through pages, referring backwards and forwards from one part of the plan to the other in order to understand it.

It is sometimes because plans are too difficult to read that they are left unread. If someone picks it up, looks at it and sees page after page of closely written script they are not likely to make the effort no matter how important it is to you.

Annual reports

No one knows a business better than the people in it but they may not be the best people to put together a presentation for external consumption. As mentioned elsewhere, experts and craftsmen should be called in to do the jobs at which we may not ourselves be skilled.

Thus the growing need for, and existence of, corporate communications consultancies. Communications specialists, design and editorial teams will come into the business, talk to people, get a feel for what goes on. They will then go away and turn the information into a brochure or report that will communicate the corporate message in a manner that is interesting, informative and attractive. Readers will want to read it.

Annual reports are generally presented to stockholders, employees and other interested parties to let them know what the company has been up to for the past twelve months. Although they must be accurate and honest, they should also be confident and positive.

Among the audiences that will read the report are potential investors, the media and general public and, not least of all, the competition. Reports should include details of:

- new product development;
- profit and loss;
- growth or contraction;
- assessment;
- plans for the future.

They need to answer questions that the target audience is likely to ask and pre-empt any possible awkward responses. They need to be clearly presented and, like all other forms of written communication, visually appealing. Photographs and illustrations of location, employees and products will give readers a more accurate understanding of what the business is all about. Some background or introductory information should be included for those who are reading about the company for the first time.

Details should be presented as graphically as possible, using tables and charts to explain patterns of change. Statistics are often thought to be confusing but they do have a great deal of value. Avoiding them can be interpreted as a sin of omission thus they should be included but in as clear a manner as possible.

Marketing and sales materials

Arthur Andersen & Co, who claim to be 'one of the world's leading professional organizations', recently advertised for two communications specialists. The jobs entailed working on publications which were considered to be 'an important element in our marketing mix'. In fact, they were looking for writers and editors but felt it sufficiently important to stress the fact that the successful candidate would 'make a crucial contribution to the impact and effectiveness of our total communications'. Now there's acknowledgement for you of the value of written communications.

Direct mail

Direct mail is used as means of marketing and selling everything from insurance to cars. Audiences must be targeted tightly, the words and designs carefully selected and produced in such a way that people will read it rather than throw it in the bin.

Incentives are usually splashed all over them to stimulate interest. Teasers, promises of wonderful gifts, discounts and prizes fall through our letterboxes every day. With the advent of hi-tech equipment, mailing lists are sold to anyone with the cash to pay for them and it is exceedingly difficult to avoid the barrage.

Making your mailshot the one that is read is extremely difficult. But there are consultants and advisers and seminars and courses and books and videos and countless other bits of paraphernalia to help. A whole new industry has sprung up. Salesmanship has grown a new arm.

Contracts

Contracts, as far as I am concerned, are one of life's necessary evils. They protect both sides of an agreement but, as I stated in Chapter 7 on Negotiations, each side is out for what it can get. We all want to protect our own interests and although we may try to let the other side in a legal agreement protect theirs as well, our own must take priority.

Lawyers are a band of people who we allow to help us in this endeavour. They represent our interests and fight for our rights. In the process, however, they make a great deal of money for themselves by creating work that may not always be absolutely essential. It is to their advantage to complicate issues and, while they are indubitably doing this in their clients' best interests, simplification is not generally a lawyer's strong point.

Twice in as many years I have been involved in negotiations that have become so protracted and costly that the contracts have been torn up and a simple exchange of letters substituted.

In both instances, the parties involved had agreed the terms of their relationship and it was only when each side's solicitors were brought in that complications ensued. Meetings, drafts, delays, investigations and debates about protection, clarification, coverage and contingency so bogged everything down that the negotiations nearly fell completely to pieces. It was only because both sides were determined to see the deals go through that they were resolved.

What had started as a straightforward agreement for one company to provide a service to the other was turned into a document of nearly 100 pages on each occasion. The bulk of each document, furthermore, was written in language that only another lawyer could understand. None of the parties in either instance felt comfortable with their own understanding.

They all became dependent on their lawyers to advise them what to think, say and do. Advice which they felt was not what they had in mind at all sometimes resulted. The lack of communication resulting from the lack of clarity of the documentation was only remedied by effective personal communication.

Contracts can also be used as a means of including details that were not discussed or agreed during negotiations. This kind of afterthought is again covered in Chapter 7 on Negotiations. But it must be stated here: read between the lines and do not sign unless the piece of paper reflects what you want it to.

Martin Cutts of Words at Work has written a version of his *Clear English Charter* specifically to cover legal documents. Both the Charter and the amendments for lawyers are given in the Appendix on Jargon.

Did you do well?

John Fletcher and David Gowing offer advice in *The Business Guide to Effective Writing* on how to verify the success of your written communication. Their guidelines can be applied to all forms of written communication, whether intended for internal or external audiences.

The answers to the following questions should all be 'Yes'.

- Does the document make a good first impression?
- Is it easy to find the answers to possible questions?

- Are all possible questions answered and, if not, is it clear why they are not?
- Is there a clear statement of purpose and is it positioned at the beginning of the document?
- Are the headings and table of contents sufficiently clear for the reader to find what he is looking for and to see what has been included or excluded?
- Does the material covered under each heading contain what the heading implies that it contains?
- Is the meaning of the document clear and unambiguous?
- Does the document sound knowledgeable and confident without being arrogant or patronizing?
- Is it written in words that anyone can understand?
- Is it laid out in a way that is clear and easy to read? Are the sentences and paragraphs short and spaced out so that they are visually attractive and effective?

The answers to the following questions should all be 'No'.

- Have you used more words, or more complicated words, than is strictly necessary?
- Will the reader have to read any passages twice in order to understand your meaning?
- Is the document monotonous or boring or repetitive?
- Does the document assume knowledge, attitudes or values that readers may not share?

The traditional Boy Scout motto, Be Prepared, will stand anyone writing a business document in good stead. If you know your audience, and know your objectives, getting the message across will be immensely simplified.

Chapter 15

Communications for Information

The biggest problem with providing or receiving information verbally is that it can be forgotten. The listener may not hear you correctly or may not entirely understand. Repeating the information or providing it in written form for easy and frequent reference overcomes the problem.

Written communication should be supported by verbal communication. As this is not always possible, the document must be written on the assumption that it is self-contained. The writer must assume that the reader will not be able to ask questions and therefore must explain every point in sufficient detail to make it unambiguous and comprehensive.

MANUALS

Manuals are written for the purpose of giving instructions. They are intended to show the reader how to make something work, or how to assemble it and how to understand it. They are, unfortunately, prone themselves to incomprehensibility. They are written by people who understand what they are explaining but often do not know how to explain to people who do not understand.

Trying to learn a new skill or a new job, or accomplish a new task without advice, teaching, or instruction of some sort is certainly possible with a certain amount of time, patience and intelligence. It is not ideal though and most of us prefer a bit of expert guidance.

There are, of course, those who prefer not to read instructions but they should still be given the option — there should be instructions available if they want them.

Instructions and technical manuals

Manufacturers of flatpack furniture often supply instructions, starting with the injunction to:

- sit down and put your feet up;
- have a cup of tea;
- stay calm;
- read the instructions through from beginning to end; *then*
- unpack the box;
- do an inventory;
- lay out all the bits in the order they will be needed.

The ease or difficulty of understanding, especially if the information being conveyed is technical, depends entirely on the skill of whoever has written the manual. Not on the person who designed the product but on the person who communicated the instructions.

Computer manuals are notoriously complex and difficult to understand by the layman. And as most of us now use computers or word processors and still come under the heading of laymen, trying to learn from the manual can be a near impossibility.

One piece of software used in my office came complete with no fewer than ten manuals. Three years later, I still don't know all that the software is capable of doing let alone being able to do it. There is a sense of euphoria and overwhelming accomplishment whenever something suddenly begins to make sense. Each obstacle that is overcome is considered a breakthrough and for a little while we can go on at a much faster rate. (Until the next barrier is reached, that is.)

And this is all, ostensibly, in English which is my mother tongue. I have also attempted to use manuals that have been translated into English from some other language. So the writer needs an extra skill. He must:

- understand what he is explaining;
- be able to explain it;
- be sufficiently multilingual to explain it in a language other than his own.

This is yet another form of international communications. But then again, perhaps anyone writing a technical manual needs to be multilingual in any case.

House style and identity manuals

Minale, Tattersfield & Partners are international design consultants specializing in corporate and financial literature, corporate identities, packaging and a range of related design services. They have produced corporate identities for such organizations as the Home Office, Central

Television, Harrods, Jewsons Builders Merchants, the Port of Dover and the House of Fraser to name but a few. Their promotional package detailing some of these states:

> When a new corporate identity has been designed, it must be implemented. Communicating the objectives of the new image and the necessary information to implement it throughout many different levels within the organization is a complex problem to handle, but the process is made easier when it starts with a well-designed corporate identity application manual.

Creating an image and formulating an identity are well and good but they must be communicated and communicated consistently. Those producing written documents on behalf of the organization must be aware of house rules and style.

In some instances there are rules about the size and position of logos on various types of stationery, be it letterheads, brochures, invoices or whatever. This kind of detail is not transmitted by osmosis. Anyone likely to need the information should have access to a style manual which clearly sets out corporate requirements.

Within one business I know, there is a standard house manual on file which can be added to at any time by any member of staff. When new procedures are established or established procedures refined, the manual is automatically updated. This is meant to help others learn or remember things that are new or not frequently required. It is also used as a training manual for new employees. Although new members of staff are supervised and talked through procedures, they are also given a copy of the manual for reference until such time as they feel comfortable with what is expected of them.

If there is no house style, perhaps someone ought to stop and ask, should there be one? Is it important for documents to be formatted consistently and, if so, shouldn't someone prepare some sample formats that others can refer to?

Nicholas Ind, in *The Corporate Image*, points out that corporate identity manuals need not be followed slavishly but that 'if an organization does want to project a coherent statement about itself, then there should be a commonality of style.'

Particularly when companies use a range of outside agencies and consultancies to fulfil their publication requirements, a consistent policy must be prepared and supplied to prevent a range of disparate interpretations.

Handbooks and employee manuals

Handbooks, employee or orientation manuals, are all designed to tell employees what the company believes and does as well as what staff are expected to do, when and how. They:

- help employees understand what the company does;

- help employees understand their roles and responsibilities, what is expected of them and what they will get in return;
- resolve any possible misunderstandings;
- explain company policy on issues of importance and interest to employees;
- explain company structure and the hierarchy that queries and complaints must pass through.

They can set out company policies, objectives and functions clearly for all to see, starting with:

- a welcome from the chairman or managing director;
- brief company history;
- outline of company structure;
- description of products and services;
- plans for the future.

Susan Brock and Sally Cabbell, in *How to Write a Staff Manual* say that among the subjects which may need to be covered are:

- conditions of employment;
- wages and bonuses;
- legislated and voluntary benefits;
- health and safety;
- company standards and rules;
- industrial relations;
- training;
- communication procedures;
- philosophy and important policies.

The best people to identify what needs to be covered in a staff manual are the staff. Interviews and questionnaires can be used to determine the general areas which need to be covered and then a draft of the manual circulated for comment. Interviews should be held with members of staff in different departments and at different levels. Questionnaires can also be distributed. In addition, moving one step up the ladder, managers generally know what their staff ought to know, do know, want to know and need to know.

Brock and Cabbell recommend asking managers:

- What are your major and/or most frequent employee problems?
- What subjects do your employees ask questions about over and over again?
- Which company policies are least understood by employees?
- Which employee benefits or privileges are most frequently asked about?

They then recommend that trial groups should consider the draft of the manual. These groups should consist of employees selected from a cross-section of departments and levels. In this way, staff in all departments and at all levels will have their views represented.

The draft manual should be distributed in advance of the meeting so that departmental discussion can take place and opinions taken by the representatives to the assessment meeting. Following the meeting, changes agreed should be made and the final manual printed and distributed to every employee.

Staff manuals, once written, should not be handed out blindly for ever more. They require regular updating, modification and additions because no company remains stagnant. An annual review and revision is highly recommended.

GATHERING INFORMATION

In addition to interviews and group discussions, forms and question-naires provide an excellent way of gathering information. Their advantage is that all of the information can be collated and analyzed simultaneously, without reference to notes and judgements that may have been made by others about responses. The recipients' answers will speak for themselves without being coloured by the interviewers' judgement.

How much to disclose

If, however, you are using a form or questionnaire you need to give some indication of the purpose of the exercise and what you are trying to achieve. How much detail you give depends on who you are giving the questionnaire to, why and what you hope to get in return.

Consumer questionnaires, for example, often ask enormous quantities of irrelevant questions because the interviewee is not supposed to know what information is actually being sought. This can serve to prevent people providing answers and information to conform with what they think the interviewer wants to know.

Personnel officers frequently use questionnaires which follow a similar pattern. They are trying to find out what job applicants' views and attitudes are without coming right out and asking them directly. They need to know how they will respond in certain circumstances and what their patterns of reasoning may be.

With this type of questionnaire, it is often advisable to ask the same question several times albeit worded differently each time it appears. Thus you can verify the information supplied.

What do you want to know?

When setting out to design a form or questionnaire, you have to decide what information you want to get and why. The next step is to order the questions logically. Determining what to ask follows the same pattern as devising a specification. You must think through all the applications and ramifications, know your objectives, then work backwards to decide what you want and need to know.

The format must also be considered. Think about the way in which the responses will be analyzed and used then decide whether it is easier to correlate short answers to multiple choice questions or free form, unlimited comments. Either way, make sure that you:

- word and space the questions clearly;
- ask one question at a time;
- leave enough space for the answers.

As with all other forms of communication, it is also essential to know your audience. You must target it very carefully in order to get the highest response rate. There is no point at all in asking people to fill in questionnaires on a subject which is of no interest or importance to them whatsoever. That is the best possible way of getting the lowest possible response rate.

Multilingual questionnaires

If you are gathering information from a number of countries, you will have to decide:

- whether one language is enough and if not, which languages and how many should be used;
- which language to send to each country for example French or German or English to Switzerland;
- is the possible variation in response rate due to languages sufficient to affect the results achieved.

Paul Gibbs, in *Doing Business in the European Community*, presents a table detailing the percentages of adults in Europe speaking various European languages. Although English is spoken by 13 – 68 per cent of those in Belgium, Denmark, France, Germany, Italy, the Netherlands and Spain, some allowance must be made for those who do not speak English or, indeed, any language other than their own. In Spain, for example, 3 per cent of adults speak German, 4 per cent speak Italian, 13 per cent speak English and 15 per cent speak French. In Italy, 6 per cent speak German, 5 per cent speak Spanish, 13 per cent speak English and 27 per cent speak French.

When an American publisher recently attempted to compile information on consultancies pan-Europe, they insisted on sending questionnaires out in English only. They believed that anyone doing business at an international level must speak English. They received a 15 per cent response rate to their questionnaires. This was far less than they had hoped for and the question had to be asked, would more people have responded had the questionnaire been in their own language?

Reports

An author of my acquaintance is very fond of repeating a lesson taught him by his first editor — 'murder your darlings,' he intoned. My friend has practised this for forty-odd years and reminds everyone he knows that it is absolutely the most important rule to follow no matter what you are writing. We have all heard about films that end up with far more on the cutting room floor than ever reaches our screens. The same applies to written communications. Unless you are writing fiction, do not use flowery language. Do not grow too fond of what you have written. Stick to the point. Do not use two words where one will do or two syllables where one will suffice.

Preparation

Before you begin to write your report, you must think about:

- the purpose of the document;
- who it is aimed at;
- who will actually use or read it;
- how you would like it to be used;
- how it is actually likely to be used;
- what you want to achieve, how and why.

Trevor Bentley, in *Report Writing in Business* maintains that you should only write a report:

- if you need agreement to a course of action;
- if you need to explain specific events;
- as a basis for discussion;
- to inform.

You should never write a report, Bentley says,

- because you have been asked to;
- if you cannot think of a good reason.

You must also do some homework about the audience. You need to know their

- level of education;
- level of authority;
- knowledge of the subject;
- interest in the subject;
- attitude towards the subject.

Structure

Reports need a beginning, a middle and an end. They must have an introduction in which the reader is told what the report is about. They must have a body in which the reader is told what you want him to know. And they must have a summary in which you tell the reader what you have told him.

Length is not important; content and presentation are. There should be short paragraphs, lots of headings and bullet points, a lack of jargon and statistics and perhaps some illustrations either in the form of stories or figures or pictures.

Subheadings, short paragraphs and sections that make their point quickly without waffle or camouflage are the ideal form for a report. Bullets and highlights should be designed for people with neither the time nor the inclination to read lengthy documents. You have to attract their attention and hook them, convincing them to read what you have taken the time and trouble to write.

Use plenty of examples to illustrate your points, for those that prefer to learn through others' experiences. These can be skipped by serious readers if they choose. Use graphics to make a visual point and dilute words or sugar coat them so they are painless to those not interested in reading.

The progression and presentation of points and arguments should be logical. Although you may jump around from one to another when drafting the document, by the time you are finished, you need to pull things together again. Do not go off on tangents.

Consultation documents

Consultation documents are actually drafts which need to be discussed before completion. They are generally put together by a committee which conducts the initial research, frequently based on a combination of interviews, questionnaires, meetings, conferences or workshops.

The committee then analyzes the information and opinions received, produces a draft document and initiates the consultation process. Proposals and recommendations are constructed and submitted to others for their opinions. Experts and individuals and groups which will be directly concerned by the outcome are then consulted before the final document is adopted. It is also sent up the ladder internally.

The feedback received is again analyzed, the document rewritten and a final draft presented. This procedure is used widely in industry but is also an essential stage for legislation or change of any sort in government.

Michael Heseltine once told an audience, during the consultation period for what became the 1988 Education Act, that the bulk of the work was being done by civil servants who knew their job. The consultation process, he asserted, was required but not actually necessary as the important decisions had already been made.

This is sometimes, but not always the case. It is during the consultation period that anyone with an opinion has the opportunity to be heard. Certainly, those preparing the draft have the hardest job but part of their job is to incorporate significant changes suggested by those being consulted. Whether you are one of those creating the draft, or one of those being consulted, this is another instance where two way communication must be encouraged rather than avoided or eliminated.

Memoranda

The difference between memoranda and letters is that the latter are personal and generally intended for one individual only. Although they may be copied to others for reference, they are primarily written to communicate with a specific individual.

Memoranda, on the other hand, are more general and provide information for a number of people simultaneously. They are set out to provide information only and do not normally expect any response.

Memoranda should be headed as follows:

- To: the names of the people to whom it will be circulated (list these one below the other for ease of reference)
- From: the name of the person who has written it
- Re: the subject to be covered
- Date:

Everyone receiving a memorandum needs to know who else has received it and who therefore has the information it contains.

Announcements

Announcements, particularly those put up on notice boards for anyone who passes to read, should be eye-catching. Presumably they are going to tell people something they do not yet know and which they need to know. They are going to convey some important message and you want to be sure that it is received.

This is the time to use a large, perhaps shocking or catchy heading, to make sure people look at it.

Do not use prose to pad it out. No one will want to know the whys and wherefores, just get to the point.

If necessary, make a list if there are several facets of your news to convey.

Space out the paragraphs and number them if you like. Use pretty or bright colours and highlights and different typefaces and exclamation marks. Use whatever tools you can find. Do whatever you have to do to get that announcement read.

Minutes and agendas

Minutes of a meeting must reflect the agenda which in its turn follows a set pattern:

- apologies;

- minutes of previous meeting;
- matters arising from minutes;
- correspondence;
- chairman's report;
- secretary's report;
- treasurer's report;
- sub-committee reports;
- any other business;
- time and place of next meeting.

Any special issues which need to be covered normally follow the sub-committee reports.

Obviously not every meeting is going to include every one of those items but committees will certainly want to know what is going on with its members and will probably include most of the items listed above. Task oriented groups or groups of people who get together occasionally in order to deal with specific issues, will find the menu less relevant although it can still be used as a guide to structuring the meeting. For example

- Apologies can be equated to an introduction of who is attending or not and why their presence or absence is important to the task at hand.

- Minutes of previous meeting can be equated to a summary of research that has been conducted prior to the meeting and is pertinent to the discussion.

- Matters arising from minutes can be equated to a discussion of the subject at hand.

- Correspondence can be related to documentation obtained to support various points of view on the subject at hand.

- Reports can be replaced by discussion although this does need to be structured in order to achieve the objective set for the meeting.

- Any other business can be related to planning a strategy and deciding on action to be taken.

- Time and place of next meeting, and whether or not one is required must still be determined.

Minutes cover every subject on the agenda and note views presented to the meeting but do not have to transcribe statements word for word. They should summarize only. For ease of reference, they should also highlight actions agreed and by whom.

Training materials

Training materials, or what Peter Sheal in *How to Develop and Present Staff Training Courses* refers to as participant handbooks, are used during and after training courses. They contain relevant information which may support the course and help to ensure that what is learned is not forgotten as soon as it ends. Training materials can take the form of:

- fact sheets;
- diagrams;
- case studies and any role play materials that may be needed;
- reprints of articles or abstracts from books which relate to the subjects being covered;
- background material about the course content and the leaders or speakers;
- background material about other participants;
- an outline of the course's aims and objectives;
- an agenda or outline of the strategy and procedures to be followed;
- an outline or recommendation for the structure of discussions and tasks including worksheets to be completed;
- quizzes and questionnaires to be used for assessment before, during and after the course;
- copies of any speeches that may be presented;
- suggestions for further work or reading.

Sheal points out that much of this material only becomes relevant or necessary during the course itself and should therefore not all be distributed at the outset. He recommends providing a folder or ring binder to each participant which can have material added to it throughout the course. A title sheet with the subject, objectives and agenda for the course should be included in the initial presentation pack, along with blank sheets for notes and comments. Section dividers to separate the various modules of the course can also be useful when referring back to course materials at a later date.

Conference materials

Conference materials can include:

- agendas;
- copies of talks to be presented;
- drafts of suggested structures for discussion groups;
- descriptions of any tasks or objectives intended to be achieved;
- background material on the subject of the conference;
- background information on speakers.

Packs containing this material, with the addition of a notepad and pen or pencil, in a neat cover labelled with the subject, date and venue of the conference, should be distributed to delegates on arrival.

Labels

Most of us want to know, when buying something, where it comes from and what it contains. There are now laws to make sure that certain information is always provided. Consumers have demanded, and now must receive, information regarding ingredients, additives, preservatives, irradiation and other treatments which their food undergoes.

Again, some people have found a way of circumventing the requirement and communicating in such a way that no information at all is provided other than to those who understand the language. Code numbers, technical terms and confusing jargon on labels have been used to conform to regulations without actually communicating.

Presentation, graphics and illustrations

At the very least, written communications should be presented in a way that is neat and tidy, word perfect, visually pleasing if not actually attractive, clear and easy on the eye, easy to read and spaced out with frequent breaks. They should also be bound into folders and not just stapled or clipped together. There should be a covering sheet and, if length justifies it, a table of contents and index. Any figures or illustrations used should be listed at the beginning. In short, they should look professional and businesslike.

Headings and bullet points, as mentioned above, should flag the subject about to be covered, rather than leaving it buried in the middle of paragraph or page. Diagrams should be used to help readers visualise the points you are making.

The use of desktop publishing to enhance the presentation and design of written communications is covered in Chapter 16. We are not all designers and sometimes people get carried away with the facilities of desktop publishing. There is an in-between stage though. Within reason, different typefaces and sizes can be used to make the document more attractive and to indicate points that need to be highlighted. Graphics and illustrations can be incorporated. Simple, basic improvements to presentation can be made by all of us if we think carefully about the types of document we find easy to read.

Reference material

Generally accepted and essential reference books which should sit prominently and accessibly on every manager's shelf include:

- at least one dictionary;
- *Roget's Thesaurus*;
- *Modern English Usage* by H W Fowler;
- *The Complete Plain Words* by Sir Ernest Gowers.

Additionally, there are books which will help you along every step of the way in your efforts to communicate effectively. Specific titles are available on leadership, relationships, training, presentation, letter writing and virtually every subject touched on in this book. There are also consultancies and organizations, such as those listed in the Directory on page 314, which will provide advice and someone to talk to. There is no need to work in isolation and no way that you will communicate effectively if you do.

Chapter 16

Fit to Print

Despite the availability of ever more sophisticated technology — interactive videos, closed circuit television, electronic mail boxes — nothing has yet satisfactorily replaced the written word when it comes to relaying information within a company or about that company to the outside world.

Among the advantages of written communication are:

- It is relatively inexpensive and endlessly adaptable — memos, bulletins, posters, newsletters, newspapers, brochures, press releases, manuals, charts, reports, leaflets.
- It can be closely targeted and tailored for a specialist readership — production department, typing pool, sales team, cricket club, warehouse staff.
- Distribution methods are flexible — to individuals at home, in wage packets, to desks or work stations, to departments or to central collection points or meeting places.
- It can be easily and quickly produced in large quantities so that important company news and announcements can reach a wide audience with the minimum delay.
- It is a great antidote to rumour and gossip, that is, industry's oldest, most potent and innaccurate communications medium — the grapevine!

Among the more serious disadvantages are:

- There is invariably too much of it; it takes time, effort and motivation to read and absorb any written material; the sheer weight of printed material which bombards us at home and at work tends to be counterproductive.

- It is often written by people with poor communication skills; computer technicians and accountants, for example, may be whizz kids at their own subjects but are invariably hopelessly out of their depth when it comes to relaying their specialist knowledge to others — annual report and computer manuals are classic examples.
- In smaller firms, particularly, the process of writing reports, memos, letters, minutes etc can take up a disproportionate amount of executive and staff time deflecting key personnel from their primary work and profit-making core activities.
- Parkinson's Law dicates that paperwork begets more paperwork which begets more paperwork.

It was all much simpler back in the days of yore. Industrial communications in a nineteenth century Manchester workshop consisted of a poster stuck on the wall citing a series of fines which would be imposed upon spinners who disobeyed company regulations!

Companies today are more enlightened, but even the most well-intentioned managers sometimes send out clumsy directives, not that far removed — in tone at least — from the autocratic workhouse poster style.

Company regulations or instructions, for example, should be presented as information not as curt commands. A bald, new directive such as:

It is forbidden to take any drinks or food whatsoever into the typing pool.

may well raise hackles. Fleshed out with the background — and just six words longer — the new regulation becomes a reasonable and acceptable statute:

Food and drink must not be taken into the typing pool as spillages can cause serious damage to wordprocessing equipment.

BACK TO BASICS

Written communication is all about providing information with clarity and precision. If you leave the reader asking

Why is he telling me this?
    or
What does this mean?

you have wasted your own and your readers' valuable time. As that prolific wordsmith, Keith Waterhouse, has observed, 'It would be interesting to know the cost to industry and commerce of incomprehensibility. Every document that has to be read two or three times before its meaning can be grasped costs money in wasted time.'

There are countless books on style, grammar, structure, editing and the supposedly correct way to set down the English language. But for most formal business purposes the simple acid test is always:

Have I made myself clear?

This is not always an easy question to answer. Take technical jargon for example. Again to quote the ever-inventive Keith Waterhouse, 'Jargon, like sex, is all right between consenting parties. It is a form of shorthand for experts communicating only with each other, in language which to the outsider is as ancient Greek.'

The problem is that, most of the time, the expert isn't even aware that he is using jargon. This becomes a serious impediment when trying to communicate with a lay audience. The best advice in such circumstances is to find a few non-expert guinea pigs to read through the text before you go public. If they understand every word, you can publish without being damned. If they find it incomprehensible, in whole or in part, then it's back to the drawing board. As anyone who makes a living out of writing will tell you, re-writes come with the territory.

Official paperwork...how to survive it

A few simple rules will ensure that writers and readers alike suffer the least irritation from outbreaks of official paperwork:

- First, always ask yourself — is this document really necessary? It may be quicker and easier to pick up the telephone. Or, it may be that there is nothing really vital to communicate at all.
- Keep it short. Even professional writers have a tendency to over-write (that's why newspapers and publishers employ editors and sub-editors). Read what you have written and then ruthlessly cut out as much you can without harming the thrust of your message.
- In long documents always provide a summary of the main points, preferably at the beginning.
- Develop a clear, jargon free, uncluttered style:
  - use one word instead of two or more, for example *'quickly'* instead of *'with the minimum of delay'*;
  - use *plain* English not flowery or mannered prose, for example 'perhaps' instead of 'perchance';
  - be grammatical but don't get hung up on split infinitives and hanging participles; if a sentence reads well and can be easily understood then it's probably grammatically correct. If the meaning can be made even clearer by breaking the rules then by all means do so. But get to know the rules first.
- Always marshal your thoughts before you put pen to paper; think about the information you want to convey, the order in which you want to say it, who will be reading it and the response you want to provoke.
- Write a draft copy, read it through with a critical eye and make sure your message is clear before you commit to your final version. If it rambles, cut out the dead wood. If it's confused or incomprehensible, start again using a fresh approach.

- Keep the reader interested. In longer documents particularly, use devices such as sub-headings, bullet points and graphics. Vary the length of sentences and try not to pack more than one thought into a sentence.

ALL THE NEWS THAT'S FIT TO PRINT...

Newsletters, newspapers and magazines are ideal for spreading company news in a palatable, user-friendly, non-officious manner.

The best of these are well-designed, bright, cheerful, newsy publications which easily hold their own against their slick, commercial, newsstand counterparts.

The worst of these – and there are still far too many – are dire in the extreme. Poorly designed and written, they are little more than a vehicle for company PR puffs and boardroom trumpeting. Their heavy-handed, patronizing attempts to dress up management propaganda in the form of news is less than convincing to their readers and of benefit solely to the nation's waste paper merchants.

Get it right and you have a superb vehicle for generating feelings of confidence, unity and pride amongst employees of even the most fragmented of companies.

Get it wrong and you can actually exacerbate feelings of alienation and mistrust. We all adopt a healthy cynicism when it comes to the transparent, vote-catching emissions of politicians. Many senior directors have a similar affect on their readers when they rush into print with thinly disguised management propaganda.

Grabbing the reader's interest

Why do so many company news publications fail? First, as any newspaper proprietor or editor will tell you, it's important to appreciate the competition.

People *have* to turn up at work and do the jobs for which they've been engaged — at least if they want to be paid. They don't *have* to read company newspapers.

It's one thing to publish a newspaper but, as Eddy Shah will testify, it's quite another to get people to read the damn thing.

All news publications compete for reading time with a huge deluge of information/media output which attacks our daily lives from all quarters. This ranges from daily newspapers — The *Financial Times* and the *Sun* — to *Practical Beekeeping*, *Computer World*, *Brass Band Monthly*, *Hot Car*, *Cosmopolitan*, *History Today*, *Viz* and the Am Dram or Tennis Club newsletter.

Add to this the bombardment of images and information from television, advertising, direct mail, social, official *and* business correspondence and you have a real job on your hands trying to hold people's attention for more than two minutes at a time.

Not all the cards are stacked against you, however. Employees are usually eager to read about important new developments such as:

- changes in pay structures;
- major new contracts which will secure their jobs;
- company successes in which they have played a part;
- union negotiations;
- the timetable for a new canteen.

And, of course, the 'gossipy' bits are always popular:

- who's getting married, leaving, joining, being promoted;
- the hidden talents of colleagues (I once interviewed a taxman who had a second career as an international concert singer!);
- the fortunes of the company's football or hockey team.

Don't try and second guess your readers. Find out at first hand what they want to read and when you've published your first edition, do a reader survey to find out what they think of it. Examine other national, local and company publications with a critical eye and canvass editors for their views and advice.

Above all, remember that company news publications will always founder if the news is massaged, manipulated and distorted by aloof and over-protective policy makers. Only if a company positively supports and actively promotes the idea of freedom of information will the company's internal media have any credibility — and readership — worth the candle. Otherwise, don't waste the paper.

Newsletters

The humble newsletter is a tremendously successful vehicle for communicating news and information. In many respects, it is probably far more useful and effective than its glitzier newspaper big brother.

Because it is simple and relatively inexpensive to produce, it can be easily tailored for specific groups — paint shop, transport, sales office, personnel, training department, social club — or any other closely targeted readership you want to reach.

Precisely because it can be localized and filled with news and chat of direct relevance to individuals in a department, club or operating unit, the newsletter is a very popular and widely read format.

In a typical four-page newsletter hard news items, that is the personnel changes, production or sales achievements, the introduction of new working practices, plant and machinery can run side-by-side with social and sports news, classified ads, births, marriages, retirements and all those human interest stories which breathe life into any publication, large or small.

Precisely because the newsletter is localized, it can be used for all the information which might get lost in a larger company newspaper, if it gets in at all. For example:

The gents loos in South Building will be out of action for the first week in June while they are being refurbished. We apologize for the inconvenience and hope you make it to the North Building in time!

Your flexible friend

The newsletter really comes into its own during times of rapid change and upheaval. Precisely because the newsletter has a simple, uncomplicated format which can be produced easily and quickly, it's an excellent medium for transmitting company-wide news flashes and 'setting the record straight' background stories at short notice.

The metamorphosis of the publicly owned Central Electricity Generating Board into first three, and then four independent companies ready for privatization, is a case in point.

The communications task was a nightmare. The enormous logistical problems and the complex cultural, commercial and technical factors involved in one of the biggest organizational changes ever undertaken anywhere in the world had to be relayed and explained to some 50,000 staff as events unfolded — and Government policies see-sawed unpredictably.

In particular, there was the need to ensure that staff did not become too alarmed by speculative articles in the external media. Says Dick Coleman, formerly Internal Communications Manager of the CEGB and now doing the same job with National Power, 'Speed was often important. Efforts were made to tell employees of developments before they learned of them from outside news media and also to make sure they understood what was going to happen — to make the future less of a shock.'

In a complex communications programme, one of the most successful sources of information about privatization, according to a staff survey, was a specially produced newsletter called *Privatization News*.

The newsletter, posted directly to employees' homes, concentrated on pushing out hard news on all aspects of privatization. The newsletter was designed to pre-empt questions about pensions, pay structure, conditions of employment, job security and a host of other matters of concern. Every issue (produced on an *ad hoc* basis as and when new developments occurred) contained a feature 'What Happens Next', trailing the changes staff could expect to see in the coming weeks.

Complementing the newsletter, a staff newspaper, *Power News*, was able to carry fuller, in-depth stories explaining the background to the news items in Privatization News.

Dick Coleman comments:

If the communications task deals with one overall subject, such as privatization, then it is worth thinking about establishing a specialist medium. I am convinced *Privatization News* was useful not only because it was widely read by families as well as by employees themselves, but also because it demonstrated we were serious about staff communications.

Production

A localized or departmental newsletter should be under the control of an enthusiastic and energetic editor, preferably a departmental manager, industrial relations person or someone able to deal effectively and confidently with staff at all levels. They must have a good writing style — not forced, pompous or humourless — and they must be allocated enough time to produce regular issues to a fixed deadline.

They should try to encourage regular contributions from company correspondents such as the sports club secretary, personnel officer, union representative or public relations manager, but in reality most of the work of chasing down stories and writing them will fall on the editor's shoulders.

Other than an attractively designed masthead in one or two colours, newsletters can be typewritten (or preferably word processed) with plenty of short stories and simple headings in a two- or three-column layout. If you want to see what other firms do, you can cadge a copy from a local company, client or supplier.

Finally, if you haven't got internal printing facilities, find a cheap, local 'instant' print shop. Get at least two or three competitive quotes and do ask your printer's advice on the most economical print methods, paper etc.

Distribution

Make sure you deliver copies quickly to all employees either by internal mail, personal hand-out or, better still, directly to their homes — but find out if that's okay with them first.

Newspapers

There are more than 2000 company newspapers in the United Kingdom, twice as many industrial newspapers as all the national, regional and local newspapers put together.

In the right hands — and that means with the aid of professional designers, editors and writers — company newspapers are potent communication tools able to build a real sense of community and purpose at all levels in the organization.

However, despite a leap in standards over the last ten years, particularly in design values, too many in-house newspapers are still little more than tub-thumping PR sheets, extolling the virtues of the company, its products and senior directors while totally ignoring the real concerns of staff and managers fermenting under the surface.

A staff newspaper should not be seen as a 'papering over the cracks' PR exercise or an extension of the company's advertising and marketing activities. The only credible excuse for the existence of a staff newspaper is for two-way communications between managers and staff at all levels in the company.

This means that management and staff should have the opportunity to express their views in fairly equal measure. It's a difficult balance to achieve but it's the only way to produce a worthwhile, readable, publication.

The professional touch

Producing a company newspaper is an expensive business and it is usually only cost-effective for companies with thousands rather than hundreds of employees.

You will need professional help from the outset, either from an outside agency or from a professional journalist within the company working in the PR or Corporate Communications department.

While enthusiastic employees can be trained to make excellent reporters, the paper needs the guiding hand of a professional who can produce crisp, punchy copy and who understands the mechanics of putting a paper together — layout, picture cropping, writing headlines, sub-heads and picture captions, copy tasting, sub-editing...and all the tricks of the trade which are used to give a paper its individual style and flair.

Design

Company newspapers come in all shapes and sizes ranging from black and white tabloid newspapers to full-colour glossy magazines and all points in between. The key element is that the format should be 'user-friendly', easy to handle and read and big enough to make a splash with important news stories, features and interesting pictures.

The biggest single design fault with most company newspapers is to cram stories and pictures into too little space. A line-up of 30 people squashed into two narrow columns on a six-column page looks awful and is a real deterrent to the reader. At some stage you will need a professional layout artist to design each story and picture individually on the page. An experienced in-house editor may be able to handle this aspect for each edition or you might need to hire someone from an agency or local paper for one or two days per issue.

For examples of excellence in company newspaper design, try and get hold of a copy of the annual British Association of Industrial Editors' *Editing for Industry Awards* booklet. Better still, join the BAIE and make a point of meeting the editors of other successful house magazines.

Desktop publishing

In recent years there has been increasing interest in the use of 'desk-top' computerized publishing systems for the design and layout of in-house publications.

There are some excellent examples of company newspapers produced on desk-top systems but there is also a great deal of confusion about the role of computers in the publishing process.

Among the uninitiated, there is a widespread belief that desk-top publishing systems will do everything down to stirring the sugar in your tea. But as Will Self, publishing director of Cathedral Publishing and a previous Editing for Industry Gold Award winner, cautions:

> Do not be deceived by all the talk of desk-top publishing into believing that a secretary or a marketing assistant can be easily retrained to lay out publications on an office-based system. Some individuals may take to it well, but the layout and design of publications is a distinct profession and the desk-top systems themselves are highly sophisticated.

BP Exploration's editorial chief, Dudley Cheale, expands on this theme:

> Myth number one is the popular belief that DTP is a panacea that magically makes all difficulties melt away. If you can't design on paper you can't design on screen, but this is a truth sometimes lost on those who expect much more from DTP than it is able to deliver.
>
> Myth number two is the conviction that DTP automatically saves money. It *can* save money. It *can* add to costs. It depends how you use it and the yardsticks applied to measure its benefits.

In BP's case, in fact, the excellent newspaper produced on a DTP system, *BPXpress*, makes the maximum use of computer technology to a mind-boggling degree. Not only is all the typesetting and layout done directly on screen, but three editions of the newspaper are published, with the help of computer links, out of offices in North America, London and Scotland.

The remarkable aspect of this operation is that any of the offices can call up stories *and* photographs from any other office in a matter of seconds. I sat and watched amazed while the London office logged into the Cleveland, Ohio's computer and called over a photograph from a large selection stored on the American system. The photograph crossed the Atlantic in seconds to appear with perfect clarity on the computer screen in London. It could then be downloaded — after suitable on-screen modifications and sizing — for use in the London edition of the paper!

Dudley Cheale adds:

> With *BPXpress* we don't save money but we make great gains in quality, flexibility, production speed and the unity of a network of editions based in London, Glasgow and Cleveland and simultaneously published ten times a year.
>
> Indeed, the whole system totally depends on DTP. In theory it could be made to work by conventional means. But the penalties — particularly in time, swapping of material and working to a common publication date — would be unthinkable. The joy of being able, in minutes, to grab a photograph — let alone an oven-ready story — from Cleveland or Glasgow has to be experienced to be appreciated!

Content

The content needs to be as varied and interesting as any national newspaper with a good balance of solid company news, human interest stories, humour, sport, competitions, feature material, picture stories, even classified ads.

It's always a good idea to vary the relentless diet of inward looking company news with stories from outside on general interest subjects. For example, an interview with Michael Fish the BBC's weather man in the Safeway magazine *Focus*, was linked to a separate piece on how weather affects people's food buying habits. An article by actor Nigel Hawthorne on his role as a senior civil servant in the popular comedy series *Yes, Minister*, afforded welcome light relief in the Inland Revenue's magazine, *Network*.

The selection, writing and presentation of stories, like design, layout and picture handling is a complex and highly skilled task and requires the input of professionals if you want your newspaper to be successful.

Much of the day-to-day news gathering, however, will be done by company 'stringers', employees appointed as official 'correspondents' to relay news about their sphere of operations, whether it be sports, personnel, marketing, administration, finance, public relations, Scottish Office etc. It's always a good idea to list these correspondents with their area of specialism and telephone numbers somewhere prominently in the newspaper.

What you are after, of course, is a dialogue, with employees involved at all levels. The best measure of success is probably the feedback in the form of letters, contributions, brickbats and accolades from readers. If you don't get so much as an indignant letter from a reader who's had his or her feathers ruffled by a provocative article, you've probably got it wrong.

Perhaps the last word on the subject should be left to Ian Wright, Internal Communications Officer with ICI Chemicals & Polymers and one of the judges on the panel for the 1990 Editing for Industry Awards.

Having judged the category: Internal Newspapers with a circulation between 7000 and up to 10,000, Ian Wright concluded

Standards varied in all aspects: weak content and average writing sometimes enjoyed good design; sometimes papers with a good balance of content and high standard of writing were let down by unimaginative and even confusing design.

The highest-placed entries achieved a happy blend of all these elements, presenting their stories on business issues, together with lively human interest material, in well-written and attractively designed publications.

Some papers obviously spent a considerable amount on colour reproduction and high quality paper, while not investing quite so heavily in the skills and resources necessary to produce papers that communicated effectively by being attractive to readers and earning their interest.

Most papers were clear about their objectives. Editorial policies ranged from the warts-and-all approach to those which equate 'fostering positive attitudes' with a parade of back-slapping success stories and little else.

The divergence between the best and the worst reveals that in a number of companies genuine communication has yet to be acknowledged as an integral part of modern business culture.

PART V

INTERNATIONAL COMMUNICATION

INTRODUCTION

Paul Gibbs in *Doing Business in the European Community* poses the very good question: 'Why are you doing business in any country other than your own?'

The obvious answer is: 'Why not?' Certainly there are a number of obstacles but they can be overcome. Largely through the use of effective communications. I do not intend to advise on the whys and why nots; that depends on your business and your circumstances. I will assume that you are doing business at an international level and are interested in the most effective way of doing it. Following the style I have adopted throughout this book, I will not tell you how to run your business. What I will do is point out some of the signposts that you should note and consider within your own terms of reference.

It is communication that has shrunk the world. And broadened the marketplace. And extended our families. There are certainly some differences when communicating with people on an international level, but many of the basic principles are the same. If you have got this far, I do not need to repeat the basics. If you are extending your network to include visitors from abroad, or are intending to work abroad or set up an office in another country, or are planning to negotiate even one contract with people from a country other than your own, please read on.

Chapter 17

Communicating across cultures

CUSTOMS AND CONDUCT

The old golden rule applies to international communications. Do not take advantage of the other person's lack of familiarity with your language or customs if you do not want them to take advantage of your lack of familiarity with their language and customs. Make sure your preparations are thorough. If others' preparations are less thorough than they ought to be, offer guidance and instruction without appearing patronizing or irritated by their lack of understanding. Courtesy should be the first rule in international communications.

Cultural rules and regulations vary from one country to another as we all know. Finding out what they are, and particularly the degree of formality that is acceptable, is one of the most important first steps you should take. A glance at guidebooks and even etiquette books would not go amiss.

There is a growing number of books specifically aimed at business people giving everything from facts, figures, holidays and dates to views on dress, the family and socializing.

The non-business aspect of business communication can be extremely significant in some places. In others, business is business and personal lives are left at the door of the office. There can also be great significance to the use of first names at different stages of relationships in different countries. It is small things that are important to know, not just the details of your business and the other person's business or the specific transaction that you are getting together on.

Honesty as the best policy

One aspect of international communications which is particularly liable to cause embarrassment is giving the impression that you understand more of the language and customs than you actually do. It is far better to admit your ignorance, or ineptitude, than to pretend fluency and familiarity. The former will be accepted. The latter, if it becomes apparent that you have misled your host, could prove extremely awkward. While the advisability of preparation cannot be stressed sufficiently, as well as some basic effort to show willing by learning at least a few simple phrases in your counterpart's language, misrepresenting the extent of your knowledge can cause you to come seriously unstuck.

Preparation v prejudging

Beware of blanket generalizations about what is acceptable and what is not, as this can lead to incorrect behaviour. One book I read cites a laugh shared when an article appeared in the press advising visitors never to show Arabs the soles of their feet.

Another describes negotiations that became protracted when each of the two people involved believed that the other was waiting for the arrival of the rest of his team. They were each under the impression that people from the other country were only able to work in teams. In fact, when they realized that they were the only people involved, they concluded their dealings swiftly and to their mutual satisfaction. Before they got to that stage, they had to discard their preconceived notions about the other's customs.

Samfrits le Poole includes a table in *Never Take No For an Answer* which compares the negotiating style of four broad groups — the Soviets, Japanese, Europeans and Americans. His tips are useful but he does stress that they are very generalized and that you must not consider them to be hard and fast rules. Not everyone conforms to a stereotype and le Poole, while presenting his list of frequently encountered characteristics, takes pains to make his readers aware that they are dealing with individuals, not societies. He recommends using the traits he cites as reference material to be considered part of the background you are gathering before doing business on an international level. Do your homework, learn what you can about the country, its customs and its people. But never forget that a country is made up of individuals and it is those individuals with whom you will be communicating.

Knowing what to expect

Samfrits le Poole also suggests a number of questions you should try to answer before dealing with people from a country other than your own:

- What is their attitude towards negotiations — is it a game? do they believe in win/win or win/lose?

- How important is it to them not to lose face?
- Are they looking at long term involvement with you or short term?
- Are you really discussing issues and packages or simply agreeing specific terms of operation?
- What is their attitude towards time? Do they like to do things quickly or at a leisurely pace?
- Do they see long pauses, breaks and silences as a natural part of life or do they feel uncomfortable if progress isn't non-stop?
- Do they ask for more and offer less than they expect to get in the end?
- Do they care what you think about them?
- Do they say no when they mean no or do they use some other expression which leaves some room for doubt?
- Do they tend to be temperamental and emotional?
- To what degree are business and pleasure mixed? Is socializing part of the deal?
- What is their attitude towards money? Towards women in business? Towards lawyers? Towards unions? Towards private deals?
- Do you know enough about their legal system? Their banking and financial structures? Their payment structures?

Being a host

While everything I have said so far about understanding other people's traditions still applies when you are the host, in that situation your own customs will take priority. Visitors will be anxious to know about you and the way you do things. They will follow your lead. They will look to you to set the style of the meetings, arrange any after-hours visits or entertainment and generally lead the way in terms of behaviour.

Barry Turner, in his book of *Readymade Business Speeches* offers a few tips on welcoming a foreign delegation:

- Make the visitors feel at home.
- Find out the names of the visitors before they arrive and make sure you can pronounce them.
- Try to greet them in their own language before subjecting them to the strains of speaking in your language for the duration of the visit.
- Introduce them to their surroundings — where the airport and hotel are in relation to your office, where your office is in relation to the town centre, where the toilets and canteen are in relation to your office.
- Introduce them to all the people they will be dealing with — and be prepared to repeat the introductions later if there are too many to take in at once.
- Prepare to meet any special needs they may have which will need to be fitted into whatever schedule you have prepared.

Turner also recommends skipping the jokes as not everyone shares the same sense of humour. On the other hand, a joke shared can be a great icebreaker so you will have to consider both the background and the individual before deciding on the relative merits of introducing the odd bit of humour to the mix.

Being hosted

One of my friends is a land surveyor, running a company that has grown, through developing an excellent reputation and network of satisfied clients, into what is now virtually a multi-national enterprise.

Rod had no intention of building an empire when he became self-employed. It took him a long time to become a manager in his own business and to adapt to life as an administrator. When he goes out on site now it is to inspect the work, maintain contact with both the client and his own team, and ensure that his standards are being met.

He has found, much to his astonishment, that his reputation is spreading to such an extent that he is working on projects in several European centres. To his further astonishment, he was recently invited to Ghana, to survey the site of a village which is being re-built to twentieth century specifications. When he got there, he found that the villagers themselves had not yet reached the twentieth century and suffered a severe case of culture shock.

He spent hours regaling us with his adventures, each experience seeming more unbelievable and unrealistic to him than the last. He told us of rituals that had to be performed to keep the snakes away from the foreign visitors, of tribal costumes and the hypersensitivity of chiefs whose status was not suitably recognized. Government officials are not trusted and are greeted with suspicion and hostility. A great deal of diplomacy is needed and when the visitors cannot speak the language but must rely on unwelcome government escorts to be their intermediaries, disaster can result. On one occasion, two of Rod's workers were forced to flee when tribesmen took exception to the arrival of yet another official jeep. They pursued the entire party with machetes. The driver and his jeep disappeared in a cloud of dust, leaving Rod's team running after them, having abandoned hundreds of thousands of pounds worth of equipment while trying to catch the jeep before the natives caught them.

Rod and his team had to learn the customs of the land at great speed in order, literally, to survive and complete their task. They were made to feel honoured at a concession made on their behalf when the chief elected to serve wine rather than goat's blood during a welcoming ceremony. When braving restaurants in the town where they were based, they stopped asking what they were eating because they preferred to accept the taste without knowing what the animal was prior to cooking.

There are lessons to be learned from Rod's encounter which was more rough and ready than some but less rough and ready than others. When you are hosting a group, you set the pace. When you are being hosted, be prepared to accept life as it comes.

Preparations

In addition to the information you will need with regard to your specific project, there are a number of basic details which are useful before setting off to visit another country. As far as possible, you will need to find out:

- the dates of public holidays;
- the details of different taxation systems, for example whether it is possible to reclaim VAT on some expenditures;
- details of currency regulations as there may be a limit on the amount you can take out;
- how to arrange payments and transfers of payments to everyone's satisfaction and in a currency that is acceptable to both parties;
- how to check, and make allowances for, fluctuations in the exchange rate;
- policies and regulations concerning health cover for visitors;
- whether you will need any vaccinations before visiting and if so, how long before departure these must be obtained;
- whether there are any visa requirements;
- whether you are sufficiently insured, for example whether or not there are exemptions or risks, against various contingencies and unexpected disasters — natural and political — remember that just because they may not be likely in your country doesn't mean they won't happen in another.

To be fully and completely prepared, you should also make detailed plans for:

- the journey;
- reception and departure.

Both of these apply whether you are going abroad or receiving visitors from abroad, particularly if there are VIPS and/or groups which need to be coordinated.

When organizing a conference or presentation in another country, details of facilities and any technical differences you may encounter are a primary factor.

Research

European standards of communication are not uniform. They have quite accurately been described as a patchwork. For all that has been said in Chapter 11 on Hi-tech Communications, having the ability to communicate is not enough. There is much that you need to know before sending a letter or fax, making a telephone call or arranging a visit. One of the most important facts, whether you are buying or selling, going into a new market or dealing with someone coming into your market, is to know something about the other country. An American publisher I recently met did not do enough research and came seriously unstuck.

As a result of all the media hype over the last few years, this publisher decided to extend its list of business titles to include a European market. They specialize in information publishing and therefore had to compile information on European businesses for listing in their directories. They also had to compile information on potential customers and plan their marketing campaign. To this end, they set up an office in the UK and commissioned a well-established, UK-based firm to help with the research. Sounds good so far? Only on paper. In practice, they did not understand that:

- not all Europeans understand English;
- not all Europeans understand any other single language;
- each country has its own postal system;
- each country has its own telephone system;
- each country has its own scale of charges and currency.

Do not misunderstand. They knew these things, they were aware of them, but they neither accepted or believed them. There was obviously a breakdown in communication because the messages transmitted from the UK to the US were not accepted.

The culture shock which ensued, when they finally began to get the message, resulted in ill-conceived projects, inaccurate budget forecasts and less successful results in compilation and information gathering than anticipated. The Americans didn't do enough research or believe the results they did get and therefore had to rethink their entire programme.

At one point, more than a year after the reunification of Germany, they asked their London representative to include listings in a new directory for companies in East Germany. There was a total misconception about the ease with which information on Eastern Europe can be obtained, whether or not the information they wanted even existed or whether the countries are sufficiently well organized to have people doing particular jobs. Most of them are so tied up with day to day living that they are still buying products and services from other countries. They have not yet reached the stage where they can offer consultancy to others.

There are numerous ways of conducting international research, and of obtaining advice and assistance on buying and selling. Computer links between European countries, for example, give daily details of public contracts being offered for tender. Chambers of Commerce and Export Clubs have been formed amongst businessmen to exchange information, facilitate transactions and just swap stories. Learning from others' experiences is a great help when forming your own network.

Finding the right contacts, checking local and business libraries for directories of existing businesses and reports, locating market research companies who will either have prepared reports or will work to your brief, are all part of the information gathering process which must precede any international transaction.

Similarly, foreign competition must be monitored by a combination of reading trade papers, national papers and, when you are in the country, trying as far as possible to understand daily radio and television news programmes.

Finding a reliable agent 'on the ground' who can keep you up to date with the market is not only helpful but, if you are thinking in the long term, absolutely essential. Do not underestimate the value of the grapevine. Having someone in the country who will keep you informed is one of the best ways of ensuring that you know what you are talking about and what you are getting into.

Language and translations

Buying a guide book that includes phonetic pronunciations of various essential phrases in a language you neither speak nor understand is highly recommended. Apart from the countless books written in this way for tourists, there are now a number of titles specifically aimed at business travellers.

If possible, find out the names of the people you will be meeting. In that way, you can learn in advance how to pronounce their names properly. If you cannot find out in advance, then make a point of finding out on meeting what they are called and try to pronounce their names in the way that they prefer. Although mimicking someone else's accent is not necessary, making the effort not to translate or bastardize their names into some variation of your own language is a sign of courtesy.

On the other hand, if foreigners cannot manage to get their tongues around your name, do not take immediate offence. Try to ascertain, from the context of the conversation, whether they are simply unable to pronounce the sounds or whether they are using deliberate mispronunciations as a tactic to emphasize the cultural and linguistic differences between you. Do not use this tactic yourself unless there is good reason.

Speaking and listening

There is a certain amount of pride involved in attempting to use a language that is unfamiliar to you. Many people will refrain from asking for clarification or admitting that they do not understand a word or a phrase. This can be a disastrous decision. You can appear foolish or simple or naive, unintentional offence can be caused or a totally inaccurate impression given.

There is, of course, something to be gained by not admitting the extent of your understanding. You can ask for phrases to be repeated, imply that you do not understand, and ask for clarification.

Not understanding a language should not put anyone at an automatic disadvantage. Although communication would be a great deal easier if we understood one another from the start, this is not always possible and extra effort has to be made when two people are using a language that is not native to one of them.

Patience is another of those basic communication skills which is particularly important in this instance. Listening to words spoken in an accent that may be new to you, or speaking to someone who may not be familiar with your accent, requires care. Without reducing the conversation to pidgin, or slowing down to a pace that is almost insulting, clear enunciation will go a long way towards helping understanding.

Comprehension

Inferences and implications can often only be picked up if you understand the nuances of what someone is saying. This is difficult enough if both people are speaking the same language and that language is their mutual mother tongue. If one is speaking in a language which is their second or third one, then misunderstandings can arise even more easily.

Everything needs to be spelled out when one of the people involved in a conversation is not a native speaker of the other's language. Just because you understand something, and know what you mean by what you're saying, doesn't mean that he does. The deliberate use of puns or innuendos that people may not understand is not appreciated.

Some people understand words of a language but are not sufficiently fluent to use it. Occasionally they don't want you to know they understand what you are saying. A television news reporter interviewed Yasser Arafat during the Gulf War. It is widely known that his English is fluent but he insisted on using an interpreter until the interviewer asked him to please respond in English.

Making the effort

Attitudes towards using a language other than your own differ widely. The British and Americans are far less fluent in any second language than people in many other countries where large numbers of the population learn English from an early age. What they find hard to accept is not only that they (the native English speakers) should learn to speak anyone else's language but that only some people in other countries have learned English. It baffles them, the Americans even more than the British, that not everyone can understand them or communicate with them on their own terms.

For some people, using their own language is often a matter of shyness or principle as much as lack of fluency. Others make as much attempt as possible to communicate in their colleagues' language as a way of showing their ability and willingness to establish a rapport.

Interpreters

Interpreters can be used when one or both sides knows a bit of the other's language but not enough to feel comfortable. Listening to the translation helps you to understand the implications of what has been said and to pick up sub-texts that you might have missed.

Watching someone's face when he is listening to an interpreter, and when he is listening to you speaking through an interpreter, may reveal a great deal.

When using an interpreter during conversation, you still need to listen to the speaker's tone. We have all seen the comedy routines where people use a lack of understanding as an excuse to speak gibberish or let loose with a steam of invective or insults, smiling all the while. An interpreter will be able to verify the content of what is being said while you are listening to the tone. Turning around a precept I have used earlier, it is not just how you say something but what you say that counts.

Interpreters attending a meeting need to be reliable and fluent in both languages being used so that you can understand what people are saying to each other and know exactly what they are saying to you. If you use the other person or team's translators rather than one you have arranged yourself, then it is just conceivable that they could be passing all sorts of messages and information to each other that you cannot understand. You need to trust your translator so that you can be sure of both the linguistic and interpretative accuracy of the translation.

Colin Robinson in *Winning at Business Negotiations* advises against negotiating through an interpreter. Apart from the obvious possibilities for misunderstanding, there is also the interpreter's own involvement which should be considered. Does he, for example, stand to gain in any way from concluding the negotiations in one way or another? Robinson's recommendation is that if you do not understand the language, you should appoint an agent and conclude your deal with him. It is then up to the agent to negotiate his own contract with locals. In that way you are both dealing with a language and customs that are familiar and you are both able to make your terms clear.

Samfrits le Poole's view of interpreters is that they keep everyone up to scratch. As you know that there is at least one member of the visiting team's group who understands every word you say and can translate it, with commentary, you are more likely to watch what you say and not take advantage of the visitors' lack of familiarity with your language.

Written communications

It is especially important to check written communications when translating or dealing with a foreign company as there is no room to clarify once you have said something incorrectly. Incorrect or inaccurate translations, at the very least, can make you look foolish. Use a good agency or someone in the country itself if you are translating anything technical or industry specific.

Proofreading written translations may prove difficult. The answer is either using two people to check one another or taking great care that the translator is reliable. You do not want to be held responsible, later, for an inadvertent misunderstanding because of an inaccurate translation.

Vocabulary and grammar in any language is a debatable issue. Often there is no clearcut right or wrong way to say something. Given a sentence or a letter to translate, two or three people could produce two or three different versions. Always remember that there are numerous ways of saying things.

Technical terms change so rapidly that translators, particularly of manuals and documents which need to be clear, precise and accurate, should be translated within the relevant country. Native speakers who have left their own country may not be sufficiently familiar with current usage, new terminology or colloquialisms.

Nonverbal communications

Body language has different meanings in different countries, for example:

- A pointing finger can be interpreted as an extremely rude gesture.
- Winston Churchill's famous V for victory, even in Britain, has an alternative, obscene interpretation.
- Continuous eye contact is considered impolite in Japan.

Different interpretations are also given to symbols in different countries. Conversely, however, a system of internationally acceptable symbols has been devised to breach the communications gap when people speak different languages. Abbreviations for country names and road signs are just two examples of this.

Telephone techniques

Chapter 9 on Telephone Techniques is equally applicable to international communications. We all have accents but when one speaker has an accent that is unexpected or unfamiliar to the other, particular attention must be paid to understanding one another. Each speaker must take pains to speak clearly and enunciate his words. You have to understand and be understood, so both the speaking and the listening parts of a telephone conversation are equally important. Each speaker must consider the other.

Nor is it unusual, with today's trends in mobility, for two people in England, for example, to have come from different countries. A Frenchman speaking to a Spaniard in English can lead to all sorts of confusion. You never know, either when placing or receiving a telephone call, what you will hear at the other end.

Networking

Communications and travel mean that there is a great deal of movement of people for employment purposes. Individuals move into and out of countries as well as between countries. If you work in France, for instance, you could meet people from Japan, Spain or anywhere else, not just France. You must be aware of this and able to communicate with multiple nationalities.

The *Guardian*, on 14 June, 1991, published a map of the world showing the number and source of foreign-born residents in the main countries of Europe. As a means of demonstrating the range of nationalities comprising the European workforce, it was extemely effective. Not only do people look for jobs in their own country and, increasingly in Europe, in neighbouring countries, but immigrants from outside the area are continuing to swell the population. Anyone seeking a job, or hiring staff, must make allowances for the cultures and languages being brought into their own melting pot. According to the *Guardian*

- Britain's main source of immigrant labour is the Caribbean, the Indian sub-continent and other Asian countries;
- France attracts Algerians, Moroccans, Tunisians and others from sub-Saharan Africa;
- the Benelux countries' influx comes from Morocco and Turkey;
- Germany gets its immigrants from Turkey, Yugoslavia, Poland, the USSR and Africa;
- Spain attracts Latin Americans and Moroccans;
- Italy pulls in emigres from the Middle East and Asia in the South, Tunisians in the middle and Moroccans flock to the Northern areas.

People change jobs as well, although perhaps less often in some countries than others. But businesses overlap and you may find the unlikeliest people in the most unexpected places. With communication making it easier for people to meet and deal with one another, to get to know one another, you may walk into a meeting in Tokyo one day and find a former colleague working for a rival company. Creating your own network, and keeping lines of communication open, means that making contacts and renewing old acquaintances is an essential face of business. Never consider a relationship over — you could meet anyone anytime anywhere. Knowing where people are, and who you can call on, may give you a head start in a new transaction. Work on the 'you never know' principle and make sure your network spreads as far and wide as you can manage.

Working abroad

Many companies opening offices in countries other than their own are anxious for information on how to recruit personnel in those countries. Their workforces are comprised of a combination of local residents and their own nationals transported to the new office to introduce established procedures. Nationals have to be taught how to communicate their own culture to locals as well as how to adapt to their new environment.

The Student Book, edited by Klaus Boehm and Jenny Lees-Spalding, has a foreword to its 1992 edition entitled, 'Before you apply, think Europe'. It advises students applying for a university course commencing in 1992 to plan ahead as, by the time they graduate, they will be citizens of Europe, not just the United Kingdom. They will be able to apply for jobs throughout Europe just as Europeans of a similar age will be competing for jobs they themselves may seek in Britain. The editors strongly advise preparing for what they describe as two linked challenges — 'to communicate effectively and fluently in the community and to compete professionally at a local level which implies understanding the national environment, including the networks which provide jobs/contracts for the boys.'

At least one British publisher has conceived the idea of an international employment directory to be used when setting up an office in a new country. Paul Gibbs' book, *Doing Business in the European Community*, covers twelve countries and details, for each:

- how to make an appointment;
- tips on how meetings are generally conducted and the etiquette involved;
- entertaining;
- women in business;
- working hours;
- public holidays;
- letter-writing;
- marketing;
- consumer preferences/differences;
- establishing a business;
- single-market efforts;
- useful addresses.

Other authors may go further and provide detailed information on those related areas that people working in a new country will need to know such as:

- cost of living;
- tax rate;
- education system.

Work related information that anyone setting up an office will require includes regulations concerning:

- unions;

- employment terms;
- equal opportunities;
- standard benefits;
- visas and work permits.

There are multiple sources of useful addresses, including associations, chambers of commerce, export clubs, and consultancies on the shelves of bookshops and business libraries. A few indicators of where to find further information are included in the Directory at the end of this book.

International communications

There are technical and psychological barriers to international communications that can be obstructive. One of the former is the problem of time zones. Jet lag makes meetings difficult when people have travelled long distances.

Hi-tech communications can also be affected. One person may be ready to send a fax or make a telephone call first thing in the morning only to realize that the person at the other end is fast asleep, having just finished a hard day's work.

Some companies may leave their machines on 24 hours a day, but others switch off for security reasons when the office closes for the day. It is possible, however, to go home and leave the timer on your fax machine set to transmit a message at an hour convenient for the recipient. Many messages are confidential and can only be sent when you know that there will be someone there to receive it. Allowance for different times must be made in these instances.

British Telecom offers a range of international brochures pointing out such difficulties and indicating ways of alleviating them. Other similar services are available worldwide.

As anyone who reads a newspaper or listens to radio or television news is aware, great debates are taking place all over the world on the subject of sovereignty. Countries that have always been independent are forming unions; other countries which have been part of a confederation are asserting their independence.

In Europe, an arbitary official date of 1992 has been set for opening trade barriers. Yet Europe as an entity does not now exist and may not exist until many years beyond 1992 if ever at all. Just as many of the Western European countries are formulating the terms of their Economic Community, Eastern European countries are breaking away from their union. Instead of fewer entities, there will be more. One of the inevitable results will be that communication can never be made uniform or consistent. There will always be different systems.

Many outsiders, particularly Americans used to a system whereby states have a certain degree of autonomy combined with a national suprastructure, have difficulty in relating to Europe as a number of individual nations. It is especially hard for outsiders to understand how

'Europe' is structured when internal agreement is still being debated and so many points are not yet settled. There are problems for member states and individuals in the various European countries when communicating with one another, let alone with the rest of the world. The mobile workforce referred to above adds yet another element which further complicates matters.

Attitude

Many people in Great Britain see the Germans and the Japanese as a threat to British industry and markets. Michael Heseltine, speaking at the Thames Valley launch of the Management Charter Initiative, stressed, and not for the first time, the need to fight against Japanese capitalism. He described a scenario whereby the British workforce became employees of Japanese owners, with managers and shopfloor workers trained by their Japanese masters and following instructions given by Japanese executives. It sounded like a modernized version of *1984*, as he drew a picture of a situation created gradually and subtly without people even realizing that it was happening.

A film I saw recently about the automobile industry took up this theme. Exactly the tale told by Mr Heseltine occurred, with Japanese families coming to live in a Midlands suburb while they transformed a money-losing factory into an efficiently run, high-production outlet. The film was intended to be a comedy and included scenes of pep talks and group calisthenics meant to show that discipline could unite the workforce and produce greatly improved results. These scenes were interspersed with domestic encounters between the Japanese and British families, mocking the difficulties they were each having in understanding the others' ways. Being fiction, it all ended happily with the culture clash being overcome and all the workers voluntarily uniting to keep the company afloat and everyone off the dole.

The film just served to highlight, through the use of comedy, an attitude that can occasionally border on the paranoid. Bill Dixon of Ford of Europe, talked about the 'Japanese threat eating into all markets in Europe and the United States' when interviewed by *Communications Week International*. He and Mr Heseltine are not alone in thinking that many of the management skills applied by the Japanese to their own economy can and will be found in the UK to an increasing extent over coming years.

Whether this is a good thing or a bad thing is a matter of opinion. Whether learning from one another, exchanging ideas, adopting one another's practises or, dare I say it again, communicating with one another, can improve our lives — business and personal — is a decision we must each make.

Negotiations

In some countries, the small talk prior to the opening of negotiations seems to go on interminably. In fact, it is an excellent way of getting to know your counterpart and for each of you to make some judgements about the other. This preliminary step in any relationship serves to make negotiations and business transactions more straightforward as each of you knows more or less what to expect from the other. By exchanging experiences, beliefs and attitudes on seemingly irrelevant subjects you have still moved towards an understanding of one another. By communicating on a personal and informal basis, you have opened the door for a smooth exchange of views on business matters.

The results are quite likely to cut through some of the formalities of business and establish a basis for a long term relationship that cannot be founded on superficial technical knowledge alone. Reading a curriculum vitae when employing someone is only one part of deciding whether or not they are right for the job. Personal contact is necessary for an informed judgement to be made. The same applies to international negotiations. Getting to know the other person, and opening the lines of communication, are an invaluable step towards successful negotiations.

Many experts on negotiations emphasize repeatedly that abbreviating the orientation period can be a wasted opportunity. Samfrits le Poole touches on this and a number of other common characteristics which differentiate nationalities as they approach the negotiating table.

- Americans and Europeans start negotiations with a very brief period of small talk and are then anxious to get down to business.
- People from Latin America, the Far and Middle East, prefer a longer orientation period. They use this as a time to gather and verify information, get to know the other side and generally create a conducive (in their terms) atmosphere.
- Russians and Eastern Europeans extend negotiations as long as they can get away with on the grounds that the longer you wait for a concession and the harder you have to fight for it, the more you will appreciate it so they take pride in treating people as supplicants and making them wait.
- Easterners tend to be comfortable with silence, Westerners uncomfortable. So while an Arab or Asian might use long periods of silence as a negotiating tactic, Americans and Europeans attempt to break the silences, often saying more, and giving away more, than they intended.
- In some Asian and Latin cultures, the word no is never used therefore the word yes must be heard in context to determine whether it means yes, no or maybe.

Saving face is important to all of us but it is more important in some parts of the world than others, for example the Middle and Far East and Latin America. In many cultures it is not only a matter of personal humiliation to be backed into a corner, it is a matter of public humiliation. Pride can force us to do things that may appear illogical or inexplicable to others. If they are of importance in our own cultures, however, they must be accepted as such and not judged by other people's standards.

Your place or mine?

The decision on where to negotiate can be influenced by the language which will be used, and customs, and your familiarity with them. Each of us naturally wants to conduct negotiations on our own territory, with our own backup staff and materials. This happens in all negotiations but is even more important when more than one country and language are involved.

There is another tacit statement made by the person who travels to another country to meet someone. The time and money spent in getting to the negotiating table are indications of willingness to reach agreement. Having taken the trouble of getting there, whoever has done the travelling has given away a clue to his interest in the deal. He is also less likely to want to go away empty handed and can perhaps be pushed into more concessions than he originally intended.

If you are the one doing the travelling, the impression of over-willingness can be countermanded by explaining, and demonstrating, that you have actually combined this trip with other purposes. A modification of the old routine 'I was in the area so I thought I'd drop in' can be used. Better yet, make sure it's true. Find other people to see, and products or services to look at, use the trip as a factfinding mission to familiarize yourself with the country. If you plan to do business there for some time to come, check out the competition, have a holiday, but make use of the trip to accomplish several tasks at the same time.

As usual, though, there is another view. If you are the one to do the travelling, you will have the chance to see your colleagues in their own surroundings and to learn more about them. You will gain valuable first-hand knowledge. There is also something to be said for appearing to be willing to make the effort and meet people in their own country. Refusing to move from your own office, or to show an interest in other people's circumstances, language and culture can give the impression not only that you are a tough business person but that you are obstinate and uncooperative.

Knowing your ground

Up until now I have largely referred to large Western, or westernized, countries. There are special tactics needed when negotiating and communicating with third world and developing nations. Speaking to people from these countries it becomes apparent that attitudes are quite different. In some places, for example, bribery is still openly accepted and anyone refusing to cooperate finds themselves rapidly reaching a dead end.

Similarly, the attitude to bureaucracy, to waiting for what seem infinite lengths of time, to being passed from pillar to post to ensure that everyone ever likely to be concerned has been approached in the correct fashion, vary enormously.

Tactics and strategy can vary as well. It may be that different issues or stages in the negotiations are handled by different people and the entire process can involve an element of musical chairs. Attitudes and approaches before, during and after negotiations are cultural and an awareness of this is part of the preparation process referred to earlier.

Finally, when you get to the contract stage, it is essential to use a minimum of two advisers, one for each language, so that everyone understands the terms thoroughly and can be sure that all documentation accurately represents what has been agreed.

The use of technology

The advantages of hi-tech communications mean that information can be transmitted by modem or fax or telephone conversations conducted from any one place in the world to any other place. Although, as I said earlier, allowance must be made for time differences, there is some type of equipment available to satisfy virtually any and every international business communication requirement.

Hi-tech communications, discussed in greater depth in Chapter 11, have special applications to international communications. Many companies regard international communications as a challenge.

- The Ford Motor company has engineers in the United States, the United Kingdom and Germany working together on designs. Their customer care subsidiary recently planned to launch a newspaper for its staff which was to be published simultaneously in four different language editions. The same stories would appear, and the page design was to be identical; only the language would change.

- A staff magazine produced by BP makes use of archives stored in Germany, England and the United States. If the designer wants a photograph of a particular subject, he can call it onto his screen from any one of the other offices within a matter of seconds.

The greater the number of businesses trading with one another, and establishing branch offices in other countries, the greater will become the reliance on technology to maintain contact between employees and between buyers and sellers.

Importing and exporting

Communication has simplified distribution systems and increased the ability to discuss specifications and orders, thereby opening markets that would not have been considered a few years ago. We now have fresh food in our shops imported from countries all over the world all year round. Component parts are made by factories in different countries then assembled in one plant often using equipment made in another country again. We all try to make the best use of labour and raw materials, then transport the finished product to some other country to sell or combine with parts made there.

Export initiatives are advertised constantly. There is an ever increasing range of services being made available, more information and grants, people advising and consulting on standards and extensive talk of closing the trade gap. Everyone is getting in on the act. There is no shortage of information, advice and material. The facilities are there and there is no reason why anyone wishing to extend their markets and conducting their business on an international level cannot and should not be able to do so. All that it needs is a system of effective communication.

PART VI

CASE STUDIES

Case Study 1

'Z International Ltd'

Among the many people I spoke to when researching this book were various managers of different departments in a large company which has recently brought several of its divisions under one roof. They have asked not to be named.

Much of what they told me was not accompanied by value judgements or opinions. But their comments, combined with my own observations, lead me to certain conclusions about the unwieldiness of their operations. They have serious communication problems internally and equally serious problems communicating with external audiences.

PASSING ON INFORMATION

Andrea is a departmental head who works at home from Friday to Monday, and in the company's offices on Tuesday to Thursday. She spends several hours travelling in each direction and fills the boot of her car with every file she is likely to need for reference. What she does not take with her, or have at her home, is any form of equipment of the sort discussed in Chapter 11. She has no typewriter, word processor or facsimile machine.

As a result, anything that needs to be transmitted to others is handwritten and taken to the office then passed to her secretary for typing.

Anything that she writes on Friday does not get posted or distributed until Tuesday at the earliest, and then only if her secretary (who is working for someone else as well and not sitting around half of the week waiting for Andrea) has time to do it.

If she is going to work at home for two days a week which are either side of a weekend then she must have the means of communicating with her office and colleagues in other companies with whom she is dealing.

283

Communicating through intermediaries

My own dealings with this company arose when I was asked to act as consultant on one of their projects. Each of the departments involved had so many responsibilities that staff were unable to cope with their workload. Hence one entire project was structured specifically for being handled by an outside agency. With, of course, the provision for frequent checking stages to ensure that the company's standards were met.

This effort to streamline communications actually produced an even more unwieldy system than that which already existed.

The checking stages involved at least three different people within the company, a lengthy process to say the least.

Nor would any of those individuals speak to anyone other than the project manager who was coordinating input from some sixty other contributors.

While this made sense as a general principle, it was taken to such an extreme stage of passing messages back and forth between people, who were often not available on the day or at the time when they were needed, that further delays were encountered.

The entire project was so complicated that meetings were inevitable and so much loaded onto each agenda that the sessions never lasted for less than three hours at a time.

Compare this with the next case study, Digital Equipment Company, where it was also decided to use outside agencies to do work commissioned and structured by internal managers. Both companies started from the same point but achieved totally different results because of the way the decision was implemented.

If Z International's project finishes on time, within budget, and to everyone's satisfaction it will largely be due to successful project management by the agency appointed.

DUPLICATING EFFORT

Again, because of the number of people involved, and their spread of locations, every telephone call or memorandum had to be circulated to a minimum of six people.

If this did not happen, someone invariably did not know something that the others did. Requests were made to make changes that contradicted others' instructions, some people were not aware of what others had asked for, time and money were spent in writing, assembling, photocopying and distributing copies of everything that everyone had said. Time and money that would have been put to far better use had they been directed towards the successful and speedy completion of the project.

SETTING THE GROUND RULES

Conflicting, incomplete and ambiguous messages characterized the entire affair.

Establishing a house style for written communications is a case in point. It emerged, several months into the project, that there was actually a house style but not many people knew either of its existence or its content. There was no manual.

One of the internal managers was assigned the task of writing up this essential document. Inevitably, over the weeks that followed, it grew as points that should have been included were added as afterthoughts.

Fair enough, we all have to start somewhere and we have to be flexible, allowing for change and fine tuning what is actually required.

What was included, and excluded, became so contradictory as to be totally inconsistent and began to negate the purpose of the manual. Edicts such as 'always put a comma between two adjectives' were later amended to read 'except...' The exceptions were so confusing and inconsistent that it became impossible to determine a hard and fast rule. Judgement was required and the agency's judgement did not always coincide with that of Z's staff.

On another occasion, a rule was laid down that 'but' and 'and' should not necessarily be preceded by a comma. Again, an acceptable point. Until it transpired that this simply meant they should not be inserted where they did not already exist. If a document written earlier by some member of Z's staff already contained such commas, these were not to be deleted.

It eventually transpired that the manager writing the manual wanted all of her instructions taken literally. If she said she wanted something done, then that is what she wanted done. She did not mean to imply that the converse should not be done.

Confusing? Unclear communications? Absolutely.

The ground rules were not sufficiently communicated at the outset. Additional responsibilities and expenses were passed onto the agency throughout the project. Each time, Z's managers explained, we thought you knew that or we assumed you knew that. They did not say what they meant, did not specify the job fully at the outset but left it, in their words, to evolve.

The trouble was that the evolution was one sided only. They passed on more and more expectations and chores, shrugging it off each time as something that they had taken as read. Unfortunately the agency had had no such understanding of the message which they claimed was not actually transmitted other than telepathically.

TALKING IT ALL OVER

Z's policy is to have departments work as teams. They have frequent meetings because team work is felt to be so valuable. Meanwhile, no one can make a decision or a move without consulting the rest of the team which means that a great deal of their time is taken up with meetings. Assuming, that is, that team members are available and not already in other meetings with other teams.

There is a certain overlap of people on the various teams running different projects. Virtually the same people attend each meeting with minor but significant changes so that some people end up attending all meetings. They get back to their desks at five o'clock to try and deal with the day's work. As a result, this work obviously does not get enough time or attention because they are too busy going to meetings.

Department managers have a longstanding weekly meeting to discuss progress on all other meetings. They have recently decided that this is now so time consuming that they are considering the introduction of a pre-meeting to prioritize their agendas.

There is so much team work that little individual work is done unless it is a task so very menial, mundane and routine that there is no excuse not to take action.

It was my observation that staff are always watching their backs and introducing new, cumbersome, unwieldy methods in order to avoid giving or taking any individual responsibility. I also feel that there was a distinct lack of initiative, with no incentive for individuals to make decisions or take responsibility. This is a classic case of too much communication preventing effective communication.

ENVIRONMENT AS FACILITATOR

Not even Z's working environment is conducive to effective communication. When the company moved to its new premises, with plans to bring as many divisions as possible onto one site, they started with empty shells of buildings. They were able to decide which departments needed to be near which other departments, which individuals rated offices, whether open plan design was better than segmented cubicles, how many meeting rooms to have, how much space was required for specific functions.

After a year or so they decided that they hadn't quite got it right and moved everyone again. Staff were consulted about their requirements and opinions on everything down to the position of telephone points and electric sockets. The discussions lasted for weeks.

Two months after what was a highly disruptive and complicated rearrangement, not everyone is satisfied that any improvement has resulted.

In a company that attempts to keep as much of its work as possible confidential, open plan offices have been retained. Conference and meeting space is at a premium which means that there are constant battles to book the few rooms available. Those managers who are unsuccessful have to borrow others' offices, pouncing on any temporarily empty space. Each area is so confined that when presentations have to be made, documents consulted or plans examined, there isn't so much as a table or work space to lay them out on.

Those with offices generally have glass walls facing into the corridor. The same applies to the conference room. Again, not conducive to the company policy of secrecy above all. No one in any other department is supposed to know what anyone else is doing. I have attended a meeting where we were asked to stand, with our backs to the wall onto the corridor, to block the view of passers by.

Basics such as ventilation and air conditioning were not designed with due consideration for those working in the building. If you open a window, papers blow all over the place. If you keep the window closed, there is a distinct lack of fresh air circulating.

ONE MAN'S VIEWS

Each of the managers I met believed that he or she was a very reasonable person. They all believed that what they were asking of others was perfectly acceptable and took any rejection as a personal affront. They had no idea what others thought of them either personally or as managers.

The outside agencies and individuals who eventually received messages from Z through the agency as intermediaries did not, in general, agree that their requests were reasonable. They were frequently considered to be so pedantic as to be totally unreasonable. Several people refused to deal with them. One contributor refused to have his name put on the end product on the grounds that Z had changed it so far out of recognition.

Part of what the agency's functions turned out to be involved diplomatic dealings as intermediary, calming frenzied contributors and trying to ensure that alterations to briefs supplied by Z were fulfilled. They also had to convey to Z, to a certain degree, the contributors' objections.

On more than one occasion, individuals or teams were pulled off segments of the project that had been declared by Z to be urgent and moved onto other segments which were declared by Z to be more urgent still. When the more urgent segment was complete, they could not understand why the originally declared urgent segment was not also complete.

None of this was specified at the outset, largely because it was not recognized by Z as a real need. Thus disputes arose later about responsiblities.

There seemed to be, and this is one woman's view, a pervading attitude at Z that if one person or agency did not want to work for them or abide by their rules, that there were plenty of other fish in the sea. Following completion of the project which I observed, I believe they will have to go fishing again before commencing their next project.

Case Study 2

Digital Equipment Company

Towards the end of 1990, Digital Equipment Company undertook a communications audit. Its purpose was to determine how the company's communications functions should work and with whom the various departments should interface.

Nine months later, the audit is virtually complete and some of the steps identified have been taken. The company has begun to implement some of the changes and made plans for the next steps necessary. They have not yet finalized the various procedures, however, or informed people outside those immediately concerned or written up their results.

Jackie Boxall, European Public Affairs Manager, was instrumental in designing and conducting the audit as well as implementing the decisions and changes. She talked me through the operation and explained what Digital hopes to achieve.

THE RESEARCH

In order to assess the way in which communications worked at Digital, and the opinions of people regarding the effectiveness of those communications, some 90 people at various levels of different departments were interviewed. The first significant finding was that some 100 man years per year were being spent in total by the company on communications work including every aspect from formal communications to brochures.

Man years, according to Jackie Boxall, are calculated by multiplying the number of hours a person is expected to work in an average week by the number of weeks in the year. In this way, time can be measured with a certain degree of accuracy. Not every person spends all of his time on specific activities but many people spend a portion of their time and this formula allows for all of that time to be taken into account. Thus:

100 man years $= 100 \times 40 \times 52$

or a total of 208,000 hours per year.

This figure represented something like double the time budgeted, therefore the audit had to find ways of pulling efforts together to be more efficient and cost effective.

In addition to internal interviews, an external agency was commissioned to talk to customers regarding their perceptions of the strengths and weaknesses of Digital's communications.

These interviews, plus reports from MORI and other routine sources of external research, were combined wtih feedback from staff interviews in order to recommend steps which would create the necessary improvements.

THE PLAN

Digital uses an organizational model which looks at the purpose of work being performed and the objectives that have been set in order to design the core work needed to achieve the objectives.

Three people, including the managing director, were asked to determine how the communications group should proceed. These discussions were so detailed that Jackie Boxall estimated that it took some 200 man years to reach a final decision.

They did come up with an idea, however, of what should be achieved and who should be interfaced with. They determined what activities would be needed, appointed managers and sent them off to build teams to design their work following guidelines which will be established by the larger group. Managers have been appointed with responsibility for:

- public relations;
- communications services including exhibitions, events and enquiry management;
- sales and marketing which is responsible for promoting specific products to specific customers;
- internal communications.

In addition, two regional communications managers have been appointed with responsibility for helping sales personnel, putting together projects that need someone on the ground, and generally pulling together the mix.

The overall objective for the groups is to decide what needs to be done and find people to do it. Outside consultants will be relied on to a far greater degree than in the past and services will be bought in. It is up to the core group to identify their requirements, create the specification, commission an agency to fulfill the objectives and liaise with them to ensure that standards are maintained. The three elements of communication which must be satisfied are:

- innovation, with particular reference to technical leads;

- choice, with particular reference to providing hardware and software consultancy and solutions;
- responsiveness, with particular reference to the services provided by Digital.

All promotions must have one of these themes.

THE CHANGES

Apart from the basic objective of streamlining operations and achieving savings in both time and money, Jackie Boxall believes that the most important accomplishment of the audit has been to flatten the management structure. By eliminating some of the intermediaries, she says, and ensuring that team members report to their group leaders, information is more generally available and easier to act upon. Instead of reporting to the marketing director, group leaders now go directly to the chairman's office. A maximum of three layers of management will be incorporated from:

deputy chairman of the company
↑
group manager to
↑
team leader to

The corporate communications manager acts as overall group manager and organizes the groups. He is responsible for making sure that the focus is on the corporate side of things rather than providing services or products. Consultancy and strategic roles need to be developed rather than detailed ground level implementation skills.

Each group has its own areas of expertise and its own projects to manage but their physical proximity prevents them working in isolation. They have frequent, informal, reference to one another as well as regular formal monthly meetings.

The reaction

In a sense, the acceptance of feedback has proved a shock to staff. During interviews with the staff involved, the quality of working life was repeatedly emphasized with priorities listed as:

- having fun;
- being involved in decision making;
- having responsibility;
- knowing who was responsible for what with minimal duplication of effort.

Having assessed the situation and agreed that group members should have more responsibility and design their own work, staff are now finding that this is not as easy as it sounds! It is time for them to put up or shut up, as Jackie Boxall says, to get involved or follow orders. Anyone who wants to be an active team member, now has the opportunity. Anyone who prefers to be told what to do will also be accommodated and assigned a task.

Digital's board of management has given the corporate communications group the go ahead to implement their plans. The groups have gone away to formulate their procedures and Jackie Boxall is about to write her report. At that point, other target audiences will be informed.

Although the audit pertains just to the UK arm of Digital, and indeed to just one aspect of the entire corporate enterprise, it has been a massive undertaking and should become a model to which other areas of the company can refer.

Case Study 3

BP Exploration Company

The following are extracts from a Green Paper on Communications published by BP Exploration in March 1990. It has been generously contributed by Roddy Kennedy, Government and Public Affairs manager. The paper sets out clearly exactly what BPX aimed to do, what it did, why and how.

THE OBJECTIVE

Review all aspects of communications to staff and assess their effectiveness; recommend new, more effective means of communication if necessary.

The transformation of BPX to a more nimble organization, whose actions are characterized by speed and decisiveness, puts a premium on effective communications. Faster asset development, the smooth transfer of technology across business units, reacting to developments in days rather than weeks or months, all require that people talk with each other — up, down and laterally through the organization. Not sharing information, or substituting piles of paper for straighforward conversation, are real roadblocks to BPX reaching its goals.

Syndicate 8 examined the current state of communications to see if both the environment and the vehicles existed for communication to play its critical role in implementing BPX's strategy. The syndicate held thirteen focus groups at key locations worldwide to assess the staff's views on whether they were getting the information they needed in a form that was timely and useful and whether they had an opportunity to express their views and ideas on how things might be done better.

THE PROBLEM

The focus group results showed that communications in BPX were poor. Staff were not getting the information they believed they needed nor were they receiving information when they required it. The credibility of management and its communications vehicles was low. Many people relied on the grapevine as their most accurate source of information. No effective vehicles for upward communications appeared to exist, which heightened staff dissatisfaction. A few comments from focus groups illustrate the extent of the problem:

- Managers don't think they have to communicate, just show videos.
- I'd like to know what's expected of you, why you're doing it and whom you're answerable to.
- ...there are as many filters up as there are down, and each filter may have an agenda that stops the information...or changes it.
- They (BPX corporate) have traded off face-to-face meetings with these experiments in communications (ie videos, consultants, questionnaires etc).

From the focus group research, the syndicate identified four salient issues:

- management credibility;
- the role of line management in communications;
- improving upward communications;
- the function of written and broadcast media.

Many focus group participants expressed doubt that their views would be accurately related to senior management. Some saw the focus groups themselves as another attempt by management to paper over the communications problem.

The group noted that attacking the credibility problem required a commitment from everyone in the organization to an open communications process. Honestly expressed views must be listened to and dealt with responsibly, and there should be no fear of retribution. Improving credibility also required a commitment to timeliness and congruence between words and actions.

THE RECOMMENDATIONS

The recommended solution involved restructuring all aspects of the communications process, from the role of line management to the myriad publications received by BPX employees. Six guiding principles were developed as a starting point:
1. Information should be shared.
2. Communications should be honest, clear, timely and relevant.
3. The preferred means of communication is face-to-face by line management.

4. A primary responsibility of every line manager is two way communication.
5. The context of decisions should be explained and questions answered in a timely manner.
6. Competitive sensitivity and personal privacy must be respected.

It was recognized that those principles represented goals to achieve with all possible speed but they also constituted a code of standards against which all communications should be measured.

Role of line management

The syndicate concluded that line management must play the leading role in communications, both upwards and downwards. It developed a formal process to facilitate this involvement, called 'Team Brief' and based on a model from The Industrial Society.

The goals of team brief included:

- provide a system for regular face-to-face communications;
- raise the profile of communications as a primary line management responsibility;
- provide people with regular, timely information on how the business is being run, issues that directly affect them and their jobs, and the part they play in achieving business objectives;
- put corporate information in a local context;
- provide an accessible channel for questions and feedback.

The recommended procedure would work as follows:

- team briefs would be held every other week, to start, beginning on Monday;
- senior executives in each major BPX location would meet with their direct reports or the next two levels of management;
- the content of the briefing should be planned in advance to be substantive and useful;
- information on business progress, policy changes, people movements and necessary actions in the coming two weeks should be included.

Some of the topics were expected to flow from a weekly conference call conducted each Friday by members of a global management group.

Handouts in the form of notes, key points or diagrams could be used; lengthy reports were to be avoided. A question and answer and discussion period was to be included as part of each brief. Any questions not answered on the spot were to be researched and responded to within 48 hours even if the answer was, we don't have an answer to that now.

Members of this first briefing would then hold team briefs with the people reporting to them. These meetings were to be held as quickly as possible, usually on the same Monday. The format was to be the same except that the information communicated was to be modified to include local of functional implications. Additional information of local relevance was also included and, again, there was to be an opportunity for questions, answers and discussion.

The purpose was not to review decisions with an eye toward changing them, but to make sure everyone understood not only what the decision was, but also:

- why it was made;
- who made it;
- when it would be implemented;
- how it would affect each manager's operations.

Notes were to be kept of the discussion so that staff feedback from each level could be passed back up the line.

The success of the team brief programme (and improved line management communications generally) would depend heavily on training. The group produced training materials on both the conduct and the content of the team brief sessions. The syndicate was also convinced that including communications in the appraisal criteria for managers was vital to assuring a more active line management role.

Upward communications

In formulating the team brief approach, the syndicate recognized its inherent facility for upward communication. The group believed this approach to be consistent with the guiding principles in that it allowed for:

- the sharing of information;
- face-to-face communications;
- a key role for line management;
- timely feedback;
- questions to be answered promptly.

In addition, as the team brief approach was designed to reach all levels of the organization, every employee was to have an opportunity to express his views through this mechanism.

Feedback was to be relayed up the management chain for action at local or regional level, depending on the nature of the issue. Staff reaction to major issues and developments which could not be dealt with by immediate line management, or which were of relevance to the business as a whole, would be passed to the global management group for discussion at the next Friday afternoon teleconference.

The group also determined that there was an important role for climate surveys and focus groups which could be useful for identifying trends and capturing underlying employee attitudes that might not be apparent in dispersed team brief sessions. For management and human resources representatives, the surveys provided feedback on areas where the company was doing well and acted as an early warning device, signalling areas of concern that might not have been adequately relayed up the management chain but could develop into major problems. Surveys could also serve as planning tools, providing information on employees' attitudes about existing conditions and preferences for future changes.

The focus groups provided helpful feedback which could be considered in designing future surveys. Participants said that the following should be explained:

- the reason for a given survey;
- why management felt the survey was important;
- what management hoped to find out;
- what would be done with the information;
- how and when the results would be communicated to staff.

They also stressed that questions should be asked in a clear, specific manner, not couched in jargon and, most important, should be obviously neutral. They should not be designed to lead respondents towards a specific reply. The focus groups felt questions should concentrate on issues on which action could be taken, not on the more vague climate of the company. Finally, surveys should be designed and conducted by outside professionals who would be objective and would protect employees' anonymity.

The group also cautioned that BPX had been 'over surveyed' in the past and that future efforts should be carefully designed, coordinated and scheduled.

Other options considered

In addition to the matters discussed above, extensive discussions and evaluations took place regarding BPX's written communications. The original draft resulting from the overall study included the principle that the sole purpose of written material was to support face-to-face communications. On reflection, the group concluded that this was not entirely true. There were many occasions when face-to-face was not a practical means of disseminating information quickly, particularly in cases of major developments which had to be publicly disclosed. In such instances, BPX had to resort to written memos or bulletins to alert staff to the news before they heard or read about it in the press.

A proposal to train a core group of communicators whose job it would be to disseminate news through the company was rejected because it removed primary responsiblity from line mangement. Likewise, with the exception of major announcements, greater use of video linkups or teleconferences was thought to be skirting line management to no apparent benefit.

The group discussed whether informal encouragement could be relied on to produce improved line mangement communications and determined that, for most managers, being a good communicator was simply too far down their list of priorities to receive the necessary attention. Nor, the group recognized, are most managers trained to be effective communicators. Therefore the syndicate turned to developing a formal system, including a training component, which resulted in the team brief programme and recommendations for the appraisal of communication skills.

The syndicate identified numerous potential upward communications methods in addition to those it recommended.

Perhaps the biggest concern the group had over the programme it recommended was whether it would result in communications that were sufficiently timely. The goal, as one member put it, is 'to beat the grapevine'. The group still had some doubts as to whether even the most successful team brief system could disseminate news of other important information to staff ahead of other sources. The group expected that timelines would continue to be an issue and that some of the programme components might have to be revisited after they were in place with an eye toward increasing their speed.

Appendices

1

Jargon

There cannot be anyone in business today who has not encountered, and been frustrated by, jargon. Words and phrases that are unnecessary, that frequently have no meaning to anyone other than the user, employed to impress or baffle, deliberately or otherwise.

Jargon is used everywhere, in written and verbal communications, and needs to be put into its proper perspective in a world of clear communications. To this end, there is growing support for the Plain English Campaign which encourages simplification of language and even offers annual awards to those who practise what they preach.

PLAIN ENGLISH

Martin Cutts, a languages graduate and journalist, is one of the campaign's founders. He also runs his own firm which will write or edit for you but also specializes in tidying words for clients. To promote his service, Cutts has produced a Clear English Charter which defines his policy for all to see.

Clear English Charter

We, this organisation's writers, will:

1. Fit our writing to the needs and knowledge of our audience, remembering that few customers understand our jargon and procedures.
2. Tell customers and colleagues clearly, concisely and courteously what has happened, how the situation stands, and what they can expect next.
3. Plan carefully our purpose and message before we write.

4. Use a reader-centred structure, perhaps with headings, lists and pithy summaries of key points.
5. Write sentences which average 15 – 20 words and include only one main idea.
6. Prefer natural word order: doer first, then an active verb.
7. Take pride in every day English, good spelling and accurate punctuation.
8. Use 'I', 'we', and 'you' to make the writing more human.
9. Cut verbiage.
10. Maintain the flow by starting some sentences with link words like 'but', 'however', 'so' and 'because'.
11. Use imperatives (commands) when writing instructions.
12. Break these principles rather than write anything silly.

A second charter, different in a few significant points, has been drawn up particularly for those perpetual proponents of jargon, solicitors and assorted legal parasites. The variations include a promise to:

• Remember that few clients are lawyers.
• Use everyday English unless technical terms are essential, avoiding legalese and Latin tags.
• Use words precisely, yet take care to be general when covering events we cannot foresee.
• Set out our reasoning clearly and leave no crack in the logic for our opponents to prise open.
• Follow precedent books which prefer plain English, but use them as guides not gospels.
• Use words to shape the situation to our client's best advantage, even if it means breaking these principles
© *Words at Work.*

Not everyone has adopted these principles, however. The *Bookseller*, the weekly magazine for the publishing industry, carried a report in April 1991 of redundancies at *Reader's Digest*. The article quoted the firm's managing director, who explained that this was 'part of the company's "regular strategic planning cycle" which aims to assess "opportunities for greater efficiency" and which on this occasion "coincided with the downturn in the market."'

The *Grocer* in July 1991 wondered what could possibly be meant by the restaurant offering on its menu 'battered fish meal'. Was it the meal that was battered or the fish? Or was it fish meal that was battered? Their reporter took the plunge, placed his order and was presented with a plate of chips, peas and fish dipped in batter.

WHAT DO YOU MEAN?

Andrew Martin, in The *Guardian* in February 1991, offered his own definition of a few frequently used business expressions.

Euphemism

- I'll just see if he's at his desk.

Translation

- I'll ask him if he wants to speak to you.

When followed by a request for the caller's name, this can be either a quite genuine offer to take a message to pass on to the person being called *or* an indication that the telephonist is signalling to the person dodging the call and asking whether he wants to speak to the caller or not. If this is then followed by:

Euphemism

- He's not at his desk right now
  or
- He's just stepped out of the room.

You can be sure that the translation is:

- He doesn't want to/can't talk to you right now but may change his mind sooner rather than later
  or
- He's in the men's room at the moment.

You can expect the worst, however, if the response is:

Euphemism

- I'm afraid he's in a meeting.

Translation

- He doesn't want to speak to you.

Martin maintains that an even more blatant brush off would be:

Euphemism

- I'm afraid he's tied up at the moment
  or
- I'm sorry but he's going to be tied up all day.

Translation

- Forget it, he does not want to talk to you
  or
- Don't call us, we'll call you.

One other, frequently encountered, expression not on Martin's list is:

Euphemism

- The specification is still evolving.

Translation

- We can't make up our minds and want to spend some more time shifting the ground rules and getting feedback from suppliers before amalgamating all the free information we can get into something that we will be forced to pay for.

Other expressions which you just know in your bones have got a sting in the tail include:

- I hear you
  or
- I take your point

both of which are invariably followed by but ... and statements of disagreement.

- With all due respect

is one of many phrases which prefaces remarks, and gives cues that create specific attitudes, particularly defensive, in the listener. Such a preface is invariably followed by the speaker explaining why he disagrees with the listener. It can often indicate a supercilious, even contemptuous, reaction to the listener's ideas which is provocative and not always constructive.

In Summary

- When all is said and done,
- at the end of the day,
- the bottom line is

that if you want to communicate, it is far better to say what you mean, and mean what you say, than to dress your words in jargon.

2

Glossary

Most of the terms which follow are frequently used in the context of communications. Current usage is not always equivalent to literal or previous definitions, however. The meanings given herein are purely and simply those relevant to business communications. They will have been encountered repeatedly throughout the book and explained further in those cases.

Many of the terms which follow also qualify as jargon. Without resorting to industry-specific terms or abbreviations, there are a number of these which would benefit from defining and debunking.

But not all jargon is useless, or meaningless. People often feel that short words should be used but are replaced by long ones just to impress. There is nothing wrong with long words if their meaning is clear. Underestimating your audience and over simplifying your language can in fact seem patronizing. It can produce a resentful and irritable audience. As with all aspects of presentation (see Chapter 3), you must gauge your audience.

The word 'jargon' generally has 'negative connotations'. Communication needs to be clear. But clear is not necessarily a synonym for simple. Not all words must be of one syllable. When General Norman Schwarzkopf used a popular American expression, bovine scatology (frequently abbreviated to BS), his meaning was crystal clear. Simplifying that expression to its monosyllabic equivalent would be totally unnecessary.

Not all of the terms below have negative connotations. Many of them are perfectly legitimate uses of language within their own frame of reference and easy to understand even if they are not always plain English. So for those interested in having the language of communications communicated, please read on.

alphabet soup Abbreviations of names, especially of organizations, can be used both as a shortcut to communication and a way of indicating familiarity with the people or organization concerned. Speeches and written material would be far longer if we had to use every organization's full name every time it came up. But the use of abbreviations also tells the audience that you know what you are talking about and want them to be aware of it. Whether or not the audience knows what you are talking about is a different issue.

audit Inventory or stock check, counting up what you have in order to decide what you need. Until recently, this term was generally associated with finance and accounts. It has now become a *buzzword*, applied to communications, skills, services and needs.

awareness Taking note of the meanings behind words, body language, others' perceptions and the general situation.

brainstorming A rapid exchange of ideas, without discussion in its early stages. Participants in a brainstorming session will have a topic and simply call out or list anything that comes into their heads on that topic. Afterwards the thoughts are discussed and either rejected or developed but the quickfire, almost stream of consciousness first stage can prove invaluable in pinpointing key issues and reactions.

buzzword A word or term currently in vogue, which is used at every opportunity and in a wide range of applications, appropriate or otherwise.

challenge Stumbling block, obstacle or problem. Some people look at problems as insurmountable potential defeats, others as an opportunity to show what they're made of. It is the latter attitude which turns a problem into a challenge.

clarity Jargon-free communications which are clear to everyone involved.

common language Words that everyone in a group understands.

common sense The ability to cut through all extraneous matter and devise a practical, sensible way of dealing with situations.

consultant An expert from outside the company brought in to look objectively at one or more aspects of the business and advise on any changes that may be necessary.

consultative document A presentation made by a selected team of experts, to an audience which will be directly and indirectly affected by the document's recommendations once implemented. This is a one-off opportunity for the audience to have its say. There are four variables involved in consultative documents which can determine their effectiveness:

- composition and objectivity of the expert panel researching, writing and presenting the document;

- length of consultative period;
- composition of audience canvassed;
- willingness and ability of the expert panel to assess and incorporate comments from the audience.

devolve   Pass the buck, spread responsibility so thinly that no single person or group can ever be held responsible. When responsibility and/or financial control for something is devolved, it is taken out of central control and passed around individual members or member organizations. In this way, a small governing or controlling group is generally replaced by several groups, a great deal of red tape, a growing bureaucracy and the increasing likelihood that the left hand will never know what the right hand is doing.

dissonance   Something that is out of tune or out of step, or disagrees with accepted wisdom.

empathy   Sympathy and understanding, putting yourself in the other person's place and trying to feel, act and react as that person would.

evolve   In its strict sense, to evolve is to change, which includes moving away from an early concept and developing that concept in greater detail. Change can be either good or bad, indicating flexibility and fairness or indicating indecisiveness.

In practice, *evolve* can also mean that policy has been changed, procedures have been changed and hence ground rules have been changed. This can be camouflage for running a business on shifting sands, never firm, and hence providing insurance against decisions that are never properly implemented. When a project or policy has evolved, it is often difficult to identify or assign responsibility.

feedback   Comments from the audience on their perceptions of what you are saying/doing.

flexible   Willing and able to change; flexibility is generally a positive attribute but taken to its extreme can be indicative of indecisiveness and weakness.

getting in touch with your feelings   Evaluating yourself, examining your strengths and weakness, likes and dislikes, goals and achievements in order to achieve self-awareness and understanding.

hidden agenda   The ideas or plans you have for a meeting or relationship which is known by you but never stated; it can sometimes be guessed at, to a greater or lesser degree, by the people with whom you are communicating. Successful communication is entirely dependent on mutual understanding which can be affected to differing degrees by the existence, and perception, of one another's hidden agenda.

human resources development   Essentially the current title for personnel management but with an implication of responsibilities that go beyond recruitment and tasks specifically related to employees' first and last days on the job. Human resources managers usually identify and implement training needs. They also maintain contact with employees throughout their time with a company and act as reference point for any difficulties or disputes.

interaction   Verbal and/or written action taking place between several parties, ie another word for communication. Interaction, like communication, may be superficial and can only be successful if all parties involved understand what is being said, verbally or non-verbally.

interpersonal   Any exchange involving two or more people; the term *interpersonal skills* implies the proviso that you communicate or interact well or successfully. When recruiting new staff, job advertisements often list as a prerequisite 'a high (or well-developed) degree of interpersonal skills' or 'the ability to interact well'.

jargon   Slang; words relating to a specific industry or project, understood only by those in the know. Jargon can develop naturally as a convenient language for those working together but can also be used to unnecessarily complicate statements that are equally well said in plain English.

KISS   Keep It Short and Simple.

language skills   The ability to write and speak well and clearly.

leading/controlling edge   One-up-manship, having the advantage, albeit slight, over other people particularly in a negotiating scenario.

listening   Not just hearing but hearing and understanding; being an active participant in communications by receiving, accepting and understanding messages being transmitted.

manipulation   Bringing others around to your way of thinking or behaving through a combination of direct and indirect methods; manipulation usually implies that the others involved would not necessarily agree with your wishes of their own accord and that subterfuge is required to achieve your ends.

negative connotations   Like a bad reputation, unpleasant aroma or flavour, certain words and phrases leave a nasty impression or association in the mind so that whenever you hear them again, an instinctive feeling of reservation, uneasiness or suspicion accompanies them.

network   Can relate to people or equipment; in either context a network is the link that exists to facilitate communication.

objectives   Aims, targets or goals; knowing where you want to go; the plans you make for reaching that point; *strategy*.

people skills/understanding   The application of communications, making your message clear to other people and making clear that their message is understood by you. Understanding a message is not enough unless the people sending the message are sure that you have received it and that your *perceptions* of their intentions are accurate. People skills particularly include assuring others that you trust them and that they can trust you.

perception An understanding of words or actions which may or may not be wholly accurate; everyone has their own perception or understanding of what other people are saying and doing. These perceptions, or impressions, are vital to establishing the degree of understanding that people share as the perception may not correlate exactly with the intention of the speaker/writer. Simply translated, this means that you are saying something with a meaning or intention different to what I am hearing.

plain English The use of the English language that everyone, regardless of their familiarity with your business or industry, can understand.

presentation The way in which something is presented to others, the way it appears to others and thus the impression it gives. Presentation can refer to the way things look, for example:

- how a person is dressed;
- how a person stands or moves;
- how an office is decorated and how tidy, comfortable or smart it is;
- how a letter or document is written, edited, proofread, designed and produced.

A presentation can also refer to a performance, that is one or more people explaining (presenting) an idea or project to other people. This can take the form of direct speech, with or without supporting material (written or visual), to a live audience or it can take the form of indirect speech perhaps through a film or video.

Material, information and impressions can be presented; people give, or make, those presentations.

responsibility Perhaps the best manager is the one willing to accept or take on responsibility. In themselves, these are two different indicators of a manager's attitude — is he a follower, willing or otherwise, or is he a leader? Either way, a responsible manager is far more likely to be concerned about a company's identity and strategy than one who avoids responsibility.

scoring points Demonstrating that your wisdom, knowledge and/or experience are superior to someone else's and therefore putting them at a disadvantage. Point scoring can be a fact of everyday business life, ensuring that you achieve or maintain the position that you feel you deserve. It is also important during negotiations, especially if you are fighting a win/lose campaign.

strategy The route you follow and the steps you take to achieve your *objectives*.

suspend judgement Request time to consider the facts and other people's opinions, to think things over, before making a decision.

terms of reference Defining the parameters of communication to ensure that *common language* is used to achieve *understanding*.

trust A belief in the validity of communications; that the audiences you are communicating to, and from whom you are in turn receiving communications, are honest and reliable, without any *hidden agenda*.

understanding Communication must include understanding; simply transmitting words isn't enough, therefore a mutual acceptance of language, jargon and objectives must be established in order to achieve understanding.

wysiwyg Pronounced whizzywig and actually meaning 'what you see is what you get'. This phrase was originally coined as a reference to computer software specifications, where precision of speech and communication was essential. Its current, broader, application implies that you literally get what you see, no strings attached, no hidden extras, nothing more and nothing less.

walking the job Keeping in touch with colleagues at all levels and knowing what they are doing. Good management training must include hands on experience, to be repeated at regular intervals, for example the supervisor or executive spending a week or so each year on the shop floor or out on the road. Bank managers and teachers may shadow industrial managers. When service companies take on a new account, the executive in charge of the project should spend some time with the client, not just in meetings but seeing at first hand how the company works. Managers who have climbed the ladder from the shop floor have far more experience, ability, sense and knowledge than newcomers to middle management and are often more able to deal with the reactions to them. Walking the job, knowing what others do, is a part of what makes us able, or not able, to communicate effectively.

Bibliography

Bishop, Peter (1987) *Computing Science*, 2nd edn NFER Nelson, Windsor.

Confederation of British Industry (1980) *Finding out the Facts about Employee Communications*, CBI Publications, London.

Frain, John (1981) *Introduction to Marketing*, Macdonald & Evans, London.

French, CS (1990) *Computer Science*, 3rd edn DP Publications Ltd, London.

Goldsmith, Walter and DC Clutterbuck, (1984) *The Winning Streak* Weidenfeld & Nicolson, London.

Harris, Nicola (1991) *Basic Editing, A Practical Course* Book House Training Centre, London.

Hurst, Ronald (1970) *Industrial Management Methods*, Hutchinson, London.

Lewis, Dr David and Guy Fielding, (1990) *The Language of Success* British Telecom, London.

MacShane, Denis (1979) *Using the Media* Pluto Press, London.

Needham, David and Robert Dransfield, (1990) *Business Studies* McGraw-Hill Book Co Ltd, Maidenhead.

Wilson, Aubrey (1984) *Practice Development for Professional Firms* McGraw-Hill Book Co Ltd, Maidenhead.

OTHER PUBLICATIONS

Business Line, Issue No 4 The Thames Valley College.

Information Exchange, July/August 1990 Management Charter Initiative, London.

IT Training, The Magazine for Training and Development Management, December/January 1990 Training Information Network Ltd.

KOGAN PAGE TITLES

Allan, Jane (1989) *How to Develop Your Personal Management Skills*, London.

Armstong, Michael (1990) *How to Be an Even Better Manager*, London.

Bennett, Roger (1988) *Managing People*, London.

Bennett, Roger (1988) *Personal Effectiveness*, London.

Bentley, Trevor J (1988) *Effective Communication for the Accountant*, London.

Bentley T J (1988) *Report Writing in Business*, London.

Bland, Michael & Peter Jackson, (1990) *Effective Employee Communications*, London.

Bone, Diane (1988) *A Practical Guide to Effective Listening*, London.

Brock, Sally & Sally R Cabbell, (1990) *How to Write a Staff Manual*, London.

Bunch, Meribeth *Speak with Confidence*, 1989.

Christopher, Elizabeth M & Larry Smith, (1989) *Leadership Training through Gaming*.

Davey, W Mackenzie & Peter Kneebone, (1989) *How to Be a Good Judge of Character*, London.

Decker, Bert, (1989) *How to Communicate Effectively*, London.

Denning, Jim, (1988) *Readymade Business Letters*, London.

Dunckel, J Parnham, E (1985) *The Business Guide to Effective Speaking*, London.

Fletcher, J A and D F Gowing, (1989) *The Business Guide to Effective Writing*, London.

Freestone, Julie and Janet Brusse, (1990) *Telemarketing Basics*, London.

Gibbs, Paul, (1990) *Doing Business in the European Community*, London.

Haynes, Marion E, (1988) *Effective Meeting Skills*, London.

Heron, John, (1989) *The Facilitators' Handbook*, London.

Hussey, David & Phil Lowe, (1990) *Key Issues in Management Training*, London.

Ind, Nicholas, (1990) *The Corporate Image*, London.

Jackson, Terence, (1989) *Evaluation: Relating Training to Business Performance*, London.

Lundy, James L, (1990) *How to Lead – So Others Follow Willingly*, London.

Maddux, Robert B, (1988) *Successful Negotiation*, London.

Mager, Robert F, (1990) *Developing Attitude Toward Learning*, London.

Mager, Robert F, (1990) *Making Instruction Work*, London.

Mandel, Steve, (1988) *Effective Presentation Skills*, London.

van Ments, Morry, (1989) *The Effective Use of Role-Play*, London.

Palladino, Connie D, (1990) *Developing Self-Esteem*, London.

Peel, Malcolm, (1990) *Improving Your Communication Skills*, London.

Peel, Malcolm, (1988) *How to Make Meetings Work*, London.

le Poole, Samfrits, (1991) *Never Take No for An Answer*, London.

Reddin, Bill, (1990) *Tests for the Output Oriented Manager*, London.
Robinson, Colin, (1990) *Winning at Business Negotiations*, London.
Schiffman, Stephen, (1989) *Cold Calling Techniques*, London.
Seekings, David, (1989) *How to Organise Effective Conferences and Meetings*, London.
Sheal, Peter R, (1989) *How to Develop and Present Staff Training Courses*, London.
Stevens, Michael, (1989) *Improving Your Presentation Skills*, London.
Stevens, Michael, (1989) *Winning at Your Interview*, London.
Stevens, Michael, (1988) *Practical Problem Solving for Managers*, London.
Turner, Barry, (1989) *Readymade Business Speeches*, London.

Directory of Useful Organisations

British Association for Commercial and Industrial
Education (BACIE)
16 Park Crescent
London W1N 4AP
Tel: 071-636 5351

British Association of Industrial Editors (BAIE)
3 Locks Yard
High St
Sevenoaks
Kent TN13 1LT
Tel: 0732 459331

British Institute of Management (BIM)
Management House
Cottingham Road
Corby
Northamptonshire NN17 1TT
Tel: 0536 204222

Confederation of British Industry (CBI)
Centre Point
103 New Oxford Street
London WC1A 1DU
Tel: 071-379 7400

Department of Trade and Industry (DTI)
1 – 19 Victoria Street
London SW1H 0ET
Tel: 071-215 5000

(There are DTI regional offices all around the country and it is recommended that you find your local office.)

EC Commission
8 Storey's Gate
London SW1P 3AT
Tel: 071-222 8122

The European Parliament Information Office
2 Queen Anne's Gate
London SW1H 9AA
Tel: 071-222 0411

The Forum of Private Business
Ruskin Chambers
Drury Lane
Knutsford
Cheshire WA16 6HA
Tel: 0565 634467

Institute of Directors (IOD)
116 Pall Mall
London SW1Y 5ED
Tel: 071-839 1233
(*Note*: The Institute's library is open from Monday to Friday, 9am until 6pm but non-members must call first to ask permission to use the library and arrange an appointment.)

Institute of Management Education
7 Westbourne road
Southport PR8 2HZ
Tel: 0704 67994

Management Charter Initiative (MCI)
National Forum for Management Education & Development
Sun Alliance House
Oxford OX1 2QE

Training Agency
TEC Promotions Unit
Room W539
Moorfoot
Sheffield S1 4PQ
(It is recommended that you find the address of the TEC for your area in order to find out what advice and assistance are available.)

Understanding British Industry (UBI)
Sun Alliance House
New Inn Hall Street
Oxford OX1 2BR
Tel: 0865 722585

Index

AB Co 101, 125, 134-6, 150-1
accountability, of management 33
advertising 178, 212, 214
advisory panels 77
agendas 60-1, 74-5, 245-6, *see also* hidden agendas
agents, overseas 269
Allan, Jane, *How to Develop Your Personal Management Skills* 66-7, 82, 84, 85-6, 96, 120
announcements 245
annual general meetings 100
annual reports 233-4
answering machines 171, 177, 200
appearance 42, 69-71, 111
apprenticeships 129
Armstrong, Michael, *How to be an Even Better Manager* 53, 83-4, 85
Arthur Andersen & Co 234
attitudes 42-3
  to foreigners 276
audience
  involvement 64
  losing your 46
audience analysis 17-23, 56-7
audio visual equipment 203
audio-visual training 127
awareness 13, 306
Banham, John 134
Bank Users Group 125
banks 124-5, 134
Bennett, Roger, *Personal Effectiveness* 76, 144, 149
Bentley, Trevor, Effective Communication for the Accountant 58-9
  Report Writing in Business 243
Bland, Michael, *Effective Employee Communications* 17, 25, 31, 56, 105
body language 64, 141, 172-3
  abroad 272
  and listening 51-3
Boehm, Klaus, *The Student Book* 274
Bone, Diane, *A Practical Guide to Effective Listening* 50-1, 52-3
Boots the Chemist Ltd 92
BP Exploration Company 279, 292-7
BPXpress 258-9
Bradford & Bingley Building Society 157
brainstorming 76, 306
branding 210-11
breathing 62-3
bribery 278-9
briefing 159
British Association of Industrial Editors 257, 314
brochures 214
Brock, Susan, *How to Write a Staff Manual* 240-1
Brusse, Janet, *Telemarketing Basics* 168-9
bureaucracy 160
Business Line 91
business plans 232-3
Business Week 192

Butterfield, Seymour Pierce 104
buyers, objectives 228

Cabbell, Sally, *How to Write a Staff Manual* 240-1
Carlisson, Jan 103
case studies 281-97
CBI 116, 165-6, 314
  Employee Relations Group 34
  Finding Out the Facts about Employee Communications 24-5, 32, 35
Chambers of Commerce 268
change
  communicating 96-7
  resistance to 118, 198
  training for 115
Cheale, Dudley 258
clarity 13, 306
clothes 69-70
Clutterbuck, David, *The Winning Streak* 94, 96
Coleman, Dick 255
Colley, A H 216
committees 76-7
common ground 13
communication
  between levels 100-6
  within and between departments 101-2
communications audit 17-37
  assessment 35-7
  consultants 25
  employee opinions 31-4, 99-100
  factors in 26-34
  implementation 34-5
  procedure 25-6
  setting up 24
  summary 36-7
  team 24-5
Communications Week International 199
community 22
  family businesses and the 92-4
companies, criteria for success 94-5
company
  external structure 19-23   Fig 1.3
  internal structure 17-19   Fig 1.1
company identity, and marketing 207-9
company image
  and marketing 207-9
  presenting 212-13
competitions 215
competitors 21, 269
complaints 97-9
  by telephone 167
  in letters 226
computer-aided design (CAD) 203
computer based training 123, 127
computer consultants 194-6
computer languages 203
computers 194-6, 202-3
  mainframe 202
  manuals 196, 238
  on-line 202

portable 30
    service for 197
    specifications 193-7
    spell-checks 193
    training 196
concessions 147
conduct, abroad 263-80
Confederation of British Industry *see* CBI
conference calls 202
conference facilities 107-8
conference materials 247
conferences 75
confidentiality 103, 188-9
conflicts 99
confrontational communications 87
consultancy 204
consultation documents 244-5, 306-7
consultative machinery 33
consumers 22
    questionnaires 241
contingency planning 49-50
contracts 234-5
    abroad 279
conversations 47
Corfield, Sir Kenneth 100
corporate communications 231-6
corporate communications consultancies 233
corporate identity 26-7, 238-9
corporate image 27-9
    'tweaking' 28
corporate strategy 27
correspondence 225-30
counter ploys 147
courtesy 263
Crookes, Phillip 91
cue cards 50
curriculum vitae 112
customers 22, 152-3
customs, foreign 263-80
Cutts, Martin, *Clear English Charter* 235, 301-2

Danzeisen, John 91, 128
Data Protection Act 193
Dawe, Roger 115, 116-17
decision making 216-17
Denning, Jim, *Readymade Business Letters* 227
design consultants 208-9
    contract 192
desktop publishing 192, 248, 257-8
developing nations, negotiating in 278-9
Digital Equipment Company 288-91
direct mail 101, 215, 227, 234
directories 215
Directory Books Ltd 77
disabled people 126
discounts 104, 215
Dixon, Bill 276
dress 69-70
Dunckel, Jacqueline, *The Business Guide to Effective Speaking* 48-9, 56-7, 66
dynamics 87-8

education 127
electronic diaries 203
electronic mailbox 30, 200-1, 202
empathy 62-3, 85, 98-9, 307
employee communications 90-113
employee manuals 239-41

employee opinions, communications audit 31-4
employee representatives, at management meetings 100
encounter groups 129
equipment
    communications 29-31
    hi-tech 199-204
equipment audit 193-4
etiquette books 263
euphemisms 303-4
Europe (1992) 275-6
evaluation, of communication 23-34
exhibitions 68-9, 214
Export Clubs 268
exporting 279-80
eye contact 46-7, 63, 68, 272

face, saving 265, 277
face-to-face briefing 32-3
face-to-face communications 39-158
facsimile machines 30, 190-1, 201, 275
failures in communication 216-17
family businesses, and the community 92-4
fax *see* facsimile machines
feedback 44-6, 218, 307
feinting 146-7
financial information 33-4
Fletcher, John, *The Business Guide to Effective Writing* 232, 235-6
flexibility 203-4, 307
Ford Motor Co 123, 279
foreign competition 269
foreign contact 261-80
formality, degree of 263
Fowler, H W 232
Frain, John, *Introduction to Marketing* 207, 215-16
Freestone, Julie, *Telemarketing Basics* 168-9
future planning 113, 114-16

Gavaskar, Sunil 122
Germany 93, 118, 276
Gibbs, Paul, *Doing Business in the European Community* 242, 261, 274
glossary 305-10
Goldsmith, Walter, *The Winning Streak* 94, 96
Goodway, Nick 104
Gowers, Sir Ernest 232
Gowing, David, *The Business Guide to Effective Writing* 232, 235-6
grapevines 31, 102
graphics 248
group dynamics 87-8, 119-20
guidebooks 263
Gummer, Peter, 'My Biggest Mistake' 56, 61

handbooks 239-41
Harvey-Jones, Sir John 93-4, 97, 115-16
Haynes, Marion, *Effective Meeting Skills* 45, 82-3, 84-5, 86, 87
Heseltine, Michael 244
hi-tech communications 190-204
    international 275, 279
hidden agendas 57-8, 64, 85, 307
honesty 186, 264
hospitality
    corporate 215
    receiving when abroad 266-7
hosting foreign visitors 265-6

house style 238-9
human resources development 109-13, 307-8
Hurst, Ronald, *Industrial Management Methods* 95

illustrations 248
importing 279-80
impressions 69-71, 212-13
incentives 104, 215
Ind, Nicholas, *The Corporate Image* 26-7, 28, 35, 97, 99, 239
industrial espionage 103
information
    communications for 237-49
    gathering 241-9
    passing it down 100-6
Ingham, Bernard 188
Institute of Public Relations 218
interaction 86, 308
interactive transmissions 191
intermediary, communicating through an 159-219, 190-9
internal communications 20 Fig 1.2
international communications 261-80, 275-80
international employment directory 274
international research 267-9
interpreters 271
interviewing techniques, media 185-9
interviews 110-11
    attribution and verification 188-9
    live versus recorded 187-8
IT Training 115

Jackson, Peter, *Effective Employee Communications* 17, 25, 31, 56, 105
Japan 105, 118, 276
jargon 231-2, 252, 301-4, 305, 308
Jenks, Brian 95, 96, 232
jet lag 275
job applicants 112-13
job satisfaction 106

Keating, Frank 43, 122
keyboard skills 121, 198, 229
KISS (Keep It Short and Simple) 8, 68, 226, 233, 308

labels 247-8
language, use of 29, 231-2, 301-4
languages, foreign 269-71
laser printers 192
lawyers 235
le Poole, Samfrits, *Never Take No for an Answer* 139-40, 142, 144, 149, 264-5, 271, 277
leaders, who are led 103-4
leadership 109
    styles 85-6
    training 119-20, 127
'leaks' 103
LECs (Scottish Local Enterprise Companies) 117
Lees-Spalding, Jenny, *The Student Book* 274
letters 225-30
    readymade 227-8
    signing off 227
    standard information 225-6
listening 50-4, 308
    active and passive 51-3
    concentration checklist 50-1
    when abroad 269-70
logos 27-8, 214

'tweaking' 28, 209
loyalty 93

Maddux, Robert, *Successful Negotiation* 142-3, 145, 146-7, 149-50
mail lists, cleaning 192-3
mail/merge software 191
management
    accountability of 33
    competences 125-6
    training 127, 198
Management Charter Initiative 128, 315
management meetings, employee representatives at 100
managers, middle 119
Mandel, Steve, *Effective Presentation Skills* 67-8
manuals 237-41
    computer 238
    employee 239-41
    identity 238-9
    in-house 197
    instructions 238
    technical 238
market research 34, 217-18
marketing 205-19
    and communication 205-6
    objectives 206-7
    stages of 215-16 Fig 12.1
marketing materials 234
marketing techniques 214-19
Mars UK 123
Martin, Andrew 302-4
MCI, *Information Exchange* 125-6
media, communicating with the 22, 178-89
media coverage 214, 215
meeting rooms 80-2
meetings 72-89
    breaks in 78-9
    chairman's role 79, 83-4
    choosing a format 75-82
    decision making 82-3
    degree of formality 78
    documentation 86-7
    participation in 84-5
    public 77-8
    seating at 80-2
    setting the style 79-80
    staff 128-9
    timing of 79
memoranda 245
messages, electronic 200
Minale, Tattersfield & Partners 28, 238-9
minutes 86-7, 245-6
modems 30
motivation 90, 104

nameplates 78
names, use of first 263
National Power 96
negotiations 133-51
    bad 139-40
    concluding 149
    with foreigners 276-8
    good 139
    last minute points 147-9
    major issues 140-2
    mistakes in 149-50
    preparing for 144-5

tactics and strategy 145-9
team 150
networking, international 273
networks 39-40, 102, 121, 201-2, 308
local area 201
wide area 201
newsletters 254-6
newspapers 256-60
Nine O'Clock News Method 8
'no', saying 277
non-verbal cues 51-3, 54, 64
note-taking 53, 87
notice boards 245

Oakley Young 26
obsolescence, built-in 154-5
offices
open-plan 107
seating plans 107
Olins, Wally 26
one-to-one communications 225-30
open communications 102-3
overseas agents 269
ownership of ideas 105
Oxfordshire, Business Education Partnership 116

packaging 208-9, 214
pagers 200
paperwork, official 252-3
Parnham, Elizabeth, *The Business Guide to Effective Speaking* 48-9, 56-7, 66
participation 105
Peel, Malcolm *How to Make Meetings Work* 88
Improving Your Communication Skills 23-4, 25
perceived value 210
perception 13, 42, 58, 99-100, 213-14, 309
personalization 191
personnel management 109-13
Peters, Tom, *In Search of Excellence* 94
PG Partners 77
Philips 192
plans, business 232-3
point of sale packs 214
posture 63, 70, 172-3
power 42-4, 47
premises 71
presentation 50, 309
training for 127
of written communications 248
presentations 55-71
conclusion 66
distribution of supporting material 61
making your point 65
preparation 56-68
research for 63-4
setting the scene 60
tools for 56
visual aids 66-8
press
handling the 180-9
power of the 179
press conferences 182-3
press coverage 178-9
repercussions 189
press pack 184
Prestel 202
pricing 209-10
printed material 250-60

Pritchett, Roger 91
private circuits 202
problems, communicating 95-6
product differentiation 210-11
proofreading 224, 272
proximity 47
PT & Sons 107
public meetings 77-8
public relations 205-19
public speaking 46-50, 124
publishing 121
pyramid training 121

qualifications 128
quality, and price 210
quality circles 105
questionnaires 241-2
multilingual 242
quotations 228-9

R S Clare 118-19
radio 187
rapport, establishing 65-6
recruitment 112
overseas 273-4
recruitment fairs 112
redundancy 97, 121, 204
reference material 248-9
rehearsals 49, 59-60, 188
Reid, Sir Bob 108-9, 121
reliability of communications 31
repetition as reinforcement 65
reports 243-4
representative training 122-3
residential courses 129
responsibility 103, 309
retraining 126
Ricoh 192
Robinson, Colin, *Winning at Business Negotiations* 137-8, 140, 146, 149, 150, 228-9, 271
role playing 83-5, 130
RSS 77
Rushworth, PJ 115

sales, negotiating 156-7
sales literature 156
sales materials 156, 214, 234
sales training 127, 157-8
Schiffman, Stephan, *Cold Calling Techniques* 155, 156, 169
seating plans, office 107
security
personal 95-7
and technology 193, 197
Self, Will 258
self-confidence 13
seller, objectives 228
selling techniques 152-8
sensitivity training 129
shadowing 129
shareholders 21, 104
Sheal, Peter, *How to Develop and Present Staff Training Courses* 67, 131, 246-7
skills training 121-2
Smith Co 124
speaker/listener interaction 52
Fig 2.1
speaking

and listening 41-54
  off-the-record 188-9
  when abroad 269-70
specifications 228-9
speeches 47-9
  preparing 58-9
  timing 62
  tips for 59
sponsorship 215
spontaneity 80
status 108-9
STC 100
Stevens, Michael, *Improving Your Presentation Skills* 67, 222
stress 105-6
suggestion boxes 105
suppliers 21-2
support services 215

team negotiations 150
technology, staff attitude to 30-1, 198
TECs (Training and Enterprise Councils) 116-17
Telecom Gold 201
telecommunications equipment 176-7
telemarketing 161-77
telephone
  answering a call 164-5
  call forwarding/diversion 201
  hiding behind the 170-1
  international calls 124, 174-6, 272
  leaving a message 165-6
  manners 171
  preparing to 162-3
  queuing 201
  receiving a call 164-8
  small talk 170
  speaking to an intermediary 169-70
  taking a message 166-7
  types of call 167
telephone skills 168-77
  training in 167-8
telephone systems 199-200
telephone techniques 161-77
telephones, mobile 30
telesales 155
teletext 30
television 187
telex 30, 201
Temple, Roger 100
Texaco Ltd 91
Thamesley College 126
Thatcher, Margaret 63
Third World, negotiating in 278-9
time management 229-30
time zones 275
Total Quality Management 119
training 91, 113, 114-32
  the business of 116-17
  cost of not 132
  cost of 131-2
  identifying needs 35, 123-32
  needs survey 130-1
  off the job 129
  on the job 129

strategy 116-23
  of trainers 127, 130
training group 129-30
training materials 246-7
training programmes 127-8
translations 269, 271-2
Turner, Barry, *Readymade Business Speeches* 265-6

understanding 13, 58, 310
unemployment 126
union meetings, managers at 100

value
  adding 91
  recognizing and communicating 91
video presentations 55
videoconferences 202
visits 215
visual aids 66-8
voice, tone of 63, 172
voice control 63, 173-4, 187
voice mail 200

Waterhouse, Keith 251-2
Waterman, Robert, *In Search of Excellence* 94
Webster, G B 115
WEKA Publishing, *Successful Model Letters...* 228
Whitaker, David 121
Wilkins, Robin 115
Wilson, Aubrey, *Practice Development for Professional Firms* 206, 210, 214, 216, 219
Winners 1990 117, 118-19
Wolff Olins 26
Wolfson, Sir Brian 116
women
  after career break 126
  in business 43-4
  working from home 204
word processors 229
working abroad 273-5
working environment 106-9
working from home 204
workshops 75
WPP 26
Wright, Ian 259-60
written communications 29, 221-60
  advantages 250
  basics of 251-4
  checking 223-4
  checklist 235-6
  disadvantages 250-1
  foreign 271-2
  organization 223
  preparation 222-3
  rules for 221-2

Xerox 192

yearbooks 215

Z International Ltd 82, 107, 283-7